T0313184

"This book sets the stage for the benefits of a lean agile strategy that has been successfully applied to administrative and supply chain operations management functions in a variety of production and service industries. In the absence of strategic sourcing and procurement, there can be a negative effect to sales and profits, because an holistic approach of a Lean philosophy is not applied.

It calls attention to an extended view on how procurement administration connects and merges with various functions, suppliers and consumers in the existing environment.

Myerson's new book entices one to explore how procurement takes on a significant role by improving information the flow of information and materials within the entire supply chain. All of which lead to best practice Lean procurement functions that reach far beyond the contractual negotiations and established crucial operational requirements, using strategic sourcing activities encompassing market research, vendor evaluation and integration."

–Dr. Joseph Mosca
Associate Professor of Management &
Decision Sciences at Monmouth University

"A book that applies Lean principles and thinking within procurement is long overdue. Although an abundance of books and articles address topics related to the supply side of supply chain management, not much is available regarding how to apply Lean within the supply organization. Paul Myerson's book addresses this important and timely need."

–Robert J. Trent, PhD
Professor of Supply Chain Management and Supply Chain Management
Program Director at Lehigh University, Author End-to-End Lean
Management—A Guide to Complete Supply Chain Improvement

"With *Lean Demand-Driven Procurement: How to Apply Lean Thinking to Your Supply Chain Management Processes*, Prof. Myerson has expertly crafted a comprehensive -easy to read-layout of the entire contemporary supply management process while breaking down key concepts, such as "Lean" and "Agile," into practical ready-to-use tools for any employer in the TLD (Transportation, Logistics and Distribution) sector.

Whether you are an industry leading employer seeking an edge over the competition or simply a curious individual looking to learn more about the latest innovations in arguably the world's most dynamic workforce and economic sector (i.e., Transportation, Logistics and Distribution), Prof. Myerson's *Lean Demand-Driven Procurement: How to Apply Lean Thinking to Your Supply Chain Management Processes* provides the clearest A to Z user's guide available to understanding and employing the smartest, most cutting edge Lean and Agile practices."

–William Bajor
East Stroudsburg University

"It's about time procurement teams harness the tangible benefits of Lean principles to take demand driven initiatives to the next level. Making a 'good buy' based on pricing incentives does not necessarily result in a great purchase for the business."

–Karin L. Bursa
Executive Vice President of Logility

"Managing a modern supply chain is not an easy task in today's fast moving economy. Costs can spike in any part of the supply chain from the raw materials area to the final delivery of the product/service to the end customer. Supply chain managers are continually looking for ways to lower costs and stay competitive looking for opportunities downstream in the supply process, but real efficiency opportunities exist at the beginning of the supply chain in PROCUREMENT. Paul Myerson's new book titled *Lean Demand-Driven Procurement: How to Apply Lean Thinking to Your Supply Chain Management Processes* presents some new and innovative Lean approaches to an often overlooked area in supply chain management for cost reduction and efficiency. His Lean concepts for streamlining the procurement area are powerful and will result in comprehensive reductions along the entire supply chain. His explanations and applications are easy to understand and often can be applied without too much change in your supply chain. In my 35 years of consulting and teaching in supply chain, I find Paul's book to a must read for all marketing and supply chain managers. It is also a valuable book in teaching new managers about the supply chain process and for university students majoring in supply chain management. Paul Myerson's is a major contribution to the field and I highly recommend it."

–Dr. Richard Lancioni
Professor of Supply Chain Management at Temple University

"If building a demand-driven network is on your strategic roadmap, then Lean procurement is in your future – even if you are not yet familiar with the term. Join Professor Myerson on a journey that rethinks what is possible in procurement and how it is already fundamentally transforming global supply chains. The result is an Agile network with connected, cross-functional and collaborative procurement processes that go beyond traditional efficiency goals to power a new level of growth, service and financial performance. Lean Procurement is a must for any executive looking to get a step-up on competition in today's fast-moving global economy."

–Ronald Kubera
SVP & General Manager at E2open

"Many companies have struggled to remain profitable in the dynamic, global environment of the 21st century which is not only highly competitive but also volatile and ever changing. Successful companies have evolved into global supply and demand networks that can effectively deal with complexity, multi-dimensional relationships and dynamic processes. Terms such as adaptive, agile, dynamic and lean have become part of the lexicon of today's supply chain executives. Paul Myerson's new text book provides insightful analysis and recommendations which can enable companies to survive and remain profitable. Professor Myerson discusses how to apply the concept of LEAN in a more holistic approach based upon continuous improvement which can lead to paradigm shifts benefiting the whole supply chain."

–Dr. John Coyle
Professor Emeritus of Logistics and Supply Chain Management
at The Pennsylvania State University

Lean Demand-Driven Procurement

How to Apply Lean Thinking to Your
Supply Management Processes

Lean Demand-Driven Procurement

How to Apply Lean Thinking to Your Supply Management Processes

By
Paul Myerson

A PRODUCTIVITY PRESS BOOK

First edition published in 2019
by Routledge/Productivity Press
711 Third Avenue New York, NY 10017, USA
2 Park Square, Milton Park, Abingdon, Oxon OX14 4RN, UK

Printed on acid-free paper

International Standard Book Number-13: 978-1-138-33716-9 (Hardback)
International Standard Book Number-13: 978-0-429-44258-2 (eBook)

Library of Congress Cataloging-in-Publication Data

Names: Myerson, Paul, author.
Title: Lean demand-driven procurement : how to apply lean thinking to your supply management processes / Paul Myerson.
Description: 1 Edition. | New York : Taylor & Francis, [2019] | Includes bibliographical references and index.
Identifiers: LCCN 2018029987 (print) | LCCN 2018032109 (ebook) | ISBN 9780429442582 (e-Book) | ISBN 9781138337169 (hardback : alk. paper)
Subjects: LCSH: Industrial procurement--Management. | Business logistics. | Lean manufacturing.
Classification: LCC HD39.5 (ebook) | LCC HD39.5 .M94 2019 (print) | DDC 658.7--dc23
LC record available at https://lccn.loc.gov/2018029987

Visit the Taylor & Francis Web site at
http://www.taylorandfrancis.com

"We cannot solve our problems with the same

thinking we used when we created them."

– Albert Einstein

Contents

About the Author...xvii

PART I   Lean Demand-Driven Procurement: Overview

Chapter 1   Introduction: Why You Need a Lean and Agile,
Demand-Driven Supply Management Process................. 3

Where to Look 4
A Lean and Agile Procurement Process Is Required..........5
Procurement Focus Areas (The Eight Wastes of Lean)......6
Applying Lean Thinking to Procurement................................8
Examples of Improvements with Lean Procurement........8
Lean Procurement is Demand-Driven 9
Lean and Technology Opportunity in Procurement.............11
Lean Procurement Strategy...12

Chapter 2   History and Importance of Procurement and
Purchasing in Adding Value to an Organization 15

Background 15
Why Purchasing Is Important..18
Integrated Supply Management (ISM) 19
Total Cost of Ownership..19
Demand-Driven Supply Chains (DDSC) Focus on Value 20
Supplier Relationship Management 22
Collaborating with Suppliers 22
Guiding Principles for SRM 25

Chapter 3   Supply Management Organization and Structure 27

Organizational Structure...27
Centralized Procurement 29
Decentralized Procurement 30

A New Operating Model for Procurement 31

   Organization..32

   Processes 32

      Sourcing Strategy 32

      Execution..32

      Ongoing Supplier and Customer Management............33

   Technology...33

   Performance Management 33

  People and Careers 34

   Certifications...35

      Education and Certifications Needed 35

Chapter 4   Procurement Strategy Development and Application 37

  Organizational and Supply Chain Strategy 37

   Mission Statement...37

      Company and Functional Objectives............................38

  Supply Chain Strategy for a Competitive Advantage............38

  Procurement Strategy 40

   Procurement Strategy—Best Practices 41

   Procurement Strategy—The Make or Buy Decision 42

   Procurement Strategy—Outsourcing 43

   Other Procurement Strategies...44

      Insourcing..44

      Near-Sourcing 44

      Vertical Integration..44

      Few or Many Suppliers...45

      Joint Ventures 45

      Virtual Companies 45

  Tailored Procurement Category Strategies 46

   Direct vs. Indirect Procurement......................................46

   Identifying Procurement Categories................................48

      A Best Practice Categorization Process 49

Chapter 5   Issues and Opportunities in Supply Management.........53

  The Global Supply Chain..53

  Growth of Globalization...54

   Global Supply Chain Strategy Development....................54

Supply Chain Integration and Collaboration 55
   Benefits to Integration and Collaboration........................ 56
   Internal Integration 56
      Sales and Operations Planning 58
   External Integration 59
      Supplier Collaboration 59
      Customer Collaboration 61
   The Internet and E-Commerce.......................................62
   Quality and Safety 63
   Other Challenges for the Procurement Executive 64
      Cost Reduction.. 64
      Digital Journey 64
      Supplier Relationships..65
      Skills Gap 65
      Outsourcing as a Strategy to Plug the Gap.......................65

Chapter 6 Lean Procurement.. 67

   Lean Purchasing 68
      JIT Purchasing Characteristics.................................... 68
      JIT and MRP Systems 70
         JIT and MRP Focus 71
         Lean (JIT) Purchasing and MRP Systems....................72
      Challenges in Implementing Lean Purchasing
      (and, More Broadly, Lean Procurement) 76
   Lean Procurement 78
      Procurement Technology and Lean 81
   The Eight Wastes..81
      Transportation Waste..81
      Inventory...81
      Motion 81
      Waiting...82
      Overproduction..82
      Over-Processing..82
      Defects 82
      Skills (or People Waste)..82
   Strategic Sourcing vs. Lean Sourcing............................... 84

PART II   Supply Management Processes

Chapter 7   Strategic Sourcing 89

Strategic Sourcing Processes 89
Lean Strategic Sourcing 94
    Seven Characteristics of Lean Strategic Sourcing 94
Lean Sourcing Journey 95
Lean Strategic Sourcing MRO–Case Study #1 96
    Challenge 96
    Approach 97
    Results 97
Sourcing as Strategy–Case Study #2 98
    Challenge 98
    Approach 98
    Results 99

Chapter 8   Procurement 101

The Procurement Process 101
    Step 1: Identify and Review Requirements 102
        Direct Procurement 102
        Indirect Procurement 103
    Step 2: Establish Specifications 103
    Step 3: Identify and Select Suppliers 104
        Vendor Evaluation 105
    Step 4: Determine the Right Price 106
        Negotiation 106
Key Metrics 107
Lean Procurement 109
    Core Principles of Lean Procurement 110
Procurement Technology 111
    Technology to Enhance Lean Procurement 112
Erskine Lean Review of Procurement–Case Study #1 115
    Challenge 115
    Approach 115
    Results 116
Scapa–Case Study #2 117
    Challenge 117

Approach...117
Results..117

Chapter 9 Purchasing 119

The Purchasing Process 119
Step 5: Issue Purchase Orders 119
Step 6: Follow-Up to Assure Correct Delivery 121
Step 7: Receive and Accept Goods.. 122
Step 8: Approve Invoice for Payment....................................... 122
Lean Purchasing 123
    Specify Value 123
    Value Stream... 124
    Flow.. 124
    Pull..125
    Seek Perfection 126
EPA Lean Review of Purchasing–Case Study #1................. 126
    Challenge 126
    Approach... 126
    Results..127
Creating a Lean Office–Case Study #2 127
    Challenge 127
    Approach... 128
    Results.. 128

Chapter 10 Material Requirements Planning (MRP) and
                Indirect Procurement 131

Materials Requirements Planning (MRP)..............................131
    MPS and MRP Calculations...132
        Lot-Sizing Techniques 134
Total Cost Minimized–How Much and When to Order...... 135
    Economic Order Quantity Model 135
        Basic EOQ Calculation..137
    Reorder Point (ROP) Models..138
        Fixed Quantity (Q) Model 138
        Safety Stock..139
        Fixed Period (P) Model 141
        Single Period Model..141

Lean and Material Requirements Planning............................142
Leaning Out MRO Inventory 143
    One-Piece-Flow and Layout 144
    5S: Workplace Organization 144
    Value Stream Mapping...145
    Standardized Work...145
    Just-in-Time 145
Gables Engineering Moves to a "Real" MRP
System–Case Study #1..146
    The Challenge..146
    Approach...146
    Results..146
Accurate Gauge Gains a Strategic Business
Advantage from MSC ControlPoint Inventory
Management–Case Study #2 147
    Challenge 147
    Approach...147
    Results..148

PART III   Tools and Techniques for a Leaner Supply Management Process

Chapter 11 Cost Management 151
Procurement Practices That Can Result in Annual Cost
Savings..151
Segment Major Purchasing Categories for Better Cost
Management..153
    Non-Critical Purchases.. 154
    Leveraging Purchases.. 154
    Strategic Purchases 155
    Bottleneck Purchases...155
Cost and Price Analysis...156
    Pricing Strategies 156
    Maximizing Customer Value..157
Negotiations 158
    Stages of Negotiation...159
    Effective and Efficient Negotiations 161

Global Energy Supplier Sees Major Increase in Price of
Parts–Case Study #1 162
    Challenge 162
    Approach..163
    Results..164
Win–Win Negotiation for a Manufacturer of Electronic
Components–Case Study #2 164
    Challenge 164
    Approach..164
    Results..165

Chapter 12 Contract and Performance Management and Ethics 167

Developing and Managing Contracts.......................................167
    Upstream or Pre-Award Activities.....................................168
        Preparing the Business Case and Securing
        Management Approval..168
        Assembling the Project Team...169
        Developing a Contract Strategy 169
        Risk Assessment 169
        Developing a Contract Exit Strategy..............................171
        Developing a Contract Management Plan 171
        Drafting Specifications and Requirements....................171
        Establishing the Form of Contract 172
        Establishing the Pre-Qualification, Qualification,
        and Tendering Procedures...172
        Appraising Suppliers..173
        Drafting Tender (i.e. Call for Bids or RFP)
        Documents..174
        Evaluating Offers..174
        Negotiation...175
        Awarding the Contract...176
    Downstream or Post-Award Activities 177
        Changes within the Contract 177
        Service Delivery Management 177
        Relationship Management 178
        Contract Administration 178
        Assessment of Risk...179

Purchasing Organization's Performance and
Effectiveness Review...179
Contract Closure...180
Ethics in Procurement, Including Contract Management 181
Codes of Conduct 182
Ethical Concepts, Principles, and Risks 182

Chapter 13 e-Procurement and Other Supply Management
Technologies 183

The Procurement Process and Technology...........................183
Automation of Procurement Documents and
Processes 183
Procurement Technology 186
Source to Pay Example...187
Standalone Procurement Solutions....................................187
Lean Procurement and Technology Case Studies...............189
Enabling Online Supplier Collaboration at Toshiba
Semiconductor Company–Case Study #1 189
Challenge...189
Approach 189
Results... 190
Clariant: Increasing Interenterprise Productivity and
Extending Its SAP Software Investment
Value–Case Study #2 190
Challenge... 190
Approach 190
Results... 190
New Purchase-to-Pay System Allows Smarter
Processes at Atea–Case Study #3 191
Challenge...191
Approach 191
Results...192

Chapter 14 Procurement Analysis, Tools, and Techniques 193

Data Analytics...193
Categories of Data Analytics...193
Analytics Applications in Procurement 194
Identifying Data Gaps 196
Focus on Category Management 197

Strategic Procurement Tools and Techniques 198
    Spend Analysis 198
    Collaborative Procurement 198
    Procurement Strategy and Plan 199
    Category Management 199
    Supplier Relationship Management (SRM)...................200
        Supplier Preferencing 201
    Supply Chain Value Analysis 202
        Value Stream Mapping (VSM) 202
    Competition..203
    e-Procurement..203
    Standard Terms and Conditions of Contract 206
    Framework Contracts and Agreements.........................206
    Preferred Supplier Lists..207
    Sustainable Procurement...207
    Total Quality Management (TQM)................................207

PART IV   Lean Ahead

Chapter 15 Global Procurement and Its Impact on the Lean
              Supply Chain 211

Growth of Globalization..211
    Factors Influencing Globalization 212
    Reasons for a Company to Globalize 213
    Lean Global Procurement..215
Becton Dickinson: Lean Global Procurement Example 216
    Process Efficiency...217
    Supplier Relationship and Risk Management....................217
    Functional Capabilities and Culture.................................218
    Continuous Improvement Programs.................................218
Global Supply Chain Strategy Development 218
Global Supply Chain Risks and Challenges........................ 220
    Questions to Consider When Going Global....................221
    Key Global Supply Chain Challenges 222
Global Risk Management 222
    Potential Risk Identification and Impact........................ 223
    Sources of Risk 223

Internal Risks 223
External Risks 224
Supply Chain Disruptions 225
Risk Mitigation 226

Chapter 16 The Future of Lean Procurement 229

People 230
Process 232
Technology 233
Still a Long Way to Go for Procurement 233
The Potential Is Out There 233
Lean Ahead with Procurement 235

Appendix A: A Lean (Philosophy) for Life 237

References 245

Index 251

About the Author

Paul Myerson has been a successful change catalyst for a variety of clients and organizations of all sizes.

Paul has over 30 years' experience in Supply Chain strategies, systems and operations that have resulted in bottom-line improvements for companies such as General Electric, Unilever, and Church and Dwight (Arm & Hammer).

Paul holds an MBA in Physical Distribution from Temple University and a BS in Logistics from The Pennsylvania State University. He has an extensive background as a Supply Chain professional, consultant, teacher (currently Instructor, Management and Decision Sciences at Monmouth University), and author.

Mr. Myerson currently writes a column for *Inbound Logistics* magazine on the topic of "Lean Supply Chain," which can be found at http://www.inboundlogistics.com/cms/article-type/commentary/the-lean-supply-chain/, as well as a blog for *Industry Week* magazine at http://www.industryweek.com/author/Paul-Myerson. He is also the author of a Lean Supply Chain Simulation Training game and training package available at http://www.enna.com/lean_supplychain. Myerson's personal website is http://www.supplychainsmarts.com

Part I

Lean Demand-Driven Procurement: Overview

1

Introduction: Why You Need a Lean and Agile, Demand-Driven Supply Management Process

Lean thinking has expanded well beyond its origins in repetitive assembly line manufacturing to encompass process- and product-focused manufacturing. Recently, it has also been successfully applied to administrative, supply chain, and operations management functions in a variety of goods and services industries.

However, while there are many books, articles, and blogs written on the basics of the "supply" side of the supply chain (i.e. strategic sourcing, sourcing/procurement, and purchasing), there hasn't been much written on those areas from a Lean perspective. This is quite surprising, considering not only that supply chain costs (primarily procurement and transportation), can range from 50 to 70% of sales, resulting in what is known as the "profit-leverage" effect (measured by the increase in profit obtained by a decrease in purchase spend), but also help drive downstream quality, productivity, and efficiency.

Many companies tend to place an inordinate emphasis on the traditional focus of reducing material costs instead of taking the more holistic approach of the Lean philosophy of continuous process improvement. Applying Lean principles to procurement and purchasing processes can identify non-traditional sources of waste, in some cases creating a paradigm shift that results in additional benefits to the entire supply chain.

This book takes a unique approach, in that it covers a combination of basic "supply management" concepts and processes (i.e. strategic sourcing, procurement, and purchasing) described in an easy-to-understand format, from a Lean perspective, using various process improvement tools, methodologies, best practices, examples, and cases. It focuses on ways to identify waste on the supply side through improved processes and in some cases, technology.

For the sake of clarity, we will define "procurement" (used in this book interchangeably with "sourcing") as the activities involved in establishing fundamental requirements, activities such as market research and vendor evaluation, and negotiating contracts. In a broad sense, it also includes the purchasing activities required to order and receive goods.

"Purchasing," on the other hand, is the specific process involved in ordering goods such as the request, approval, and creation of purchase orders and the receipt of goods.

WHERE TO LOOK

If you were to ask someone who knew a bit about Lean thinking how they defined Lean procurement, they would probably say that it's about increasing productivity for procurement staff so they can spend more time on value-added activities rather than administration. While that is certainly true, in this book we will extend the view to how it connects and interacts with other processes, functions, suppliers, and customers, as today, procurement plays an important role in improving the flow of information and materials throughout the entire supply chain.

It is important to establish best practice Lean procurement functions that go beyond contract negotiation and establish crucial operational requirements, utilizing strategic sourcing activities such as market research and vendor evaluation and integration.

Inventory management and sourcing supply chain decisions are directly linked to a company's financial performance and can therefore affect a company's cashflow and profitability.

A procurement organization needs to consider:

- The prevention of production disruptions due to inventory or material shortages, while remaining flexible to meet changes in customer demand or cope with market volatility.
- The trade-offs of inventory carrying costs and customer service levels.
- Optimal buying quantities that consider the trade-offs of inventory carrying cost and volume discounts.
- Moving from reactive to proactive procurement operations.

A Lean and Agile Procurement Process Is Required

Furthermore, in today's global, dynamic economy, it is beneficial for companies to operate a supply chain, and supporting procurement process, that is both Lean and Agile. Using Lean and Agile in combination is known as having a hybrid supply chain strategy.

A hybrid supply chain strategy may be appropriate for a company attempting to become a "mass customizer"—producing progressively smaller batch sizes (sometimes as little as one item) specific to customers' sometimes unique needs.

A Lean supply chain focuses on adding value for customers, while identifying and eliminating waste—anything that doesn't add value for the customer. Being Agile and responsive, on the other hand, implies that your supply chain can handle unpredictability—and a constant stream of new, innovative products—with speed and flexibility.

An Agile strategy uses a wait-and-see approach to customer demand by not committing to the final product until actual demand becomes known (also referred to as postponement). For example, this might involve the subassembly of components into modules in a lower-cost process, with final assembly done close to the point of demand in order to localize the product.

An Agile supply chain must be responsive to actual demand, and capable of using information as a substitute (to some degree) for inventory through collaboration and integration with key customers and suppliers.

On some occasions, either an Agile or a Lean strategy might be appropriate for a supply chain. But many companies will probably face situations where a hybrid strategy is a better fit. If so, they need to carefully plan and execute the combined strategy with excellence, which is often easier said than done, because it involves a lot of moving parts. As in so many aspects of supply chain and operations management, there is more than one way to accomplish this goal.

One example of a company using a hybrid strategy in its supply chain is Zara, a Spanish fashion designer and retailer. Zara directly manufactures most of the products it designs and sells, and performs activities such as cutting, dyeing, labeling, and packaging in-house to gain economies of scale. A network of dedicated subcontractors performs other finishing operations that cannot be completed in-house.

As a result, Zara has a supply chain that is not only Agile and flexible, but incorporates many Lean characteristics into its processes.

Some semiconductor manufacturers incorporate a hybrid strategy using a flexible manufacturing and distribution model. Subcontractors perform distinct manufacturing processes at separate physical locations. This hybrid approach taps a virtual network of manufacturing partners and requires responsive, flexible, and information-driven sourcing, manufacturing, and distribution functions—in many ways, the opposite of Zara's strategy of shifting processes in-house.

Many organizations can find some form of hybrid supply chain that works well for them. In today's ever-changing, volatile, and competitive global economy, it may often be in a company's best interest to operate a supply chain that is both Lean and Agile (Myerson, 2014).

Procurement Focus Areas (The Eight Wastes of Lean)

In general, many Lean manufacturing tools and methodologies can be applied in all areas of the supply chain to improve product quality, reduce lead-time, and reduce working capital. Specifically, waste in procurement processes can also be identified and reduced in the same way as waste in manufacturing, creating both tremendous savings and process improvements.

Examples of waste or non-value-added activities in procurement and entire supply chain organizations can be found in all eight categories of waste (easily remembered by using the name "TIM WOODS"; Figure 1.1).

You can zero in on these opportunities in procurement by focusing on the eight wastes below:

- Transportation: Excess paperwork and transporting materials and component inventory around a facility more than would be otherwise needed.
- Inventory: Ordering inventory or services early or in excess due to poor visibility or inaccurate information in material requirements planning (MRP) systems, which in turn may be driven from inaccurate end item forecasts.
- Motion (or movement): Walking, bending, or searching. Includes manual inventory tracking and control, having internal material not directly located close to where it is needed.
- Waiting: Personnel, material, system, and tool waiting or delay. This includes employees waiting for deliveries, approvals, data, or correct materials and services to arrive. This also can include waiting for

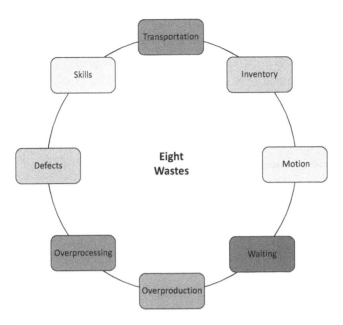

FIGURE 1.1
The Eight Wastes of Lean.

supplier performance measurement results, or the processing of purchase orders and contracts.

- **Overproduction:** Excess paperwork in process due to purchase order processing bottlenecks. Ordering materials without internal customer need, as well as having more work-in-process or finished goods inventory than necessary to meet demand adequately.
- **Over-processing:** This can often be found in developing quotations, purchase order processing, order acknowledgements, and invoicing. It can result in information being held up; for example: guidelines that require too many competitive bids, more approvals required than necessary to proceed with issuing purchase orders, etc.
- **Defects:** This waste refers not only to the quality of materials, but also to paperwork errors requiring rework and supplier errors. This also includes information from a material or service requester not efficiently received or processed (e.g., missing or wrong standards and no confirmation from supplier on purchase orders), or incorrect, or of poor quality.
- **Skills:** Staff spending too much time on administrative tasks rather than on continuous improvement, and thereby missing opportunities to increase the supply chain surplus through collaboration with

internal and external supply chain partners. This would include unsynchronized processes resulting from frequent changes to decisions already made, long lead-times, and wrong material delivery schedules. It can often be the result of the lack of, and proper support (training and otherwise) for, a true Lean culture that should permeate an organization.

APPLYING LEAN THINKING TO PROCUREMENT

Designing and implementing a Lean procurement process can significantly change the way a company does business.

For example, having a standardized process to source materials or parts, and using just-in-time (JIT) inventory policies can help with the balance sheet to minimize variability in the entire supply chain. Suppliers that are selected and assessed the same way will have the same reliable purchasing structure and can be more easily integrated into flexible production processes giving companies a competitive advantage.

Examples of Improvements with Lean Procurement

Organizations can use a variety of Lean tools to identify and reduce or eliminate waste, such as:

- Value stream mapping ("VSM") diagrams the flow of materials and information from customer to supplier through your organization separating value-added and non-value-added activities. A VSM of internal procurement and purchasing processes can create a future state that is both streamlined and improved.
- Quality at the source, based on the concept of performing quality checks at every stage of a process, can allow early supplier integration and problem-solving competence by expanding the viewpoint to the total cost of quality.
- One-piece-flow, or batch size reduction, can be created by establishing local suppliers to assist with flexible manufacturing and supply chain strategies for shorter inbound transportation distances and consistent deliveries to help smooth demand fluctuations.

Ultimately, companies expect their procurement and purchasing organizations to provide materials and assemblies on time, and to meet their demands. By applying these Lean principles to procurement and purchasing processes, businesses will experience multiple benefits throughout the supply chain.

For example, one consulting firm found the following results at various clients after applying Lean principles to their respective procurement processes:

Lead-time: Implementing inventory reporting and accuracy standards allowed for faster decision-making and ordering, thereby reducing lead-time for non-standard items by four hours (50%).

Optimizing an insurance company's claims process decreased average throughput time from nine business days to just under four business days (56%).

Quality: Optimizing and standardizing a B2B data exchange process decreased supplier-caused defects 98% over the entire process.

Lean materials requirements planning (MRP) solutions helped inventory reconciliation to be minimized to an annual activity, increasing inventory data quality.

Optimizing an insurance claims process decreased errors by 98% over the entire process.

Costs: Inventory accuracy improvements from a Lean MRP solution reduced inventory by $3.3 million (www.fourprinciples.ae, 2016).

LEAN PROCUREMENT IS DEMAND-DRIVEN

Traditional manufacturing and distribution was forecast-based and sales-driven, with product "pushed" through the supply chain to the market.

This can cause an unstable supply chain due to what is known as the "bullwhip effect" (Figure 1.2), where demand variability increases as one moves up the supply chain away from the retail customer, and small changes in consumer demand can result in large variations in orders placed upstream. Eventually, the network can face very large swings, as each organization in the supply chain seeks to solve the problem from its own perspective, leaving inventory shortages or excesses, and often resulting in increased cost and poorer service.

MANUFACTURER   WHOLESALE   RETAILER   CONSUMER

FIGURE 1.2
The Bullwhip Effect.

A demand-driven supply chain, on the other hand, is:

1. Driven by customer demand where products are "pulled" to market by customers: The companies in a supply chain work more closely together to sense and shape market demand by sharing information and collaborating with each other. By doing so, they achieve greater and more timely visibility into demand.
2. Flexible and responsive: Minimizing the effect of long material lead-times by adopting postponement strategies.
3. Efficient, with waste minimized in the procurement cycle: Without Lean procurement, buyers spend the much of their time on non-strategic processes like tracking down order statuses, purchase order entry, and maintaining individual spreadsheets for analysis. Often as a result, they miss opportunities for mutually beneficial supplier negotiations and process efficiencies.

To reach the goal of a Lean, demand-driven supply chain, one can focus on these characteristics and try to come up with improvements, from either the "demand side" or the "supply side."

On the demand side, companies try to get a better sense of actual market demand and in some cases, can attempt to shape it as well through various tools such as promotions, discounts, everyday low pricing, etc.

On the supply side, companies try to become more flexible and Agile to be able to use more of the actual demand, thus becoming less reliant on forecasts.

In this book, we will discuss ways for companies to integrate demand and supply initiatives and techniques into their procurement strategies.

LEAN AND TECHNOLOGY OPPORTUNITY IN PROCUREMENT

While cost reduction is always an area of focus for procurement along with an improved and more efficient process using Lean techniques, technology can help to enable a Lean procurement strategy to reap the full reward.

According to a 2016 Deloitte Global CPO Survey, a growing number of companies are adopting innovative procurement technologies to increase efficiency in these uncertain times.

Most procurement executives said they are investing heavily in innovative technology solutions. For example, 70% said they were investing in self-service portals, 45% said they were investing in cloud-based computing, 42% said they were investing in mobile technologies, and 16% were investing in social media technology.

Spend analysis is the largest focus for technology investments (38% of executives saying this area is most likely to receive investment in the survey), followed by contract management (37%), e-sourcing tools (30%), supplier relationship management technology (29%), and requisition-to-pay solutions (24%).

However, this must be tempered by the fact that the majority of procurement organizations do not have a clear digital strategy in place, with 60% of procurement executives stating that they hadn't yet formulated such a strategy.

Also, and surprisingly, while involvement in risk management and mitigation is a growing area of focus for procurement executives, only 25% are involved in it now.

This lack of focus in a digital strategy and a low level of risk management and mitigation involvement can result in significant disadvantages to an organization in today's volatile global supply chain (McAvoy, 2016).

Ultimately, Lean tools such as value stream mapping, 5S-workplace organization, visual workplace, kaizen, standard work and the use of technology are a means to an end. The focus should be on strategy, leadership, culture, and people first, before implementing the appropriate tools and technology.

LEAN PROCUREMENT STRATEGY

Strategic sourcing, as opposed to Lean procurement/sourcing, is a term that has been around since 1990s and is a systematic, data-driven approach to enhance a supply base and improve the overall value proposition. It focuses on analyzing spend, inventory data, holding costs, and personnel expenses to find opportunities for savings, and considers geopolitical and financial risks for suppliers based on product or service type. This is, in many cases, followed by supplier rationalization to obtain volume discounts and improve product and service delivery.

Strategic sourcing and Lean procurement philosophy don't necessarily conflict. In fact, a Lean procurement strategy requires a long-term commitment to combining elements of strategic sourcing with Lean principles.

Strategic sourcing is more of an initial step to identify long-term supply partners and coordinate purchasing efforts with operations and manufacturing. In a global supply market, conditions change, and companies need to regularly go to the market to identify, qualify, benchmark and select global suppliers with the greatest capability and competitiveness.

So, what might a Lean procurement strategy look like? At the very least, it should focus on the following objectives:

- Collaboration with key functional areas: Lean sourcing involves the creation of a strategy for future success through internal collaboration (for example, purchasing and operations working more closely together). This is accomplished by streamlining procurement operations and purchasing while at the same time improving financial performance.
- Identify and implement sourcing savings: Use Lean kaizen strategies to reduce costs in areas such as logistics management through consolidating shipments, improved inventory planning and management, and cost analysis. Lean sourcing relies on effective, sustainable cost reductions that don't reduce quality or reliability, balancing sourcing and operations requirements.

- Improve quality and reduce waste: Lean sourcing relies heavily on reducing waste in all forms, including wasted time, efforts, and capital. These issues can be addressed by improved compliance and process improvement and standardization.
- Achieve ongoing additional cost reduction and process improvement opportunities through collaboration with supply partners: Lean sourcing involves collaborating with suppliers to develop better contract terms, optimized transport costs, and a stronger and more effective supply network minimizing the chance for disruptions.

Lean procurement organizations need to understand and select suppliers based upon a multitude of factors that influence total enterprise cost, both tangible and intangible.

The elements of total enterprise cost include:

- Sourcing supply cost, quality, service, and risk factors.
- Tariffs, trade, and duties.
- Logistics cost, quality, service, and risk factors.

Organizations that have gone down the Lean procurement path have learned to combine aspects of Lean and strategic sourcing.

Lean factors to consider include:

- Supplier integration and demand management
- Reduce product complexity
- Synchronized processes
- Part standardization; SKU rationalization
- Reduced inventory
- "Pull" most products
- Joint product design
- Collaborative cost take-out

Strategic sourcing factors include:

- Company-wide approach
- Proactively managing supply risk
- Total cost of ownership/total cost request for quotes (RFQs)
- Global reach

In summary, Lean procurement provides opportunities for process improvements and savings through cost reduction, eliminating wasted time and efforts, and improved cost analysis, and can improve contract compliance and develop better, sustained partnerships with suppliers and other business partners (Burns and Reisman, 2005).

Now that we have a general understanding of what this book and Lean procurement are about, it is important for us to understand a bit about the history of procurement before delving into mechanics of the actual processes and how they can work in a Lean environment.

2

History and Importance of Procurement and Purchasing in Adding Value to an Organization

In historical terms, purchasing—referred to more commonly nowadays in a broader sense as procurement or sourcing—was thought of as the act of finding, acquiring, or buying goods, services or equipment from an external source. Today, it has gone from its origins as a transactional, clerical function which is highly focused on cost, to a more strategic sourcing or procurement view which is critical to an entire organization's profitability and gives them a competitive advantage in today's global economy.

BACKGROUND

In late 1890s the purchasing function didn't usually have its own department, except in some railroad organizations who designated it the "supplying department." Through the early 1900s purchasing was considered to be a clerical work (Figure 2.1).

During World War I, the Great Depression, and World War II purchasing function increased due to the importance (and scarcity) of raw materials, supplies, and services needed to keep the factories and mines operating.

During the 1950s and 1960s, purchasing continued to gain stature as the techniques for performing the function became more refined and as the number of trained professionals increased. However, purchasing agents were still basically order-placing clerical personnel serving in a staff support position.

FIGURE 2.1
History of Procurement.

In the late 1960s and early 1970s, purchasing personnel became more integrated with a materials system. As materials became a part of strategic planning, the importance of the purchasing department increased.

In the 1970s, the oil embargo and the shortage of almost all basic raw materials brought much of business world's focus to the purchasing arena.

The advent of just-in-time (JIT) purchasing techniques in the 1980s, with its emphasis on inventory control and supplier quality, quantity, timing, and dependability, put more competitive pressure on suppliers and made purchasing an important part of an organization's overall competitive strategy.

The 1990s brought us supply market globalization on a completely new scale. By the late 1990s, purchasing had begun its transition into strategic sourcing, looking at suppliers as partners, and long-term contracts become more common with strategic suppliers. This was the beginning of the strategic sourcing concept. Supply management's involvement in identifying and evaluating outsourcing options required the profession to become proficient in the management of complex third party services.

The paper-based supply chain organization started giving way to e-based approaches with an increase in the speed at which purchasing transactions could be completed, which was further accelerated by the growth of e-commerce.

In the 2000s, purchasing continued to shift its primary focus on cost to broader terms, hence the commonly used more strategic terms of procurement and sourcing.

Today, procurement professionals are critical to the success of organizations, having a significant impact on the bottom and top line, with some companies having "C-level" executives with titles such as "Chief Procurement Officer" (CPO).

Some of the most widely used developments today include:

- Spend analysis: Assessment of a company's current spend. (That is, what is bought where?)
- Low-cost country sourcing: Assessment of the supply market. (That is, who offers what?)
- Improvements in procurement technology: ERP systems, e-procurement, etc.
- Procurement outsourcing: Procurement and vendor management of indirect materials and services (commonly referred to as indirect procurement) are typically the most popular outsourced activity.

- Total cost of ownership: Total direct and indirect cost to provide goods or services.
- Advanced strategic sourcing: Development of a sourcing strategy that determines what to buy where when considering a specific demand and supply situation, while minimizing risk and costs.
- Data-mining and benchmarking: To improve negotiations with suppliers (products, service levels, prices, geographical coverage, etc.)
- Lean and Agile procurement: Implementation of improved supply processes that minimize waste and maximize service and flexibility Rowat, 2009).

WHY PURCHASING IS IMPORTANT

Purchased materials, components and services make up a great deal of the supply chain spend for most organizations. It is a very visible and important component of supply chain management.

This significant spend results in a "leveraging" effect, as any dollar saved on procurement contributes the same to the bottom line as a much larger and often unattainable increase in sales. This will vary based upon an individual company's profit margin.

Table 2.1 illustrates this through an example of a business that is evaluating two strategic options:

1. Reduce its supply chain costs by approximately 7.7% through more effective negotiations with a vendor; or
2. Increase sales by 25%, which will most assuredly also add to its sales and marketing costs.

TABLE 2.1

Supply Chain Leveraging Effect

	Current	Supply Chain Improvement Option	Sales Increase Option
Sales	$1,000,000	$1,000,000	$1,250,000
Cost of materials	$650,000 (65%)	$600,000 (60%)	$812,500 (65%)
Production costs	$150,000 (15%)	$150,000 (15%)	$187,500 (15%)
Fixed costs	$100,000 (10%)	$100,000 (10%)	$100,000 (8%)
Profit	$100,000 (10%)	$150,000 (15%)	$150,000 (15%)

We can see the leveraging effect of the supply chain, as the relatively small cost decrease contributes as much to the bottom line as the 25% sales increase (which is difficult to accomplish in any economy).

While the procurement cost reduction in this example has impressive results, we should keep in mind that "you can only get so much blood from a stone." That is where Lean techniques, which will be discussed later, can have a significant impact. Through Lean, a team-based form of continuous improvement which focuses on the identification and elimination of waste, we can create a "paradigm shift" that can make process (and cost) improvements that were not previously thought to be possible.

Besides the cost impact of improved procurement processes and techniques, supplier capabilities can add significant value to the final product as well.

INTEGRATED SUPPLY MANAGEMENT (ISM)

Today, organizations realize that they must work to effectively manage the domestic and international supply of products and services into, through, and out of their firms to customers. Ultimately, effectively integrated supply management results not only in lower costs, but also higher product quality, better customer service, and higher profits for the organization, their suppliers, and their distributors.

While companies are traditionally arranged into functions, it doesn't mean that they should operate in a silo. When they do, there is a tendency to sub-optimize whereby functions such as procurement will focus more on material cost, traffic focuses on minimizing transportation cost, manufacturing wants to minimize work-in-process inventory, sales will maximize service, etc. In an ISM environment, everyone communicates and collaborates with the same goal of maximizing customer service at the lowest possible cost.

TOTAL COST OF OWNERSHIP

Furthermore, today there is more of a focus on total cost of ownership or "TCO," which is the purchase price of an asset plus the costs of operation. When deciding among alternatives in a purchasing decision, buyers should look not only at an item's current purchase price, but also at its long-term price, which is its total cost of ownership. The item with the lower total cost of ownership typically adds more value in the long term.

Companies (and individuals) should consider total cost of ownership when purchasing assets and making investments in capital projects, using costs that are usually found separately on a company's financial statements. TCO analysis includes both the initial purchase price as well as all of the direct and indirect expenses.

One example of a business investment that requires thorough analysis of the total cost of ownership would be investment in computer systems. On top of the hardware purchase price, there are additional costs that might include software license fees, customization, installation, transition costs, employee training, security costs, disaster recovery planning, ongoing support, and future upgrades. These costs should be used to compare the advantages and disadvantages of purchasing the computer system, as well as its long-term benefit to the company.

DEMAND-DRIVEN SUPPLY CHAINS (DDSC) FOCUS ON VALUE

In Chapter 1, it was mentioned that in demand-driven supply chains (DDSC), which are truly focused on customer value and not just cost, supply-side improvement initiatives generally lessen reliance on the forecast by becoming more Agile with faster response times.

Consumer packaged goods (CPG) and high-tech industry have been leaders in DDSC. The types of initiatives taken in those industries on the supply side include:

- Shortening planning cycles and freezing short-term planning periods.
- Smaller batch sizes and more, quicker changeovers.
- Late stage differentiation/postponement.
- Demand prioritization.
- Upstream inventory visibility/supplier collaboration.
- Consumption-based pull planning.

In order to deploy the mechanisms listed above, there are some capabilities manufacturers need to have to become more demand-driven:

Multi-tier connectivity and collaboration: Information is critical when implementing a DDSC, whether it is downstream to distributors and retailers, upstream to contract manufacturers and suppliers, or both. Organizations need to coordinate the design, manufacturing and supply of complicated and long lead-time end products within their supply chain network, requiring visibility and collaboration to the extended supply network. CPG companies use such technology to access point-of-sale (POS) data from various retail customers to improve forecasts, while high-tech companies can use it to share demand and supply plans within the extended supply chain.

Data timeliness and granularity: To become demand-driven, companies need to collect and share data on demand and supply frequently and increase the detail of the data that they analyze. For example, supply-constrained high-tech manufacturers require visibility into finished goods in the distribution network and work-in-process inventory at plants, while CPG companies need visibility into SKU (stock keeping unit)-level detail on items in stores, and in distribution centers.

Agility and flexibility: Flexible manufacturing capabilities such as short changeover times, temporary labor and external capacity, and the ability to produce small batches cost-effectively make it easier to respond quickly to volatility in demand, a key to DDSC success. Agility is also important within the extended value chain.

Fast re-planning and what-if analysis: Demand volatility and same-day fulfillment require fast re-planning and simulation. Furthermore, these models are extending upstream and downstream to supply chain partners to accomplish multi-tier re-planning.

Alignment of metrics and incentives: Performance metrics and incentives of all supply chain participants should be aligned so that everyone achieves the targeted service at the lowest cost. A supply chain that is siloed internally (functionally) and externally is unlikely to achieve success. Best practice DDSC companies focus on the end-to-end process, and develop a balanced scorecard of metrics to achieve overall competitive advantage and to maximize supply chain surplus, which is the total profit shared by all the stages and intermediaries. The greater the supply chain surplus, the more successful the supply chain.

The demand-driven supply chain concept is relevant to all industries with many commonalities in the core information technology and operational capabilities needed. However, the road to get there can be different for each industry, with varying degrees of emphasis placed on demand-side and supply-side initiatives (Lipton, 2013).

SUPPLIER RELATIONSHIP MANAGEMENT

One particular strategy that is used to help ensure that purchased materials add value to the final customer is through what has become known as "supplier relationship management" (SRM). SRM is a strategy used to maximize interactions with third party organizations that supply goods and/or services to an organization by creating closer, more collaborative relationships with key suppliers to identify and obtain new value and reduce the risk of failure.

SRM has no set organizational structure as it can range from an individual relationship manager to an entire team or office, possibly with an executive sponsor.

An agreed upon governance model for managing SRM should be created, and include internal and supplier sponsors, representatives from various functions—for example, procurement, engineering, operations, quality, logistics, etc.—to review meeting schedules and conflict resolution procedures.

The types of meetings held in an SRM model include supplier summits, executive strategic meetings and operational reviews.

The true benefit of SRM comes from utilizing the ideas and expertise of key supply partners and converting much of it into product and service offerings for customers.

Collaborating with Suppliers

A 2014 Deloitte Global CPO (chief procurement officer) survey found levels of supplier collaboration and restructuring on the increase with 77%

of CPOs in some industries actively driving innovation with suppliers; yet the vast majority rated the effectiveness of their strategic supplier collaborations as poor or mixed.

Deloitte felt that there was a need to look beyond traditional procurement-centric perspectives on supplier management and look more closely at how relationships with key partners should be managed in a strategic and holistic manner. They recommended the following:

Traditional perspectives on supplier management are lacking a clear framework and alignment: In traditional supplier relationships, the interaction between various functions of a company and its suppliers tend to be more tactical and operational. These types of relationships tend to lack internal and external transparency.

A growing global supply network involves more complexity and risk which can result in a vulnerable network lacking global visibility.

The SRM approach requires company-wide commitments combined with a clearly defined process. This type of structured framework to manage supplier relationships reduces complexity, and increases transparency internally as well as externally.

Establish mutually-beneficial relationships with key suppliers: SRM establishes collaborative and relationship-building activities with critical supply partners in addition to supplier performance and contract management activities that add value to the company.

Benefits include reduced costs and efficiencies through long-term relationships, better supplier risk management and compliance, innovation, continuous improvement.

Create sustainable value with SRM processes (Figure 2.2): Organize around core processes of:

1. Supplier segmentation: Categorizing suppliers based on a defined set of criteria to concentrate on relatively few strategic suppliers.
2. SRM governance: Requires alignment within the organization, internal governance processes and assigned ownerships of supplier relationships.
3. Supplier performance management: Set-up and tracking of a few important mutually agreed upon operational measures. Any significant variances must be resolved by identifying root cause and corrective measures.

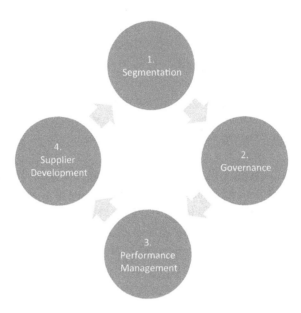

FIGURE 2.2
SRM Processes.

4. Supplier development: Establishment of value creation activities such as joint business development, input on improving current or new products, etc.

Ensure conformance with supplier audits to manage supply risks: Supplier audits allow for the identification of non-conformances that might negatively affect financial stability, compliance with legal requirements, quality and value, and the traceability of products and services.

Overcome challenges of establishing SRM: The process of establishing an SRM program in itself can be quite difficult. Deloitte recommended five key steps help organizations to overcome these challenges. They are:

1. Select the right partner: It is not just about strategic and financial fit. Think about other things such as compatibility of corporate culture, for example.
2. Align internally and externally: Common understanding of requirements and initiatives looking to the extended supply chain.
3. Establish mutually beneficial relationships: Strive for "win–win" types of negotiations, and train employees on conflict management, problem solving, and networking skills.

4. Select meaningful KPIs and share information: Identify mutually-defined strategic objectives, be specific on how those goals should be measured, and communicate in "real time" when possible.
5. Commit to change: Realize that there will be changes within each partner organization which require a mutual commitment.

Move from strategy to action: Generally, you can start internally by identifying and mobilizing key stakeholders, or conducting an external survey with key suppliers—these are known as "voice of the supplier" or "VoS" surveys—to support deployment and measure progress (Deloitte Consulting GmbH, 2015).

Despite the existence of SRM in many companies today, we still see the occurrence of supply failures such as Boeing's Dreamliner lithium battery issue which caused worldwide groundings of aircraft, and unlabeled horse meat finding its way into beef products in the UK, both examples of failure to control supply chain quality, and of poor supplier management.

Guiding Principles for SRM

So, what can we do to avoid these types of disasters? Atkinson (www. fourpillars.co, 2012) suggests some guiding principles for successful supplier relationship management below:

- Keep in mind that SRM is about the creation of post-contract value from key business relationships.
- Successful supplier relationships have an outcome that can be measured in value terms and is as much about driving up day-to-day operational performance as innovation and joint value creation, so it is important to focus on the basics.
- SRM requires a detailed analysis of the specific supplier relationship, before the strategy can be determined, and needs to be integrated with sourcing and category management processes. It is about aligning the whole enterprise around the task of managing a specific supplier based on a clearly-documented relationship strategy.
- Although it involves collaboration with strategic suppliers, it can still be adversarial (i.e. not necessarily "win–win"), as well as rigorous and process-focused. However, contracts must be structured to ensure each party enthusiastically implements the agreement.

- To get started in an SRM program, it is best to implement a small number of SRM pilot projects successfully, rather than attempt a full implementation, as resources may spread too thinly, resulting in failure.

According to Atkinson "organizations that deploy SRM successfully report additional value benefits of 2% of total spend, right through to 40%+ from specific key relationships."

In order to leverage the potential value that the procurement function offers a company, there has to be a strategic and organizational fit with the rest of the company which will be covered in the next chapter.

3

Supply Management Organization and Structure

The procurement function is critical to the success of a company with a goal of sourcing the best quality items, at the best price, at the right delivery time allowing manufacturing to produce and ship quality items to the customer.

ORGANIZATIONAL STRUCTURE

If the procurement organization is structured poorly, it can lead to higher costs for materials and poor quality of finished goods, negatively impacting customer satisfaction.

In the case of smaller businesses, the purchasing process may be simple, but it still must operate efficiently and effectively. A small business may only have one purchasing professional, but they will usually have a personal relationship with vendors and act quickly when issues arise to make sure that materials arrive when they are required, in the proper condition, and at the correct price.

As a business grows, the need for a formal structure will then emerge. Formal structure allows the responsibilities for different functions and processes to be clearly allocated to different departments and employees. With this clarity of responsibility comes the authority to control. The design of the structure should aim to implement the organization's processes as efficiently and effectively as possible, and to facilitate the working relationships amongst its various functions. Ideally, it must balance the need for order as a command structure with the need for flexibility and promoting creativity.

The size and activities of the procurement function in a single business unit organization will depend on a number of factors, such as the size of the organization and the nature of its businesses. Obviously, in small- and medium-sized organizations where the supply staff consists of only one or two individuals, the staff is expected to be flexible in terms of their capabilities and skills. In fact, in small companies, it is not unusual to see procurement responsibilities shared by a variety of individuals for whom procurement may even be a secondary responsibility.

The idea emerged of assigning a professional the responsibility of procurement, and a separate function was created. Specialization will occur as the organization gets larger and can afford to hire additional procurement personnel. Figure 3.1 provides an example of a procurement organization in a typical medium-sized single business unit company staffed by procurement professionals with clearly defined responsibilities in four general areas of specialization: sourcing, materials management, administration, and supply research.

In recent years, procurement has undergone a transformation whereby organizations are adopting best practices for the purchase of raw materials, component and office supplies. This has caused a shift from an exclusive focus on cost to one that includes strategic considerations.

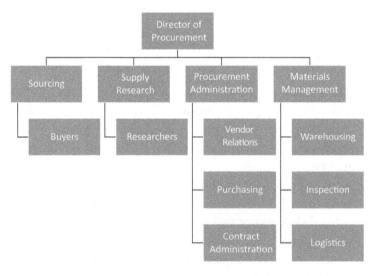

FIGURE 3.1
Procurement Department Organizational Structure.

At least at the executive level, the function is becoming more centralized as CPOs interact with and are accountable to finance and operations in a collaborative environment.

Globalization, compliance pressures, supply market risk, and procurement automation have simultaneously elevated the visibility of the procurement discipline within companies and increased supply management challenges. Many CPOs report to a director, or directly to the chief executive officer (CEO) of their company.

Centralized Procurement

In many cases, larger companies with multiple facilities and divisions utilize a centralized procurement structure with all the purchasing staff reporting to procurement executive to gain economies of scale and purchasing leverage. The centralized organization will consolidate the purchasing requirements for the entire company.

With a single procurement organization, the company can better control and leverage the total spend of the company when negotiating with vendors by committing to buy in larger volumes.

In larger organizations, centralized procurement organizations allow staff to specialize in one area, with less duplication and, potentially, a lower headcount. For example, a purchasing clerk could work with vendors who provide steel products only; on the other hand, if they were in a smaller company, they would have to work with vendors from many industries.

Other advantages of centralized procurement may include:

- The services of an efficient, specialized and experienced purchase executive can be obtained.
- Economy in recording and systematic accounting of materials.
- Transportation costs can be reduced because bulk quantities of materials are purchased.
- Helps to minimize the investment on inventory.
- Centralized procurement avoids careless purchases, reduces duplication of efforts, and helps to maintain uniformity in purchasing policies.

Disadvantages of centralized procurement may include:

- High initial investment may have to be made in purchasing.
- Delay in receiving materials from the centralized store by other departments.
- In case of an emergency, materials cannot be purchased from local suppliers.
- Defective materials often cannot be replaced on a timely basis.
- May not be suitable if branches are at different geographical locations far from vendors.

Decentralized Procurement

Organizations with many locations often use a decentralized procurement model. Decentralized procurement refers to all departments and branches purchasing materials independently to fulfill their needs. In such a situation, there is no one manager who has the right to purchase materials for all departments and divisions.

This model can be successful where the culture of the organization is such that each location acts as its own profit center, or has a business that is different from other locations. For companies that have acquired businesses that may not be similar to their core business, the decentralized purchasing structure would be a better fit. Local procurement organizations often have closer ties to local vendors and can react quickly when required, versus a national vendor who may not be able to offer the same response.

Disadvantages of decentralized procurement may include:

- Organization loses the benefit of bulk purchasing.
- Local procurement staff may lack specialized knowledge.
- Chance of over- and under-purchasing of materials and more safety stock required.
- Greater chance of ineffective control of materials.
- Lack of proper cooperation and coordination among various departments.

Many companies try to utilize a mix of centralized and decentralized procurement, where, for example, facilities have the purchasing responsibility for certain critical production items, but the central purchasing organization has the task of purchasing non-critical items (Murray, 2016).

A NEW OPERATING MODEL FOR PROCUREMENT

According to a Booze & Company white paper (Houston and Hutchens, 2009), the average company leaves unrealized savings of 5–10% of its total spending on the table due to inherently flawed or incomplete procurement operating models.

There are many reasons for this, such as: they may not include the processes, tools, or resources needed to fully execute the desired sourcing strategy; they may not be properly connected to organizational decision-making and corporate planning processes; decision-making authority and accountability may not be clearly defined; or the IT systems that enable them may be fragmented.

To avoid these problems and deliver on purchasing's cost, quality, and service commitments, Booze & Company concluded that organizations must evaluate and design their procurement operating models along four fundamental dimensions: organization, processes, technology, and performance management (Figure 3.2).

While most procurement organizations are good at one or more of the operating model dimensions, very few have fully developed and aligned all four of them.

The concept is that by using this view companies can better see gaps in their current operating models and address each of the four dimensions.

FIGURE 3.2
Today's Procurement Operating Model.

Organization

While the question of whether procurement should be centralized or decentralized is important, an organization should first determine how to structure procurement's various roles in corporate, business unit and functional-level purchasing. There is a delicate balance between leveraging purchasing power with the need to have flexibility in business units, functions, and regions.

When specific business units or functions purchase complex, business-critical, non-standardized items, they themselves should conduct most of the sourcing and procurement activity, and central procurement can play a support role.

In the case of products or services that are less business-specific but still must be somewhat customized (e.g. maintenance, repair, and operational needs) corporate procurement can play a facilitating role on behalf of a wider variety of business units or functions.

For purely standardized purchases not critical to business success (e.g. travel, office supplies, and utilities), corporate procurement can completely manage the entire process.

Processes

Best practice procurement organizations have defined and disciplined processes at every level across the entire procurement life cycle. These processes fall into three general categories: sourcing strategy, execution, and ongoing supplier and customer management, all of which will be discussed in more detail later in the book.

Sourcing Strategy

Sourcing strategy processes can offer a lot of value to a company since they determine spending patterns, requirements for products and services, relationships with suppliers, and supporting contractual terms and internal policies.

Execution

Procurement execution processes, on the other hand, include activities such as requisitioning, purchase orders, goods receipts, and invoicing, and establish structured, easily understood and used systems and tools to streamline execution and manage compliance for end-users.

Procure-to-pay processes, the process of obtaining and managing the raw materials needed for manufacturing a product or providing a service, should be mined for value, as consolidating and streamlining them can reduce a company's total spending by 1–5%, yet many companies don't look too closely at the processes.

Ongoing Supplier and Customer Management

These days, ongoing supplier and customer management has moved to a more collaborative relationship mindset with companies working closer with vendors to satisfy both parties' needs. This type of relationship requires much more involvement from the perspective of procurement professionals to attain cost savings, service, quality, and innovation goals.

Technology

The objective in any approach to a procurement technology system is to enable purchasing transactions and give decision-makers at all levels relevant and actionable information in a predictable and accessible manner.

The reality is that many procurement systems today were built for financial reporting and budgeting purposes, and don't necessarily offer enough procurement performance data, or help to facilitate procurement transactions. However, these existing IT infrastructures can be used in combination with various add-on systems to help in this matter, such as web-based applications for easily integrating functions into the procurement system such as supplier portals and interfaces to manage the procurement process through purchase order and payment.

The result of this action can improve transaction accuracy, timeliness, and compliance to improve spending analyses supporting supply and demand management decisions.

Performance Management

A best practice performance management process should look at both cost savings and value-added activities generated by procurement programs versus specific objectives, and also help with goal setting, joint accountability, and continuous improvement.

Tools such as procurement dashboards, budget data, and continuing assessment against global benchmarks can help measure, set, and refine realistic and reachable performance goals.

The right procurement model can result in cost reduction, the ability to better focus resources, enhance value from supplier collaboration and innovation, and better capture contractual commitments (Booze & Company, 2009).

PEOPLE AND CAREERS

Of course, any organizational model is only as good as its people, which is especially important in the case of procurement, as its visibility is growing with chief procurement officers (CPOs) becoming increasingly important members of the boardroom. Not only does it involve reducing costs and reporting on any savings achieved, but it is responsible for other benefits such as:

- Negotiating multi-million dollar contracts.
- Enabling the introduction of innovative new processes.
- Managing major offshoring operations.

Despite the opportunities, there is a shortage of college graduates looking to enter the profession.

Salaries are competitive with other functions such as marketing, finance and human resources. Furthermore, board level appointments were up 33% in the USA and 15% in Europe in 2012. Another benefit in this field is the early exposure to senior-level stakeholders and performance tends to drive career progression.

Furthermore, procurement can involve a wide variety of different projects which may require analytics and rapid cost savings, while others may require a more hands-on approach. Types of projects in procurement can go from benchmarking to designing more effective supply chains.

One particularly appealing aspect about a career in procurement is the variety of sectors it can involve and the fact that it is outward-focused, requiring collaboration with colleagues from these various sectors.

To be successful, individuals should have strong presentation and analytical skills and be able communicate their ideas in a range of formats to many different types of audience (Allen, 2012).

Certifications

The requirements for procurement careers vary from company to company, but a bachelor's degree in business is typically a starting point—although this is not always required for an entry-level position, especially if one has a certification, as will be discussed shortly. The starting point is usually a position such as assistant buyer or purchasing clerk that can lead up the corporate ladder to purchasing manager, then director of purchasing and beyond.

Continuing education is important for advancement in all industries, especially if one wants to truly add value to an organization. Professional certification is increasingly valued, particularly for those new to the field. Seminars offered by professional societies are popular among purchasers, as are college courses in supply management.

Education and Certifications Needed

The requirements for purchasing managers vary from company to company, but a bachelor's degree can be a good way to get started in the field. Many universities today offer a major or minor in supply chain and logistics management, but even a more general bachelor's degree program in business or economics can provide you with the knowledge and skills needed to work in the purchasing field. The position of purchasing manager is usually attained by first gaining experience in lower-level positions, such as assistant buyer or purchasing clerk.

If one did not major in supply chain management, but has an interest or works in the field, a certificate can be beneficial to one's career. The leading certification used to be the certified purchasing manager (CPM) designation, which was offered by the Institute for Supply Management (ISM), but this is being replaced by the Certified Professional in Supply Management (CPSM) designation (www.ism.ws). You can gain the CPSM title after completing an accredited bachelor's degree program, three years of supply management experience, and a three-part examination.

The American Purchasing Society (www.american-purchasing.com) offers two additional designations: Certified Purchasing Professional

(CPP) and Certified Professional Purchasing Manager (CPPM). You can earn these designations after proving that you have sufficient education, professional experience, and ethical standards, and then passing the required examination.

A third organization, the American Production and Inventory Control Society (www.apics.org), offers both the Certified in Production and Inventory Management (CPIM) program, which confers the CPIM designation after completion of the program and a passing score on the examination, and the Certified Supply Chain Professional (CSCP) certification, which is awarded after sufficient educational and professional experience and a passing score on the exam.

If you are interested in working in procurement for a government agency, there are two designations offered by the Universal Public Procurement Certification Council (www.uppcc.org). These include the Certified Public Procurement Officer (CPPO) and Certified Professional Public Buyer (CPPB) designations, which are also awarded after sufficient educational and professional experience and a passing score on the exam.

Most of these certifications require work-related experience, a certain level of education, and successful completion of some type of exam (learn. org, 2014).

It is important to note that structure should always follow strategy, the topic of which is covered in the next chapter.

4

Procurement Strategy Development and Application

As purchased materials, components, and services make up a great deal of the supply chain spend for most organizations, resulting in the leverage effect discussed in the first chapter, it is a very visible and important component of supply chain management. Therefore, it is critical to spend considerable time on developing a strategy for your organization.

ORGANIZATIONAL AND SUPPLY CHAIN STRATEGY

If an organization can identify what adds value for their customers and deliver it successfully—while at the same time eliminating activities that don't add value for the customer, thus creating waste—they will have established a competitive advantage, which is the purpose of a strategic plan.

Mission Statement

In order to do so, you must first establish a broad mission statement, supported by specific objectives for your business. A mission statement is a company's purpose or "reason for being" and should guide the actions of the organization, lay out its overall goal, provide a path, and influence decision-making.

It does not have to be lengthy, but should be well thought out and touch on the following concepts:

- **Customers**: Who are our customers?
- **Products or services**: Major products or services.
- **Markets**: Where do we compete?
- **Technology**: What is our basic technology?
- **Future survival, growth, and profitability**: Our commitment towards economic objectives.
- **Philosophy**: The basic beliefs, core values, aspirations, and philosophical priorities of the firm.
- **Self-concept**: Identify the firm's major strengths and competitive advantages.
- **Public image**: What is our public image?
- **Concern for employees**: Our attitude toward employees.

Company and Functional Objectives

The mission is a broad statement, but this should then lead to specific objectives with measurable targets that a firm can use to evaluate the extent to which it achieves its mission.

In a typical medium- to large-size organization, individual functions/departments may have their own mission statements, but most will at least have goals and objectives that tie to the company's overall mission statement and objectives (see example in Table 4.1).

SUPPLY CHAIN STRATEGY FOR A COMPETITIVE ADVANTAGE

Historically, supply chain and logistics functions were viewed primarily as cost centers to be controlled. It is only in the past 20 years or so that it has become clear that it can be used for a competitive advantage as well.

To accomplish this, an organization should establish competitive priorities that their supply chain must have in order to satisfy internal and external customers. They should then link the selected competitive priorities to their supply chain and logistics processes.

TABLE 4.1

Sample Company and Supply Chain Mission Statements and Objectives

Company Mission Statement	• To manufacture and service an innovative, growing, and profitable worldwide electronic business that exceeds our customers' expectations
Company Objectives	• Growth in earnings per share averaging 8% or better per year • Return on employed capital of 20% or better • 25%+ of sales from products that are no more than four years old
Supply Chain Department Mission	• To collaborate with suppliers to develop innovative products from stable, effective, and efficient sources of supply
Supply Chain Department Objectives	• Supplier order fill rate of 95% • Supplier order fulfillment lead time of four days • Supplier on time delivery of 99%

Krajewski et al. suggest breaking an organization's competitive priorities into cost, quality, time, and flexibility capability groups.

Cost Strategy: Focuses on delivering a product or service to the customer at the lowest possible cost without sacrificing quality. Walmart has been the low-cost leader in retail by operating an efficient supply chain.

Time Strategy: This strategy can be in terms of speed of delivery, response time, or even product development time. Dell has been a prime example of a manufacturer that has excelled at response time by assembling, testing, and shipping computers in as little as a few days. FedEx is known for fast, on-time deliveries of small packages.

Quality Strategy: Consistent, high-quality goods or services require a reliable, safe supply chain to deliver on this promise. If Sony had an inferior supply chain with high damage levels, it wouldn't matter to the customer that their electronics are of the highest quality.

Flexibility Strategy: Can come in various forms such as volume, variety, and customization. Many of today's e-commerce businesses such as Amazon offer a great deal of flexibility in many of these categories (Krajewski et al., 2013).

In many cases, an organization may focus on more than one of the above strategies, and even when focusing on one, it does not mean that they will offer sub-par performance on the others; just not, perhaps, "best in class."

PROCUREMENT STRATEGY

As previously mentioned, in the past, procurement was more transactional in nature and therefore typically used a more tactical approach to sourcing. Purchasing decisions were primarily based on price and delivery times. In fact, procurement was not fully incorporating the corporate strategy in its buying decisions.

Today, procurement has taken a more strategic approach and needs to work more closely with the various silos that are present in each company. In "best practice" companies today, they try to find ways to provide more value to the company.

To achieve these types of goals, procurement must contribute to, and should be aligned with other functions, as well as overall corporate and business strategies (i.e. priorities and goals) of an organization.

This is impacted by the external environment, especially customer demand and stakeholder expectations, as well as internal resources and capabilities which provide the company with the ability to create value.

As mentioned earlier, in many organizations, the primary focus of the procurement organization is cost reduction, which perhaps should be one focus, if the company has a cost reduction strategy. However, in today's competitive world, where most companies don't only focus on cost as a strategy, there tends to be more focus on value creation while not ignoring cost and waste reduction. In that way, it can help with not only the bottom line, but the top line as well, through key performance indicators (KPIs) such as quality, response time, lead time, etc.

In general, moving towards Lean procurement will help you increase total value. While concepts like just-in-time (JIT) are Lean tools that focus on inventory—which is a waste, as will be covered in detail in Chapter 6: Lean Procurement—there are many other areas in procurement that can benefit by:

- Improving the procurement process itself as well as workflows, thereby reducing time and eliminating waste.
- Reducing/lowering costs while improving the quality of products and services.
- Improving the performance and responsiveness of suppliers.
- Increasing the focus on those activities that add value to the firm.
- Enhancing procurement's strategic rather than transactional focus.

Furthermore, the implementation of supply chain technologies (Chapter 13) can help make procurement more Lean by streamlining and automating procurement processes, including spend analysis, savings tracking, sourcing, contract management, and procure-to-pay to boost process efficiency. At the same time, technology can allow all business stakeholders to collaborate efficiently—internally and externally—and optimize savings opportunities.

Procurement Strategy—Best Practices

According to an AT Kearney Assessment of Procurement Excellence www.atkearney.com, 2011), value chains are bending so rapidly that procurement professionals are more important to business strategies than ever before.

In the early 1990s, procurement was primarily a back-office function—i.e. requisitions, bidding, order placement, receiving, and payment—and more recently has shifted its resources toward value-adding activities, with nearly three-quarters of staff members now devoted to strategic activities, with nearly two-thirds of procurement functions reporting to a C-level executive today.

In the study they identified 13 companies that demonstrate consistently high levels of procurement performance and are strategic contributors to their businesses.

They found seven characteristics that the leaders shared. They were:

1. **Align with the business**: Leaders understand that the procurement strategy must align with overall business goals. They engage with traditional functions such as transportation and engineering but also engage with R&D, marketing, finance, customer support, and legal.
2. **Contribute to the top and bottom lines**: They contribute to innovation, integrate suppliers into the new product development process, reduce time-to-market for new products, and create new business opportunities with suppliers, and are twice as likely to affect the bottom line by increasing the total value of purchased goods, collaborating with key suppliers, and improving working capital.
3. **Manage risk systematically**: Procurement leaders excel at managing risk by using tools such as risk impact analysis, financial risk management, and disaster-planning as ways to protect against unforeseen threats.

4. **Use supplier relationship management (SRM) consistently**: SRM, the process of strategically planning for, and managing, all interactions with third party organizations that supply goods and/or services to an organization to maximize the value of those interactions, is used more consistently, thus helping to prove that a structured process drives strategic value through improvements in innovation and growth, better managed risk, and improved supply chains.

5. **Tailor category strategies** (discussed later in this chapter): Leaders use more advanced methods to tailor their approaches to each situation.

6. **Adopt technology**: Leaders have more control over what they spend because they have technology that allows for more visibility into spending, standardized data, and are able to track and report spending by supplier and category. Also, most leaders are fully automated with real-time access to data, and are far ahead in adopting technology to support contract management and compliance.

7. **Win the "war for talent"**: Leaders are more forward-looking and aggressive in their approaches to recruiting and retaining top talent, such as establishing relationships with leading university supply chain programs, using online collaboration technologies, and offering part-time work and flexible hours.

Procurement Strategy—The Make or Buy Decision

One of the first decisions to make in the supply management process, at least strategically, is the question of "make or buy," which is the choice between internal production and external sources.

A simple break-even analysis can be used to quickly determine the cost implications of a make or buy decision in the following example:

If a firm can purchase equipment for in-house use for $500,000 and produce requested parts for $20 each (*assume there is no excess capacity on their current equipment*) or they can have a supplier produce and ship the part for $30 each, what would be the correct decision: make (assume with new equipment), or buy (i.e., outsource production)?

To arrive at the correct decision, a simple break-even point could easily be calculated as follows:

$$\$500,000 + \$20Q = \$30Q$$
$$\$500,000 = \$30Q - \$20Q$$
$$\$500,000 = \$10Q$$
$$50,000 = Q$$

As the breakeven point is 50,000 units, the answer is that it would be better for the firm to buy the part from a supplier if demand is less than 50,000 units, and purchase the necessary equipment to make the part if demand is greater than 50,000 units.

Procurement Strategy—Outsourcing

Many companies choose to outsource activities, resources, and entire business processes for a variety of reasons that include not being viewed as a core competency, high taxes, high energy costs, excessive government regulation, and high production or labor costs. Outsourcing can also sometimes involve transferring employees and assets from one firm to another. Logistics (especially distribution and transportation) is always a good candidate for outsourcing, as are manufacturing and assembly.

There are many benefits of outsourcing that include:

Focus on core activities: Outsourcing non-core activities helps to put the focus back on the core functions of the business, such as sales and marketing.

Cost savings: The lower cost of operation and labor makes it attractive to outsource.

Reduce capital expenditures: Outsourcing frees an organization from investments in technology, infrastructure, and people that make up the bulk of a back-end process' capital expenditure.

Increased flexibility: Outsourcing can improve an organization's reaction to fluctuations in customer demand and changes in technology.

There are also many disadvantages or risks to outsourcing such as:

Security risk: There is always the risk of losing sensitive data and the loss of confidentiality.

Loss of management control of business functions: You may no longer be able to control operations and deliverables of activities that you outsource.

Quality problems: The outsourcing provider may not have proper processes or may be inexperienced in working in an outsourcing relationship.

Loss of focus: The outsourcing provider may work with many other customers, and therefore may not give sufficient time and attention to your company. This may result in delays and inaccuracies in the work output.

Hidden costs and legal problems: This can occur if the outsourcing terms and conditions are not clearly defined.

Financial risks: Bankruptcy and financial loss cannot be controlled if the outsource partner is, or becomes, financially unstable.

Incompatible culture: The culture of the outsourcing provider and the location to which you outsource may eventually lead to poor communication and lower productivity.

The individual company will ultimately have to make the decision after determining the probability of both the risks and rewards of outsourcing.

Other Procurement Strategies

Insourcing

There is also an opposite, more recent trend in outsourcing and off shoring (the relocation by a company of a business process from one country to another) where companies are starting to perform tasks that were previously outsourced themselves and develop facilities back in their home locations, as the results of outsourcing were not exactly as expected (e.g. poor quality or low productivity). This is known as "insourcing."

Near-Sourcing

There has also been a recent trend for US companies called "near-sourcing," strategically placing some, or all, operations close to where their end-products are sold. An example of this occurred in 2011–2014 primarily a result of a spike in energy costs (i.e., transportation), making it more economical to produce closer to home, such as in the Caribbean or Mexico.

Vertical Integration

A concept similar to insourcing, but used to develop the ability to produce goods or service previously purchased, is known as "vertical integration." The integration can be forward, towards the customer, or backward, towards suppliers and can be a strategy to improve cost, quality, and inventory, but it requires capital, managerial skills, and adequate demand.

However, it is sometimes more effective for a company to rely on the expertise and economies of scale of other vendors rather than trying to become vertically integrated.

Few or Many Suppliers

Companies can choose to go with many suppliers or few suppliers for some materials or products as a supply chain strategy.

Many suppliers: This strategy is used for commodity products in many cases where price is the driving decision factor and suppliers compete with one another.

Few suppliers: In this strategy, the buyer establishes a longer-term relationship with fewer suppliers. The goal is to create value through economies of scale and learning curve improvements. Suppliers are more willing to participate in just-in-time programs (JIT: a strategy to reduce in-process inventory and associated carrying costs which will be discussed later in the Lean chapter of the book, Chapter 6) and contribute design and technological expertise. The cost of changing suppliers in this strategy is high as you tend to have "all your eggs in one basket" and may have invested heavily in this relationship as a result.

Joint Ventures

Joint ventures are formal collaborations between two companies to reduce risk, enhance skills, or reduce costs, or a combination of all three. A business entity is created by the two companies and typically has shared ownership, shared returns and risks, and shared governance.

An example that ended in 2011 was a 50/50 joint venture between Johnson & Johnson and Merck handling the OTC product lines Pepcid, Mylanta, and Mylicon.

Virtual Companies

Virtual companies rely on a variety of supplier relationships to provide services when needed. They usually have very efficient performance, low capital investment, flexibility, and speed. An example of this is Vizio, a company that became the largest-selling brand of LCD television in the US in 2010, with only around 200 employees at the time. They used contract manufacturing and creative distribution with the result that a relatively low-cost generic TV could be produced with minimal need for employees or capital.

TAILORED PROCUREMENT CATEGORY STRATEGIES

A supply strategy is a proactive plan for acquiring and managing a group of goods or services. It outlines how the enterprise intends to ensure cost-effective, responsive, reliable, and high-quality supplies to meet current and future needs. It should be developed before there is a requirement.

Best commercial sourcing practice entails the development of supply strategies for all key goods and services prior to actual procurement.

Supply strategies should be tailored to varying characteristics of purchases, including the characteristics of the product, its importance and technology, supplier preferences and power, the strategic importance of the purchase, the buying power of the purchaser, and the cultures of the buyer and the supplier.

Best practices today involve analyzing spending, segmenting it into major commodity groups based on their value to the enterprise and their vulnerability, and prioritizing them for initial purchasing and supply management efforts. This starts with identifying direct versus indirect spend categories.

Direct vs. Indirect Procurement

When discussing requirements, especially as applied to goods manufacturing and distribution, it should be made clear that procurement activities are often split into two categories (direct and indirect), depending upon the consumption purposes of the acquired goods and services (Table 4.2).

The first category, direct, is production-related procurement, and the second is indirect, which is non-production-related procurement.

Direct procurement is generally referred to in manufacturing settings only. It encompasses all items that are part of finished products, such as raw material, components, and parts. Direct procurement, which is a major focus in supply chain management, directly affects the production

TABLE 4.2

Direct vs. Indirect Procurement

		Types		
		Direct Procurement	**Indirect Procurement**	
		Raw Material and Production Goods	**Maintenance, Repair and Operating Supplies**	**Capital Goods and Services**
Features	**Quantity**	Large	Low	Low
	Frequency	High	Relatively high	Low
	Value	Industry specific	Low	High
	Nature	Operational	Tactical	Strategic
	Examples	Resin in plastics industry	Lubricants, spare parts	Resin and plastic product storage facilities

process of manufacturing firms. It also occurs in retail where "direct spend" may refer to what is spent on the merchandise being resold.

In the case of retail, direct procurement items are managed in "categories" which is a retailing and purchasing concept in which a group of products purchased by a business organization or sold by a retailer are broken down into groups of similar or related products, known as product categories (examples of grocery categories might be: laundry detergent and toothpaste).

In contrast, indirect procurement activities concern "operating resources" that a company purchases to enable its operations (i.e. maintenance, repair, and operating or MRO inventory, which are maintenance supplies, spare parts, and consumables used in the production process, as well as capital spent on plant and equipment). It comprises a wide variety of goods and services, from standardized low-value items, like office supplies and machine lubricants, to complex and costly products and services, like heavy equipment and consulting services.

The source for requirements can come from materials requirements planning (MRP) systems via planners and purchase requisitions from other users in the organization. A purchase or material requisition is a document generated by an organization to notify the purchasing department of items it needs to order, the quantity, and the time frame that will be given in the future.

During this step, purchasing will review the paperwork for proper approvals, check material specifications, verify the quantity, unit of measure, delivery date and place, and review all supplemental information.

Identifying Procurement Categories

A procurement category (direct or indirect) can be defined at any level above a single procurement. To have a truly efficient procurement process, it is important to segment your buy into categories, as they can improve procurement processes and increase productivity. The categories will vary according to the size and type of organization and the supply market.

Procurement categories allow you to:

- Develop targeted strategies for the best way to procure similar goods/ services.
- See the procurement spend across your organization.
- Generate large discounts.
- Establish aggregated supply processes to cover a category with many transactions.

The procurement categories identified should be broad enough to take advantage of market competition—in general, ten or so categories should be sufficient to cover a significant amount of your organization's spend. However, a category of goods or services may have sub-categories where there is a need for greater differentiation per below:

Category: a group of goods/services with common supply and demand drivers and suppliers.

Sub-category: a logical sub-grouping within a category with similar goods/services/market characteristics.

The process for identifying categories involves mapping and ranking an organization/business unit's spend data. Mapping and identifying procurement spend categories should be done by employees with knowledge and insight of the spend and procurement activities of the organization.

Furthermore, procurement categories can change over time. For example, memory sticks probably would be categorized under stationery, as they are currently supplied at a competitive price by general stationers. In the past, they were only procured from IT-oriented suppliers.

A Best Practice Categorization Process

The categorization process occurs in coordination with the organization's procurement strategy. The steps to defining procurement categories are:

Step 1: Locate appropriate spend data: Spend data should be detailed enough to identify individual procurement activities. A year of accounts payable data should cover different patterns of spend (seasonal or otherwise) that may occur at particular times of the year. Other sources of data may include information from contracts, business unit inputs, budgetary processes or suppliers who are managing a contract for a category of goods or services.

Data sourcing and analysis should be carried out by people with specific skills and expertise. One reason for this is that in some cases, as transactions may not be described in financial data, it may be necessary to investigate further to categorize appropriately.

Step 2: Remove non-supplier line items: This would include any non-supplier items found in accounts payable data such as wages, balance transfers and any spend that is not covered by the organization's procurement policy.

Step 3: Group spend data into categories: Analyze data at the transactional level and group items together on the basis of like spend. This might include considering similarity of use, suppliers, and characteristics. "One-off" transactions that are unique may not be easily grouped, and may be put in their own category.

Besides traditional categories shown in Table 4.2, others may include energy, commercial and professional services, catering services, construction and engineering, facilities, financial services, IT and telecoms, logistics/freight, marketing/marketing services, outsourced services, and travel, to name a few.

Step 4: Are sub-categories beneficial?: Sub-categories allow you to further group similar goods and services so that you can develop targeted strategies that apply across the group, as opposed to developing a strategy for individual procurement activities.

Step 5: Group procurements into sub-categories where it is helpful: When creating sub-categories, base groupings on the criteria in Table 4.3.

Step 6: Perform a common sense check of categories and sub-categories: To make sure that categories and sub-categories are the optimal size and composition, you should ask yourself:

- Is there a statement describing the purpose/composition of each category and sub-category?
- Are categories and sub-categories sufficiently different in their purpose and composition?
- Are most procurement activities easily located into a category and sub-category (if needed), with the possible exception of unique "one-off" procurement events?
- Can you further aggregate procurements into larger categories that are still meaningful and manageable?
- Are the categories understandable to stakeholders?

If the answers indicate that more work is needed to refine and improve categories, you should continue to work on your categories to ensure they are useful and meaningful to your organization.

TABLE 4.3

Category and Sub-Category Criteria

	Intent of Level	Criteria to Consider
Category level	The similarity of goods/ services as suggested by their characteristics and use in the organization	Similar suppliers Similar use Similar characteristics/purpose Similar form (small transactional goods, services, construction, large single item procurements)
Sub-category level	An additional level that allows organizations to enhance value-for-money and efficiency of procurement outcomes	Similar supply market dynamics Similar impact of demand aggregation Similar indirect impacts Similar level of substitutability with other goods/services Similar criticality to core business (similar level takeover of customization)

Step 7: Document procurement categories and sub-categories: Include the categories in your organization's procurement planning process (State of Victoria, Australia, 2014).

One reason that strategies need to be living, breathing documents is that things (internally and externally) continually change, which is the topic of our next chapter on issues and opportunities in supply management.

5

Issues and Opportunities in Supply Management

There is a variety of factors that can be looked at as both challenges and opportunities in supply management for organizations. Major ones include the global supply chain, collaboration and integration, internet and e-commerce, sourcing strategies, and quality management. These factors can contribute to the bullwhip effect discussed in Chapter 1, and can have a negative impact on service, profitability and growth if not managed properly.

Organizations can ignore these factors at their own peril. Forward-looking companies address them head on, and in many cases, turn them from negatives to positives.

THE GLOBAL SUPPLY CHAIN

In the late 1980s a considerable number of companies began to integrate global sources into their core business, establishing global systems of supplier relationships and expanding their supply chains across national boundaries and into other continents around the globe.

The globalization of supply chain management in organizations had the goals of increasing their competitive advantage, adding value to the customer, and reducing costs through global sourcing.

In addition to sourcing globally, many companies sell globally and/or compete with other companies that sell globally.

Ultimately, global supply chain management is about sourcing, manufacturing, transporting, and distributing products outside of your native country. It ensures that customers get products and services that they need and want faster, of high quality, and more cost-effectively either locally or from around the world.

Thus, we can define global supply chains as worldwide networks of suppliers, manufacturers, warehouses, distribution centers and retailers through which raw materials are acquired, transformed, and delivered to customers.

GROWTH OF GLOBALIZATION

In recent years, we have seen a change in how firms organize their production into global supply chains where companies are increasingly outsourcing some of their activities to third parties and are locating parts of their supply chain outside their home country (known as "offshoring").

They are also increasingly partnering with other firms through strategic alliances and joint ventures, enabling not only large companies, but also smaller firms and suppliers, to become global. These types of global business strategies have allowed firms to specialize in "core" competencies to sustain their competitive advantage.

This is not just limited to outsourcing manufacturing and supply chain operations, but also includes business process outsourcing (BPO) and information technology (IT) services that are supplied from a large number of locations as well as other knowledge-intensive activities, such as research and development (R&D).

Global Supply Chain Strategy Development

Today, in most industries, it is necessary to develop a global view of your organization's operations to survive and thrive. However, many companies find it difficult making the transition from domestic to international operations, despite the fact that there have been significant improvements in transportation and technology over the past 25 years.

To be successful in the global economy, a company must have a supply chain strategy, part of which is a procurement strategy, as discussed in the previous chapter. This should include significant investments in enterprise resource planning (ERP) systems and other supply chain technology to prepare them to optimize global operations by linking systems across their businesses globally, helping them to better manage their global supply chains.

In general, organizational strategies must be supported by the supply chain, and in some cases result in supply chain segmentation based upon product lines, sales channels, etc.

It is no different when discussing a global supply chain. In general, an organization should have their global supply chain set up to maximize customer service at the lowest possible cost.

In Chapter 15, we will discuss the topic of global procurement strategy development in detail.

SUPPLY CHAIN INTEGRATION AND COLLABORATION

To help combat the negative effects of the bullwhip effect, "best practice" companies strive to integrate and collaborate with key customers and suppliers to gain visibility into their supply chain.

Supply chain integration refers to the degree to which the firm can strategically collaborate with their supply chain partners and collaboratively manage the intra- and inter-organization processes to achieve the effective and efficient flows of product and services, information, money and decisions (Figure 5.1). The objective of this integration is to provide the maximum value to the customer at low cost and high speed.

Integration is not the same as collaboration, as integration is the alignment and linking of business processes and includes various communication channels and connections within a supply network. Collaboration, on the other hand, is a relationship between supply chain partners that is developed over time. Integration is possible without collaboration, but it can be an enabler of collaboration.

In today's ultra-competitive environment with volatile demand and shorter and shorter lead times with an ever-increasing amount of customization, both internal and external collaboration as described below can mean the difference between success and failure.

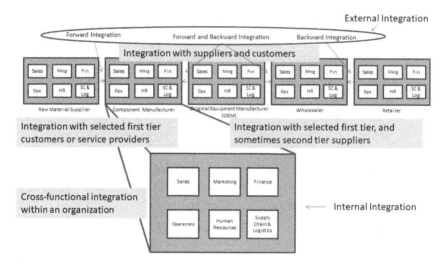

FIGURE 5.1
Major types of integration.

Benefits to Integration and Collaboration

Increased connectivity and collaboration between companies and their trading partners create many benefits for both suppliers and customers such as:

- Higher inventory turns.
- Lower fulfillment (transportation and warehousing) costs.
- Lower out-of-stock levels and improved customer service.
- Shorter lead times.
- Early identification of changes to demand and improved market intelligence.
- Visibility into customer demand and supplier performance.
- Earlier and faster decision-making (www.sap.com, 2007).

Internal Integration

Understanding the entire supply chain of an organization begins with understanding its internal processes (Figure 5.2) as an integrated firm presents a united front to customers, suppliers, and competitors.

As the saying goes, a chain is only as strong as its weakest link so it is critical that there are good communications, policies and procedures that

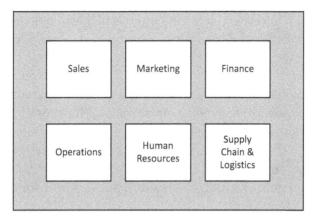

FIGURE 5.2
Internal integration.

link not only the internal supply chain processes with each other but also with the other major functions within the organization.

In general, purchasing, operations, and logistics are responsible for delivering the product to the customer. Purchasing is a gatekeeper for process inputs, operations transform raw materials into the final product, and logistics is responsible for physical transfer and delivery.

Internal supply chain integration is therefore a process of interaction and collaboration in which manufacturing, purchasing and logistics work together in a cooperative manner to arrive at mutually acceptable outcomes for their organization.

It is important to integrate communications and information systems so as to optimize their effectiveness and efficiency, and this can be achieved by structuring the organization and the design and implementation of information systems where non-value-adding activity is minimized, costs, lead-times, and functional silos are reduced, and service quality is improved.

Many organization's today use process improvement tools such as Lean and Six Sigma (and the combination of the two known as "Lean Six Sigma") to analyze existing organizational structures, eliminate non-value-adding activities, and implement new work structures so that the organization is optimally aligned.

An integrated enterprise resource planning (ERP) system is a key enabler of internal integration, often exposing remaining non-value-added activities in the organization, and allowing for better communication and collaboration through a common database.

In summary, internal integration needs more than a system and proper organization. It also needs:

Shared Goals: Refers to the extent to which the manager of each key function (purchasing, operations, and logistics) is familiar with the strategic goals of each of the other two focal functions.

Cooperation: Measured by the frequency of requests from other focal functions fulfilled by the members of each focal function.

Collaboration: Defined as the frequency at which a member of a key function actively works on issues with members from the other key functions.

Sales and Operations Planning

One popular tool for internal collaboration which is also used to some degree for integration with external processes is known as "Sales and Operations Planning (S&OP)." S&OP is an operational activity that generates an aggregate plan (i.e., for product or service families or classes) for the production process for a period of 2 to 18 months. The idea is to ensure that supply meets demand over that period, and to give management an idea as to material and other resource requirements that are required and when they are required, while keeping the total cost of operations of the organization to a minimum.

Sales and operations planning (S&OP) allows you to introduce collaborative information into the decision-making process, and when used as part of your collaborative efforts, enables better communications between cross-functional internal groups and trading partners, both customers and suppliers.

Globalization and outsourcing generate a lot of information that can impact an organization's decision-making process both internally and externally to the enterprise. As a result of this, a comprehensive S&OP process is even more important. The S&OP process makes sure that your business is continually managed to meet organizational strategies, goals, and commitments, despite ongoing changes in your environment.

This topic is so important that S&OP has recently been expanded using what is known as an integrated business planning (IBP) model. IBP is a business planning process that extends the principles of S&OP throughout the supply chain, product and customer portfolios, customer demand, and strategic planning, to deliver one seamless management process.

External Integration

On a broader basis, external or inter-organization integration (Figure 5.3) involves the sharing of product and service information and knowledge between organizations in a supply chain. Like internal integration, it also requires shared goals, cooperation, and collaboration to work successfully.

This enables all stages of the supply chain to take actions that are aligned and increase total supply chain surplus (i.e., the difference between revenue less the cost of producing and delivering the product to the customer).

It requires that each stage in the entire supply chain share information and take into account the effects of its actions on the other stages.

If the objectives of the different stages conflict with each other or information moving between stages is delayed or distorted, lack of coordination will result, leading to the bullwhip effect described earlier in Chapter 1.

Successful collaboration relies on the development of mutual trust between you and your partners, as well as the willingness to share information (electronically and manually) that can benefit all the members of your collaborative team. The goal is to treat all suppliers, outsourcing partners, customers, and service providers as an extension of your organization.

Supplier Collaboration

Some of the types of supplier collaboration include:

Vendor managed inventory (VMI): A family of business models in which the buyer of a product provides certain information to a supplier (vendor) of that product, and the supplier takes full responsibility for maintaining an agreed inventory of the material, usually at the buyer's consumption location (generally a plant, warehouse or store). Two VMI applications are:

1. **Kanban**: A signal-based replenishment process used in Lean or just-in-time (JIT) production that uses cards or other visual signals, such as a line on a wall, to signal the need for replenishment of an item.

   Using collaborative technologies, the *kanban* process allows customers to electronically issue the *kanban* replenishment signals to their suppliers who can then determine requirements and see exceptions.

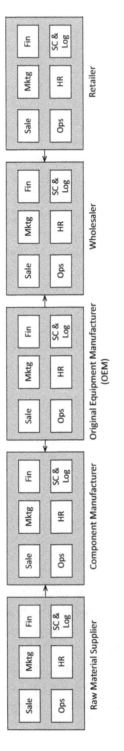

FIGURE 5.3
External integration.

2. **Dynamic replenishment**: This is a process whereby suppliers compare customer forecasts or production schedules with their own production plans to match supply and demand. It allows suppliers to adjust to changes in customer requirements or supply shortages.

Invoicing processes: Automating invoicing and related processes give the visibility to the vendor of the entire supply side including purchase orders, releases, supplier managed inventory, *kanbans*, and dynamic replenishment.

Outsourced manufacturer collaboration: When managing outsourced manufacturing relationships or contract manufacturers, you must shift your focus from owning and organizing assets to working collaboratively with partners.

The collaborative efforts should help simplify processes such as product development and reduce manufacturing costs and improve reaction to response to customer demand.

Any efforts to automate these processes should support information sharing, collaboration, and monitoring activities that are needed to effectively manage the relationship with a contract manufacturer.

Customer Collaboration

Customer collaboration involves receiving the demand signals and automatically replenishing the customer's inventory based upon actual demand. This is seen primarily in consumer products and other industries that have downstream distribution systems that extend to retailers.

This type of integration and collaborative effort enables manufacturers to shift from a "push" system to a demand "pull" supply chain, while combining both forecasts and actual customer demand.

Collaborative replenishment processes are more responsive than purely forecast-based processes, as they are driven largely by actual customer demand and also provide visibility in out-of-stock situations so that manufacturers and retailers can react more quickly. Examples of these are quick response (QR) and efficient consumer response (ECR) where manufacturers and retailers collaborate on forecasts and inventory replenishment through shared information and responsibility. Point of sale (POS) information can add visibility across the entire supply chain as well, when included in a collaborative replenishment process.

Another type of customer collaboration which focuses on forecasts is known as collaborative planning, forecasting, and replenishment (CPFR), which is a trademark of the voluntary inter-industry commerce standard association (VICS). It is an outgrowth from some of the earlier customer replenishment initiatives such as QR and ECR.

In general, CPFR is an attempt to reduce supply chain costs by promoting greater integration, visibility, and cooperation between trading partners' supply chains. It combines the intelligence of multiple trading partners in the planning and fulfillment of customer demand.

Figure 5.4 shows collaborative or vendor-managed inventory configurations in terms of the level of sophistication or complexity. Levels 1 and 2 have been implemented in various industries, and would include programs such as QR and ECR. Levels 3 and 4 are more advanced and would include CPFR-like programs.

THE INTERNET AND E-COMMERCE

E-commerce is the transaction or facilitation of a transaction in products or services using computer networks, such as the internet. As technology, e-commerce, and globalization become more intertwined, buyers and sellers are increasing their integration and collaboration, as well as the

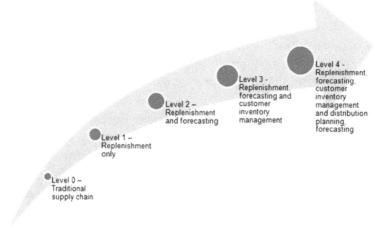

FIGURE 5.4
Types of collaborative or vendor-managed inventory in supply chains.

speed with which they conduct sales transactions. E-commerce has altered the processes, timing, and technology of business-to-business (B2B) and business-to-consumer (B2C) commerce. It has affected pricing, product availability, transportation patterns, and consumer behavior globally.

A major "best practice" in supply chain management is for organizations to work closely together, in long-term relationships that increase the competitive advantage of the supply chain as a whole.

Utilizing e-commerce can not only help every enterprise in the supply chain reduce their production costs, shorten demand response time, and time to market, but also can provide overall service, quality, and value for customers.

Benefits of e-commerce to the supply chain include:

- Lower cost.
- Better customer service.
- Quick comparison.
- Teamwork.
- Information sharing, convenience, and control.
- Enhancing techniques such as total quality management (TQM), JIT, etc.

Chapter 13 will delve further into the subject of e-procurement and other supply management technologies.

QUALITY AND SAFETY

The pressure on manufacturers to produce high-quality products that are safe is an increasing challenge. Product recall cases can damage a company's reputation and is expensive to its bottom line.

If you rely on overseas suppliers to determine that quality standards have been met, you may not know about problems until after orders arrive. One way to prevent that is to conduct quality inspections before the packaging leaves the country of origin. Another option is to train suppliers in how to comply with your quality standards, such as teaching them the quality control methodology you want them to use, and then holding them accountable for following it.

When suppliers fail to comply with quality, environmental, and safety standards, it can be detrimental to your company's relationships with customers. It is important to make sure suppliers understand both the standards and your expectations, and give them a reasonable period to come into compliance. Regular audits of major suppliers are critical and it may be worth hiring a third party auditor to verify that proper practices are being followed.

Consumers expect quality products, regardless of whether they are branded or private label, and hold retailers accountable for supplier quality. At the same time, compliance is increasing in complexity, as governments and consumer bodies have established greater regulatory measures and quality standards. Corporate social responsibility is no longer an option, as labor, environment, and product quality directly impact both brand image and the company's bottom line.

OTHER CHALLENGES FOR THE PROCUREMENT EXECUTIVE

Other challenges for procurement executives as pointed out in a Deloitte 2016 Global Chief Procurement Officer (CPO) study were:

Cost Reduction

The number one challenge is cost reduction. According to Deloitte's study, 74% of CPOs are citing cost reduction as a strong business priority for the upcoming 12 months. This is driven by a general trend of margin improvement and operating cost reduction, up 15% to almost 50%. Regardless of the tactics employed, CPOs have continued to deliver the numbers for their businesses, with almost 90% meeting or exceeding their saving plans.

Digital Journey

The importance of technology in procurement continues to grow at an increasing rate. Technology can drive efficiencies and streamline processes. It also results in fewer costly errors, enables better service quality, allows for faster decision-making, and lowers the administrative overhead associated with procurement. But perhaps most importantly, technology provides relevant data. The more you know, the better you can make decisions, control spend, and manage operations. In other words, investing in technology in procurement can contribute to cost reduction. Despite this importance, 60% of procurement departments lack a digital strategy. In conclusion, emerging technologies are presenting opportunities for improved value creation and better transactional efficiency.

Supplier Relationships

Another challenge for CPOs is improving their relationships with suppliers. The study from Deloitte mentions that CPOs are suffering from the impact of weak supplier relationships. Consequently, CPOs are focusing much more heavily on supplier collaboration and 29% of CPOs surveyed in the Deloitte study are planning to invest in Supplier Relationship Management (SRM) systems over the next 12 months.

Skills Gap

In the research, CPOs responded that their teams do not have the skills or capabilities to deliver their procurement strategy. In addition, investment in talent development has not yet been prioritized. There is even a decline in spend on training over the past years. In 2015, 29.5% of the surveyed CPOs spent less than 1% on training budgets. Also, just under half of CPOs felt that attracting talent has become even more difficult over the last 12 months. How can CPOs plug the skills gap?

Outsourcing as a Strategy to Plug the Gap

A trend identified by Deloitte is a sustained push toward outsourcing as a way of plugging the capability gap. There is a shift from outsourcing solely for lower-value tasks where the cost/value equation for internal resources was difficult to argue, to those considered more strategic and "core." The business case behind this holistic approach is clear—lowering the internal costs, synergies from technological set-up costs, improving supplier relationships and plugging the skills gap (Deloitte, 2016).

In today's world, when operating in a global economy with shorter product life-cycles and changing market demands, many leading-edge companies are now embarking on a Lean journey, where their supply strategy can support a company's Lean philosophy. This is covered in our next chapter.

6

Lean Procurement

As mentioned in Chapter 1, using Lean thinking principles creates opportunities in internal procurement and purchasing processes, and externally, downstream with customers, and upstream with suppliers.

Internally, there may be opportunities to improve and streamline procurement and supply management processes, as well as to implement practices to improve efficiencies and performance, eliminate wasteful activities, and reduce total cost.

Externally, Lean principles can involve better integration and collaboration with key customers to improve forecast accuracy, thus reducing costs and improving service levels, and with suppliers to ensure they meet established product and service performance requirements.

In many organizations, the primary focus of the procurement organization is cost reduction, which should perhaps be one of its focuses if the company has a cost reduction strategy. However, in today's competitive world, where most companies don't focus only on cost as a strategy, there tends to be more focus on value creation, while at the same time not ignoring cost and waste reduction.

In general, moving towards Lean procurement will help you increase total value. While concepts like just-in-time (JIT) are Lean tools that focus on inventory waste, there are also many other areas in procurement that can benefit by:

- Improving the procurement process itself as well as workflows, thereby reducing time and eliminating waste
- Reducing/lowering costs while improving the quality of products and services
- Improving the performance and responsiveness of suppliers

- Increasing the focus on those activities that add value to the firm
- Enhance procurement's strategic rather than transactional focus

Furthermore, the implementation of supply chain technologies can help make procurement Leaner by streamlining and automating all procurement processes.

Having a Lean, flexible sourcing strategy can not only reduce costs and increase efficiency but also serve as a competitive advantage to an organization to help increase the top line.

One of the oldest and most common applications of Lean is often found in the more transactional purchasing process, so that is where we will start the discussion on Lean procurement.

LEAN PURCHASING

As has been mentioned in Chapter 1, the terms purchasing, and procurement are frequently used interchangeably, but they have different meanings.

Procurement involves the process of selecting vendors, establishing payment terms, strategic vetting, selection, the negotiation of contracts, and actual purchasing of goods. Procurement is concerned with acquiring all of the goods and services, and is where purchasing is located.

Purchasing, on the other hand, is a subset of procurement and generally refers to the transactional aspect of buying goods or services. Purchasing often includes receiving and payment activities.

Lean thinking can be applied to the purchasing function, as its core concepts have had a significant effect on profitability in almost all industrial settings. The key Lean principles which focus on people, efficiency, and the elimination of waste have a direct effect on the purchasing function.

JIT Purchasing Characteristics

To be able to maintain low inventory levels, it is critical that replenishment lead times be as short as possible. A Lean purchasing philosophy attempts to reduce lead times for order completion.

A comparison between traditional and Lean purchasing approaches is shown in Table 6.1.

TABLE 6.1

Traditional vs. Lean JIT Purchasing

	Traditional Purchasing	**JIT Purchasing**
Order quantities	Based on trade-offs between ordering and carrying costs	Based on small lot sizes for production
Delivery schedules	Infrequent, primarily because of high ordering costs involved	Frequent because of small lot sizes and low ordering costs
Delivery windows	Relatively wide	Very narrow
Delivery lead times	Relatively long and relaxed	Stringent and reduced significantly
Parts quality	Responsibility of the quality function in the organization	Responsibility of the supplier
Supplier base	Fairly broad	Considerably smaller

Implementation of Lean purchasing assists the function in its major objectives of improving the quality of incoming materials and supplier delivery performance, and reducing lead times and the cost of materials. Some of the benefits are:

1. Reduced inventory levels: Lean purchasing ordering in smaller lot sizes facilitates reduction in inventory levels and related inventory holding costs.

   Toyota, having used a JIT philosophy since after the Second World War has been able to have inventory turns up to 60 or more times per year, compared to American auto industry rates of 5 to 8 times.

2. Improved lead time reliability: Compared to traditional purchasing approaches, delivery lead and reliability times under the Lean system are considerably shorter, which requires a more integrated partnership with key suppliers.

   This typically results in higher levels of customer service and lower safety stock requirements for the company, with accompanying reduced working capital requirements.

3. Scheduling flexibility: Lean requires scheduling flexibility, both internally and with suppliers, to reduce purchasing lead times and set-up times, offering unique competitive advantages to firms by making them capable of adapting to changes in the environment more quickly.

4. Improved quality and customer satisfaction: Lean purchasing results in improved quality and corresponding levels of higher customer

satisfaction by producing and purchasing in smaller quantities (affecting fewer items), and using various Lean techniques such as quality at the source (a concept in which each employee, department, and/or other party must ensure the quality of every product) internally and with vendors. Quality at the source itself utilizes Lean techniques such as standardized work, self-checks, visual management, mistake-proofing, and continuous improvement. Good quality incoming materials also results in savings associated with less rework and scrap.

5. Reduced costs of parts: As relationships between suppliers and manufacturers become less transactional and more of a long-term partnership in a Lean system, the opportunities to conduct an extensive value analysis and focus on reducing the cost of parts purchased also increases.

   In fact, it's not uncommon for supplier costs to be reduced by over 10% when adopting a JIT system in cooperation with their customers.

6. Synergies with suppliers: A Lean purchasing program involves close technical cooperation between manufacturing and design engineers with suppliers. Due to smaller lot sizes and frequent delivery schedules, suppliers get quick feedback regarding any potential manufacturing or design problems and can make engineering changes take effect sooner because of the reduced inventory levels reducing supplier quality issues at the same time.

   As Lean purchasing reduces physical inventory levels, resulting in lower inventory holding cost, it can also reduce labor cost in store rooms, lower material handling, clerical and administrative costs, less manufacturing waste and reduced depreciation of handling and storage equipment resulting in a Leaner more profitable operation.

JIT and MRP Systems

Just-in-time (JIT) and material requirements planning (MRP) are different but complementary concepts used in material planning and control and both help organizations to reduce order costs and inventory-holding time, which increases a company's cashflow.

In general, MRP is a resource planning system that focuses on the future, and is time phased, while JIT, on the other hand, does not provide for much in the way of forward-thinking (i.e. it is reactive).

JIT systems are dynamically linked system (i.e. focused on the current, 'real' usage, where parts of the production system are 'connected' with the use of Kanban's), and hence better when applied for items with short lead times. MRP, which is not linked, tends to be better suited for longer lead time items.

JIT is one of the major tools (and really, philosophies) of Lean which is directed primarily at reducing flow times and inventory levels of material, components and information within a system as well as response times from suppliers and to customers based upon the "pull" of customer demand. It accomplishes this by receiving inventory only as it is needed in a process based upon actual and forecast demand as opposed to more traditional systems which "push" inventory downstream based purely upon forecasts, typically in large lot sizes.

An organization driven by a Lean philosophy can improve profits and return on investment by reducing inventory levels, reducing variability, improving product quality, reducing production and delivery lead times, and reducing setup costs.

As we know, the cost of raw materials has traditionally been a serious concern of top management as material cost as a proportion of total cost of the end-product has risen sharply and is as high as 70–80% in some cases. Consequently, the role of the purchasing function in a manufacturing organization has become increasingly important.

JIT and MRP Focus

The function of purchasing is to provide a firm with component parts and raw materials at the right place, right time, right price, and in the right quantity.

A JIT system focuses on reducing both raw materials and work-in-process inventories, and requires that the right materials are provided to work stations at the right time. As materials are made available as needed in JIT, inventory shrinkage and redundant functions, including inspections, are reduced. Although inventory and supplies are kept at a minimum, the reliability of materials' availability is increased.

MRP also reduces the work in process (WIP) inventory, while eliminating material shortages by increasing the reliability of materials' availability (described in more detail a little later in this chapter).

Both JIT and MRP enable companies to plan for the long term, which enables a manufacturer to plan labor and facility use more effectively. Both systems also reduce lead-times and past-due orders.

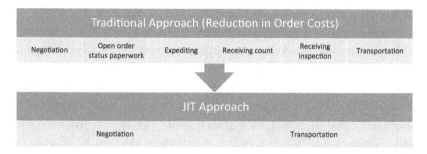

FIGURE 6.1
JIT vs. Traditional Purchasing.

A comparison of critical elements associated with Lean purchasing using JIT (sometimes with MRP) tools and traditional purchasing approaches is shown below in Figure 6.1.

One of the most crucial elements of the JIT system is small lot sizes. Traditionally, long and infrequent production runs, often due to having long changeovers and long lead times, have been considered beneficial for the overall productivity of a manufacturing organization. However, long production runs usually lead to high levels of raw material and finished goods inventories, one of the major wastes identified in Chapter 1.

Under traditional purchasing practices, the lead time is made up of the following components: paperwork lead time, manufacturing time for supplier, transportation lead time, and time spent on receiving and inspection.

Lean (JIT) Purchasing and MRP Systems

MRP has been around since the 1960s and was created by Joseph Orlicky of IBM as a concept of planning and time-phasing the procurement of parts and materials (dependent demand) tied to the forecast (independent demand) requirements from the master production schedule. It was the first use of computers to generate the supply orders, which can be quite a task, as many finished goods items can be made from hundreds, if not thousands, of parts, components, sub-assemblies, and raw materials. This was great for large manufacturing companies, saving a lot of time spent on manual order point systems. MRP was developed at a time when most companies used a demand "push" mentality, well before today's customers began demanding shorter lead times and smaller quantities.

Lean-type thinking became prevalent in the 1980s and focused operational management on timing production rates to actual market consumption. It uses replenishment signals known as "kanbans" that summarize customer demand up the supply chain (known as a demand "pull" system). Lean processes can have trouble dealing with extreme variability and can be difficult to use in mixed-mode manufacturing environments with resources shared across multiple products with unique demand rates. Lean can also lack visibility into the actual flow of materials through the supply chain, especially if it is focused only on the manufacturing operation.

In general, typical thinking on MRP versus JIT is that MRP is usually best for companies with many product options, frequent engineering changes, and a variable product system, and JIT is best used in environments with fewer product options, engineering and product mix changes, and less variability in demand levels.

The reason for this type of thinking is that MRP and Lean view inventory a little differently. MRP typically uses finished goods inventory to meet future customer orders, while Lean attempts to produce as needed, "just-in-time," meaning producing to order, not to stock.

Not surprisingly, MRP and Lean also look at the production process differently. Companies using MRP try to steer clear, to some degree, of small lots of a finished product because of cost inefficiencies (i.e. they don't have Lean processes). Manufacturers using Lean concepts, however, are more open to small order batches, as they have minimal machine set-up times.

In a white paper entitled "Lean Finds a Friend in Demand Driven MRP," Ptak and Smith (2012) found that MRP and Lean can indeed work together, even though each has its own objectives.

MRP objective: Visibility of the total requirements and status picture across the enterprise.

Lean objective: Align efforts and resources as close as possible to actual demand.

Both also have weaknesses:

- Lean tends to rely on replenishment kanbans that aren't connected (or visible) to the plant, or the enterprise and supply chain level.
- MRP, as it uses complex rules for demand, and supply orders can impede flow.

They suggest that users should have the ability to define where to place critical "decoupling points" that dampen variability, compress lead times, and minimize working capital. It then uses priority signals to launch and manage the replenishment of these positions using sales orders instead of forecast orders.

When combining the two objectives of visibility and alignment, both of which are conducive to flow, MRP software companies and users can find common ground with Lean manufacturing proponents. Before that, there are a few ways that MRP software needs to change.

An article entitled "Three Ways Manufacturing Software Can Adjust to Lean Principles" (www.shmula.com, 2012) described how

> proponents of MRP software believe that today's complex manufacturing challenges require formal planning tools to get an accurate picture of the production requirements. Lean advocates, on the other hand, argue that these planning tools actually get in the way of accurate planning because they're too slow and transaction-intensive to pace to actual consumption, or adjust to demand fluctuations.

The article

> described three main ways that manufacturing software can evolve to adapt to the demands of Lean manufacturing. Each way focuses on bringing Lean principles front and center of manufacturing software packages.
>
> 1. **Make Value Stream Mapping a Core Software Component** - ... Modeling how information and materials flow through a shop floor will allow manufacturers to more easily identify production bottlenecks.
> 2. **Monitor Cycle Times Intensely** - The most important metric to know in manufacturing is how long it takes for materials to arrive on the dock and to leave in a completed product. To improve cycle times, these times need to be monitored and tracked. A subset of monitoring and tracking cycle times is keeping track of production status [and production capacity].
> 3. **Locate Key Places to Add or Remove Inventory** - While there's ample functionality in manufacturing software for determining what to stock and how much to stock, there is little functionality to

help manufacturers figure out where to stock. Functionality that can tell a manufacturer where ... [within the plant, supply chain and distribution network to place stock buffers] ... will help them identify the best places to protect against volatility, which will ultimately help avoid product shortages.

Benton and Shin (1998) also discussed the integration of MRP and JIT (used synonymously with Lean in this and many cases). They hypothesized that this is a result of the evolution of the production planning system used to support JIT implementation in the U.S. (as well as implementing MRP in Japan) to take advantage of both systems and improve overall performance.

They felt that there were three factors that have contributed to this "hybrid" type manufacturing environment:

1. A multitude of operating problems found when implementing JIT manufacturing techniques.
2. Organizations' (and researchers') better understanding of the compatibility between the two systems.
3. The combination of MRP flexibility in long-term capacity planning and JIT's agility in daily production.

I think that, in totality, the above-mentioned papers point out the fact that MRP can be used in conjunction with Lean, but must be linked through manufacturing execution systems, as MRP is more suitable for planning. Rather than change MRP to be a Lean system, it must be connected (and configured) to what is actually going on in the shop in terms of Lean tools, such as lot size, lead time reductions, kanbans, etc.

JIT and MRP–Advantages of Working Together

Both JIT and MRP enable companies to plan for the short and long term, which enables a manufacturer to plan labor and facility use more effectively. Both systems also reduce lead-times and past-due orders and attempt to limit waste and lost time in the production process.

MRP is more agile when unexpected orders are received, or schedule adjustments are needed. This type of system depends on accurate data entry, tracking, and analysis. When utilized properly, advantages include reduced per unit cost of production, improved capacity allocation, and better response to changing market demand.

Employing MRP along with JIT and incorporating them into an advanced planning and scheduling (APS) system can also result in a more optimal process flow, where realistic contingency plans can be constructed by utilizing what-if scenarios. A manufacturing firm can, thus, always remain proactive, rather than reactive, when problematic situations develop.

Challenges in Implementing Lean Purchasing (and, More Broadly, Lean Procurement)

As attractive as the Lean philosophy in general, and specifically in purchasing, might initially seem, it can be quite difficult to implement.

Some of the common problems associated with implementing the Lean system are as follows:

1. Lack of cooperation from suppliers: Many U.S. firms involved with just-in-time manufacturing find that they have serious problems with some of their suppliers, as the suppliers see little incentive in adopting a JIT approach, when the primary benefits of the program go to the buyer.
2. Lack of top management support: Implementation of the Lean philosophy requires a cultural change in the organization.

    Lean cannot be implemented successfully without total support from top management, as an estimated 50%+ of Lean initiatives in U.S. manufacturing firms have failed, and in many cases, firms did not receive total support from top management in their efforts to implement the just-in-time manufacturing system.
3. Lack of employee readiness and support: Many firms lack support from their employees; as a result, in many cases, of lack of training, as well as the lack of management support mentioned previously.

    In many cases, the lack of employee support can be due to employees being required to change their existing work habits, or because they interpret the new system as being a threat to their jobs.

Also, a Lean system requires most employees to assume more problem-solving responsibilities on the job, which may lead to additional frustration.

4. Lack of support from design engineering personnel: Design engineering creates technical specifications for the materials a company buys, and on some occasions (up to 39% in one survey), the purchasing function in an organization does not receive adequate support from the engineering functions. In this case, it makes it hard for purchasing to advise suppliers on material quality design options.

5. Low product quality: If suppliers fail to provide materials of adequate quality on a regular basis, production slow-downs and stoppages will occur, which can be amplified in a JIT environment where there isn't much, if any, inventory cushion.

6. Lack of support from carrier companies: The purchasing function of some major firms spend large amounts of money moving materials in and out of the factory. However, many companies don't work closely with carriers to develop long-term relationships for highly consistent delivery schedules that lower costs for the buying firm. In fact, many buyers, especially in SMEs (small to medium size enterprises) have traditionally accepted terms offered to them by the carriers regarding their inbound freight, or buy material with "delivered" terms with minimum information on the carrier or freight costs.

7. Lack of communication: An effective just-in-time system requires integration of important functional areas such as purchasing, manufacturing, quality, production, and transportation. A lack of proper communication among these areas can be a major obstacle to the implementation of such a system.

   To help avoid this problem, the purchasing function needs the support of top management for leadership and support.

8. Lack of Lean culture: In many cases, the key to the successful implementation of the Lean system is the development of a Lean culture.

   Companies like Toyota and Honda have a Lean culture with a focus on team-oriented activities which is suitable to the implementation of a Lean system and provides for better manufacturer–supplier relationships. However, it is important to note that every company has to tailor a Lean system to fit their own company's existing culture and processes, similar to what Dupont has done with the recent creation of the "Dupont Production System" (DPS) which led to a four-fold increase in annual gross value of improvements delivered by their Integrated Operations: more than $1 billion per year from 2009–2012 (Benton, 2009).

LEAN PROCUREMENT

Procurement (also known as "sourcing" and "supply management") is the process of managing a broad range of processes associated with a firm's need to acquire goods and services in a legal and ethical manner that are required to manufacture a product (direct items), or to operate the organization (indirect items), the foundation of which is provided by the purchasing function. Per Figure 6.2, the procurement process typically includes the functions of determining purchasing specifications, selecting the supplier, negotiating terms and conditions, and issuing and administrating purchase orders.

Preparing and managing purchasing documents involved in this process has always been a time-consuming process. Most firms have streamlined the document flow process using Lean and other process improvement techniques to reduce the paperwork and handling required for each purchase.

As we know, supply chain costs can be a significant percentage of a company's sales, depending on the industry it is in, with much of it from the procurement process, so it is not difficult to see why it is an area of interest, in terms of looking for waste.

Lean sourcing, or procurement, is a different way of looking at, and working with suppliers, much more than just JIT. There is a greater use of partnerships and alliances, as well as a greater need for coordination and collaboration, often utilizing some of the technological tools mentioned previously for accuracy, timeliness, and efficiency.

Traditional supply chains are managed more on a cost basis, negotiating with many suppliers. While this may still be effective in some instances

FIGURE 6.2
The Procurement Process.

(e.g. commodities), Lean procurement is all about long-term partnering with fewer, longer-term suppliers, with less reliance on low-cost bidding. Motorola, for example, has eliminated traditional supplier bidding by adding emphasis on quality and reliability, and in some cases may sign contracts that are in place throughout a product's life cycle (Heizer and Render, 2011). In this way, the relationship can be mutually beneficial. The value is created by economies of scale and long-term improvements (see Table 6.2).

As a result of this type of relationship, where trust is very important, suppliers are more willing to get involved in JIT partnerships, and share in the design process and be willing to contribute technological expertise. For example, when Cessna Aircraft opened a new plant in Kansas, they set up consignment- and vendor-managed inventory programs with some select suppliers. One supplier, Honeywell, was allowed to maintain avionic parts onsite. Other vendors who participated kept parts at a nearby warehouse to supply the production line on a daily basis. This was a "win–win" situation, as Cessna was able to execute JIT inventory replenishment for parts and their suppliers gained better insight into Cessna's production requirements, and could offer suggestions for product improvements, thereby strengthening the relationship (Heizer and Render, 2011).

TABLE 6.2

Lean Supply Chain Characteristics

Characteristic	Traditional Supply Chain	Lean Supply Chain
Suppliers	Many	Few
Interactions	Confrontational	Collaborative
Relationship Focus	Transactional	Long-term
Primary Selection Criteria	Price	Performance
Length of Contract	Short Term	Long-term
Future Pricing	Increased	Decreased
Lead-times	Long	Short
Order Quantities	Large Lots	Small Lots
Quality	Extensive Inspection	Quality at the Source
Inventory (Supplier and Customer)	Large	Minimal
Information Flow	One-way	Two-way
Flexibility	Low	High
Product Development Role	Small	Large (Collaborative)
Trust	Limited	Extensive

Some suppliers may be somewhat hesitant because of issues such as having too much reliance on one customer, shorter lead times, smaller order quantities, etc. As a true partnership, the customer must be willing to work with the supplier and share costs, training, and expertise so that they are not just "passing their problems upstream." Of course, you need to always have a back-up plan, and only single source (i.e. one supplier for an item) where there is very little risk involved (e.g. commodity-type item, easily substituted part, etc.).

There are many Lean opportunities in procurement including:

- JIT, such as in the Cessna example above. There may also be a potential application for vendor-managed inventory (VMI), where a supplier manages its customer's inventory of parts and supplies.
- Batch size and lead-time reduction: Producing smaller quantities of items more frequently, thus reducing inventory and cycle time.
- Blanket orders: Where a customer places a single purchase order with its supplier containing multiple delivery dates scheduled over a period of time, in many cases at predetermined prices.

As they say, "if you can't measure it, you can't improve it." This applies to all of the applications mentioned in this book. By performing "Lean assessments" and "supplier reviews," you can determine how Lean your supplier is and what progress has been made towards that goal.

Besides process improvement in the procurement process itself, the benefits of electronically generating and transmitting purchasing-related documents include:

- A virtual elimination of paperwork and paperwork handling.
- A reduction in the time between need recognition and the release and receipt of an order.
- Improved communication, both within the company and with suppliers.
- A reduction in errors.
- Lower overhead costs in the purchasing area.
- Purchasing personnel spend less time on processing of purchase orders and invoices, and more time on strategic value-added purchasing activities.

Procurement Technology and Lean

There is a variety of technology available today to help an organization automate and improve their various procurement processes; this will be discussed in Chapter 13.

Needless to say, many industries are adopting technology to automate supply processes, bringing themselves significant bottom-line benefits through greater productivity, visibility, and cost efficiency. In fact, e-procurement—the business-to-business purchase and sale of supplies and services over the Internet—provides the opportunity to increase efficiencies in business transactions and enhances negotiation leverage for firms. Use of technology is a key metric used to benchmark companies as a measure of the maturity of their procurement organizations.

THE EIGHT WASTES

By considering the eight wastes mentioned in the first chapter (i.e. "TIM WOODS"), we can quickly find areas of potential waste in the S2P (Source-to-Pay) process.

Transportation Waste

Where are invoices coming from and going to, what is their final retention place, and are there steps and hand-offs that could be eliminated and/or automated?

Inventory

Is there a large backlog of purchase orders or contract requests, and if so, are there ways to consolidate purchases in collaboration with the business areas creating the purchase orders?

Motion

How many times is the document exchanged between the supplier, legal counsel, and the contracting/sourcing agent during contract negotiations, and are there ways to reduce or eliminate these exchanges?

Waiting

Is there a long wait time for the agent while other parties are reviewing contracts, and if so, are there ways to negotiate terms that can involve all parties simultaneously?

How are your sourcing, contracting, and purchase order approval workflows managed? For example, do employees routinely wait for manager approval to process or finish work, and are there technology or policy changes that could streamline these approvals without giving up control?

Overproduction

What categories of spend are being strategically sourced and are you focusing on the highest value, most critical opportunities? How many reports are being published to support the management of the S2P process, and are there ways to automate the production and publication of these reports?

Over-Processing

Are the legal and/or business terms unnecessary, causing extended negotiation periods, and if so, is alternative boilerplate language available to satisfy requests to modify template language? How many reviews take place on a given contract, sourcing event, or purchase order, and are all required? Can authority be increased to reduce unnecessary oversight?

Defects

What percentage of contracts or purchase orders are changed, and if significant, can collaboration with the business areas decrease the need to amend contracts or purchase orders?

Skills (or People Waste)

People are a company's greatest resource and when their time is misallocated or wasted, that potential may be lost. [Williams, 2013]

Value stream mapping (VSM) is a Lean method for analyzing the current state, and designing a future state for the series of events that take a product or service from its beginning through to the customer. When used in conjunction with the eight wastes mentioned above, as well as other Lean tools, such as one-piece-flow and quality at the source, VSM can be a very powerful tool in any area of procurement or purchasing (see example in Figure 6.3).

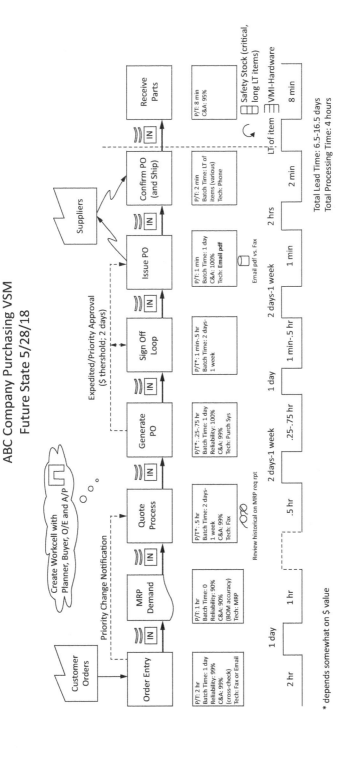

FIGURE 6.3
Future State Value Stream Map.

It is very helpful when analyzing standard business processes, such as those found in procurement, to highlight process waste and reduce lead-times. It can be particularly effective where large amounts of processing is carried out, as in the case of purchasing teams which can benefit from this approach, as a traditional purchase order may go through several stages of processing (creation, validation, approval, etc.) in its life-cycle, and can be subjected to various non-value-adding activities.

STRATEGIC SOURCING VS. LEAN SOURCING

Strategic sourcing, popularized by a number of consulting firms in the late 1980s and early to mid-1990s, is an approach to supply chain management that formalizes the way information is gathered and used so that an organization can leverage its consolidated purchasing power to find the best possible values in the marketplace. The process of strategic sourcing involves developing channels of supply at the lowest total cost, as opposed to the lowest purchase price. It expands upon traditional purchasing activities to include all activities within the procurement cycle, from specification, to receipt of, and payment for goods and services.

As such, it was able to achieve tremendous savings for many of its users, since a company's purchasing costs can range from 50–70% of every sales dollar. While this gave adopters a short-term "home run," it didn't focus on other costs, and somewhat neglected longer-term, collaborative relationships with suppliers.

To go after these additional opportunities, some of these purchasing organizations began to coordinate their efforts with supply chain and operational executives inside their organizations, which is now evolving into Lean sourcing.

On a strategic level, Lean sourcing provides four key benefits to organizations:

1. Greater buy-in from key functional areas, including operations and purchasing which care about both cost and performance.
2. Improves chances of implementing identified sourcing savings.
3. Improved quality and reduced waste.
4. Additional cost reduction opportunities via collaboration with supply partners.

Lean strategic sourcing can be implemented through:

Strategizing for collaboration and redesigning processes: Collaboration is vital to Lean sourcing and is achieved by streamlining procurement operations and purchasing in order to improve financial performance.

Implementation of cost-cutting methods: Lean sourcing takes advantage of kaizen strategies, and one way it can be achieved is by improving logistics management, such as by taking control of, and consolidating, shipments and cost analysis.

Better cost-cutting methods: It is important to have a focus on cost-cutting that does not compromise on quality or reliability, and provides a balance between sourcing and operations.

Waste reduction: Lean sourcing relies on reducing waste in all forms, including time, efforts, and funds through improved compliance and process improvement initiatives.

Collaboration with supply partners: A critical component of Lean sourcing is collaboration with suppliers to develop favorable contract terms, optimize transport costs, and create a supply network that minimizes the chances for potential disruptions.

Ultimately, Lean sourcing success requires that organizations:

Create a Lean sourcing process that can be mapped and communicated to all team members. Open communication facilitates fairness and buy-in across the company, and cross-functional input provides a common understanding of the sourcing processes, as well as issues that impact the company, enabling solutions which address problem areas.

Develop project milestones, deadlines, and target dates to get the job done. Accountability tends to drive results.

Create a team member incentive structure and compensation plan tied to process outcomes. One of the first questions asked (or thought of) is often, "what's in it for me?". It is therefore important to develop bonus structures and cash compensation that are both focused on the job at hand, and awarded back to employees that identify and help implement cost reduction initiatives.

Take a global perspective but factor in risk. Consider global markets for certain product categories but be sure to model potential risks (e.g. longshoremen strikes, late deliveries, etc.), as well as mitigation strategies for risks with the biggest potential impact and likelihood of occurring. [Aptium Global, 2005]

It is now a good time to explore the major supply management processes discussed in this chapter (i.e. strategic sourcing, procurement, and purchasing) in more detail, with a bit of a Lean perspective.

Part II

Supply Management Processes

7

Strategic Sourcing

Strategic sourcing should not be confused with simply using centralized procurement to leverage volume buying. In fact, it is a systematic and fact-based approach for optimizing an organization's supply base and improving the overall value proposition, and is the process of taking advantage of purchasing opportunities by continually reviewing current needs against such opportunities.

In its broadest sense, strategic sourcing expands an organization's focus to the supply chain impacts of procurement and purchasing decisions, with the goals of achieving large and sustainable cost reductions, long-term supply stability, and minimization of supply risk.

The approach, first established by General Motors in the 1980s and now a common business purchasing tool, is founded on a detailed understanding of the spend profile of the organization, as well as that of the supplier market. This understanding is continually updated in order to deliver ongoing improvements to the organization's sourcing and procurement performance.

STRATEGIC SOURCING PROCESSES

A seven step strategic sourcing process developed in 2001 by consulting firm A.T. Kearney has stood the test of time and, with variations, has become best practice. The result of this process may be savings in cash (typical savings range between 4 and 20%), greater added value from the suppliers, and/or time and aggravation saved on a previously time-consuming and unwieldy exercise.

The seven steps or processes within this best practice strategic sourcing process are:

Step 1: Profile the category: This helps you to understand your organization's internal spend for categories of products, while at the same time researching the external market.

A category is made up of a number of products from similar vendors that can be grouped together in a competitive sourcing process. For example, a bicycle company might purchase different tires for different bikes from different manufacturers, in which case it makes sense to group the total spend on tires together into one category to identify savings potentials.

The types of analysis involved in this step include:

Spending analysis: Identifies your organization's total spending with a vendor(s) and is done in advance of contract negotiations.

Needs analysis: Develops an understanding of specifications and needs for the product, and, if applicable, the current supplier's performance, and any enhancements that they would like to see in the product.

Supply market analysis: It is important to then research the external supply market and the market pressures the supplier faces. This includes understanding your vendors' pricing structures to be potentially used later in the process as a negotiating tool.

Step 2: Select the sourcing strategy: It is important to understand how the product (or service) that you are sourcing aligns with your company's overall strategy, especially where you would place the product within a category positioning matrix (Figure 7.1).

This also ties into a Lean philosophy through the various approaches used where, for example, a strong relationship and integration with the supplier might be necessary (i.e. strategic items), and in other cases, a more streamlined purchasing process might be a priority (i.e. non-critical items).

Once you have decided how it aligns with your corporate strategy, you are able to decide on which sourcing strategies you wish to utilize (Figure 7.2). These strategies generally fall into two major categories of (1) exercise power, and (2) creating advantage. While the creating advantage strategy is more in alignment with a Lean strategy, the exercise power strategy can't be ignored in some situations and, in fact, in some cases, both strategies

Leverage	Strategic
Characteristics: Competitive market, high expenditure levels, commodity type items **Approach:** Use competitive marketplace to reduce total cost, and consolidate volume as a negotiation tool	**Characteristics:** No true substitutes, usually single sourced, high product differentiation, and key to core business **Approach:** Ensure availability of supply, focus on relationship building, process integration and innovation
Non-Critical	**Bottleneck**
Characteristics: Low expenditure, small % of expenses, and not key to core business **Approach:** Simplify and streamline purchasing process, reduce number of suppliers and simplify ordering	**Characteristics:** No true substitute, usually single source, not core to business and lack of availability will cause problems **Approach:** Search for alternatives and strengthen relationships

Business Impact

Supply Market Complexity

FIGURE 7.1
Category Positioning Matrix (Source: A.T. Kearney, 2001).

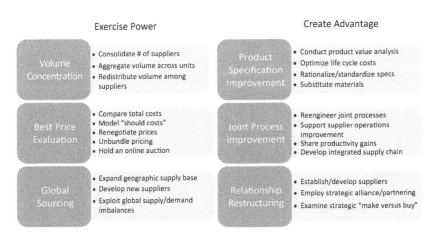

Exercise Power

Create Advantage

Volume Concentration
• Consolidate # of suppliers
• Aggregate volume across units
• Redistribute volume among suppliers

Product Specification Improvement
• Conduct product value analysis
• Optimize life cycle costs
• Rationalize/standardize specs
• Substitute materials

Best Price Evaluation
• Compare total costs
• Model "should costs"
• Renegotiate prices
• Unbundle pricing
• Hold an online auction

Joint Process Improvement
• Reengineer joint processes
• Support supplier operations improvement
• Share productivity gains
• Develop integrated supply chain

Global Sourcing
• Expand geographic supply base
• Develop new suppliers
• Exploit global supply/demand imbalances

Relationship Restructuring
• Establish/develop suppliers
• Employ strategic alliance/partnering
• Examine strategic "make versus buy"

FIGURE 7.2
Sourcing Strategies (Source: A.T. Kearney, 2001).

may work together where a company can gain a competitive advantage through volume leverage (e.g. cost), but still work to develop the supplier in a mutually advantageous way.

Step 3: Generate the supplier portfolio: This step uses the needs analysis from Step 1 to develop your criteria for supplier selection to widen your supplier base, and identify all viable suppliers, including small and/or new ones that might have more favorable contract terms.

A variety of means can be used during this step, such as interviewing key suppliers and industry leaders which will eventually lead to submitting requests for information (RFIs) to potential suppliers.

It is important for a company to select potential suppliers for their portfolio carefully. A supplier's inability to meet selection criteria can result in significant losses for the organization. The business reputation and performance of the supplier must be evaluated, and financial statements, credit reports, and references must be checked carefully. The use of agents, who are familiar with the markets and stakeholders, can also be beneficial to this process. Organizations may select more than one supplier to avoid potential supply disruptions, as well as create a competitive environment.

Step 4: Select the implementation path: Creates an execution strategy for choosing short listed suppliers.

The traditional route taken by many procurement departments is to conduct a request for proposal (RFP) where the prospective buyer states their requirements and asks suppliers for a proposed offer (if there is only one viable supplier to consider, the best approach may be to negotiate directly with them, without issuing an RFP). Typically, it requires vendors to complete a standard pricing matrix to compare all offers. A set of criteria and weightings for evaluating the completed RFPs is then developed, commonly referred to as the "factor weighting method." Electronic RFP tools can be useful in speeding up the process and simplifying the analysis of responses.

Suppliers that get through the RFP process will then participate in negotiations, which may be conducted face-to-face or possibly by way of the internet (e.g. reverse auctions and e-auctions). Internet negotiation, which works best when there are at least three suppliers whose products are broadly similar, can compress time in the process. No matter which method is used, there are then final contract negotiations to be concluded with the successful bidder.

Step 5: Negotiate and select suppliers: One of the keys to successful negotiations is careful, detailed preparation, starting with assembling your negotiation team. You will need to develop the team's objectives and roles. Roles on a negotiation team may include the leader, a senior authority, a technical expert, a user, and an observer (note-taker), for example.

When developing a negotiation strategy, information is key including information from your RFPs and your needs analysis, as well as current knowledge of the supplier marketplace.

It is important to know your current bargaining position which includes your most desired outcome (MDO), your least acceptable agreement (LAA), and your best alternative to a negotiated agreement (BATNA, which is the most advantageous alternative course of action a party can take if negotiations fail and an agreement cannot be reached), and what concessions you are prepared to give.

Have a contingency plan including your best alternative to a negotiated agreement (BATNA), and decide in advance if you are willing to walk away from a deal if it doesn't meet your LAA. In any case, you should never concede anything without getting something from the supplier in return.

At the end of the negotiations, you need to have everything in writing to avoid future disagreements, and to finalize a contract.

Step 6: Integrate suppliers: In the case of a new supplier, you will need to:

- Identify transition issues.
- Consider the organizational implications and required changes.
- Create new processes and procedures if necessary (for example, how will charge-backs be handled?).
- Create a transition/implementation plan.
- Communicate changes to users.

Step 7: Monitor the supply market and supplier performance: Work with the supplier is only beginning once the contract is signed. It is also important to stay abreast of your supply market conditions as things may change.

The contract should state performance metrics that you have agreed upon with your supplier, such as joint process improvements, meetings, and reporting. It should be agreed as to what procedures will be put in place to monitor agreed upon metrics (Clegg and Montgomery, 2005).

LEAN STRATEGIC SOURCING

Kearney's assessment of excellence in procurement (AEP) study (2011) found that corporate procurement functions are becoming a more vital, strategic tool resulting in better governance to improve performance both internally and externally. Many of the findings tie directly or indirectly with a Lean philosophy by focusing on the top-line, not just the bottom-line, as well as concentrating more on customer value.

Kearney found that leading procurement organizations are playing an active role in developing and executing top-line strategies for growth, while still being held accountable for bottom-line efficiencies. Many companies have processes, methodologies, and technologies that take advantage of their power in the supply base.

Many leading companies are starting to develop long-term category management strategies, where collaboration with key suppliers is used to create value. Performance management, knowledge and information, and human resources are key to a successful procurement organization. As a result, it pays to invest in new ways to measure performance, sophisticated technology to embed best practices, and expanded professional skills.

Seven Characteristics of Lean Strategic Sourcing

The survey identified seven "best practice" characteristics in companies, most of which support a Leaner supply chain, demonstrating consistently high levels of procurement performance and are strategic contributors to their business. They are:

1. Align with the business: Leaders in the survey understand that the procurement strategy must align with overall business goals and go beyond the traditional areas (transportation, IT, engineering) to engage with R&D, marketing, finance, customer support, and legal.
2. Contribute to the top- and bottom-lines: 75% of the leaders say they contribute to innovation, integrate suppliers into the new product development process, reduce time-to-market for new products, and create new business opportunities with suppliers.

3. Manage risk systematically: Procurement leaders focus on managing risk, as most use risk impact analysis, financial risk management (such as hedging), and disaster-planning as ways to protect against potential threats.

4. Use supplier relationship management consistently: Leaders felt that a structured process can increase strategic value by pointing to improvements in innovation and growth, better-managed risk, and more Agile, flexible, and efficient supply chains. They put a lot of effort towards managing strategic suppliers, expanding the supply base into new markets, monitoring compliance and risk management, performing joint initiatives, and developing suppliers' capabilities.

5. Tailor category strategies: Leaders in the survey tend to tailor their approaches to each situation, but more complex categories require closer collaboration with suppliers.

6. Adopt technology: Procurement leaders have technology that allows for more visibility into spending and supply chain activity. They also tend to be automated, and have adopted technology needed to support contact management and compliance.

7. Win the "war for talent": Leaders tend to be more forward-looking in their approaches to recruiting and retaining top talent. They tend to have more sophisticated recruiting approaches and use online collaboration technologies and offer part-time work and flexible hours for their diverse, dispersed workforces Blascovich, Ferrer, and Markham, 2011).

LEAN SOURCING JOURNEY

Ultimately, Lean sourcing requires a long-term commitment to combining elements of strategic sourcing with Lean principles. As it is not a destination, but a journey, there are stages of maturity along the way. Figure 7.3, below, is an example of a Lean sourcing maturity model.

The model shows the relationship of developing a Lean philosophy that can be integrated and work hand-in-hand with strategic sourcing over time. Companies that apply basic tools and techniques typically have a "push" type system and are focused primarily on price. World class companies on the other hand, take a more global approach to sourcing

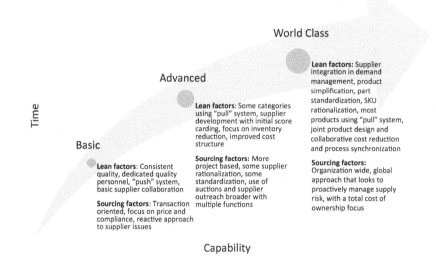

FIGURE 7.3
Lean Sourcing Maturity Model (Source: Aptium Global, 2005).

while managing risk, and have a total cost of ownership focus. They typically employ collaborative "pull" systems focused not only on cost reduction, but process improvement and waste elimination (Aptium Global, 2005).

The following case studies show some examples of how strategic sourcing can be combined with a Lean, efficient, and Agile philosophy to improve the top- and bottom-line.

 LEAN STRATEGIC SOURCING MRO–CASE STUDY #1

Challenge

A large publicly traded mining and minerals processing corporation with 44 locations across 24 U.S. states and Canadian provinces was trying to preserve profit margins during a turbulent economic period and rising supply costs.

While the company had a central reporting system, individual plants independently made many of the purchasing decisions, so the company found it difficult to leverage their entire spend and to coordinate contracts.

Approach

After an initial cost analysis, an executive committee decided to focus on their maintenance, repairs, and operations (MRO) spend. In the past, the company didn't have the resources to adequately analyze all the purchasing information, due to the inconsistent records of entries from the various plant locations. To overcome this obstacle and gain strategic sourcing expertise, the executive committee engaged Source One, a provider of procurement and supply chain solutions to help. The goal of the project was to have more competitive pricing by leveraging their corporate spend, strategic relationships, and marketplace competition.

The project included 14 MRO spend categories, including general mechanical supplies, fasteners, electrical/electronic components, safety supplies, and lubrication products. The consultant conducted a spend analysis and created a baseline spend report which identified historical purchasing patterns, and revealed possible sourcing strategies that could be examined.

The consultant then proceeded to determine which spend categories presented potential savings opportunities. For each category, Source One conducted a market assessment and spend analysis. The client and consultant agreed that they should conduct a full sourcing project in each of the 14 categories.

Results

Through the introduction of competition, utilization of strategic relationships with supplier conglomerates, and extensive negotiations, Source One managed to produce average annual savings of 14% by helping the client to improve their plant purchasers' ordering, inventory, and reporting methods.

The client, various suppliers, and consultant achieved supplier rationalization and successful implementation of new pricing and purchasing processes in each category. Better performance and compliance metrics that were implemented helped the client company to develop better systems for understanding, monitoring, reporting, and controlling their spend for each product category. The consultant continued to ensure the success of the initiative through internal process and supplier auditing well after completing the implementation phase.

The collaborative team not only reached the initiative's primary goal of creating cost savings without any major disruption of the client's business processes, but also implemented the tools, insight, and relationships necessary to continuously improve their sourcing procedures. As a result, the client company has ongoing cost savings as well as better reporting systems, improved supplier relationships, and better control over their total spend (www.sourceoneinc.com, 2017).

 ## SOURCING AS STRATEGY–CASE STUDY #2

Challenge

An $18 billion manufacturer transformed its procurement process from a transactional cost center to a source of strategic advantage, while saving $500 million at the same time.

The Fortune 200 manufacturing company had grown through an aggressive acquisition policy, but did not integrate various businesses. The company's decentralized structure gave it flexibility and an entrepreneurial culture, but without a focus on minimizing costs. The board of directors realized that significant costs savings could be achieved by leveraging their $9 billion annual procurement spend, especially with commodities used across its manufacturing operations. However, as they didn't have the expertise to build a consolidated purchasing program on their own, they needed specialized help to develop the processes and create the organizational structure that would make a difference. They brought in consultant Pricewaterhouse Coopers (PwC) to assess the value they could achieve with a leveraged purchasing program.

Approach

PwC proposed a three-phased plan to: (1) assess the client's procurement capabilities and potential savings; (2) build new processes and a centrally led procurement organization, including pilot commodity testing; and (3) transfer control of the new procurement operation back to the client.

The first phase assessed the company's global commodity spend to identify opportunities for significant savings and an evaluation of their procurement capabilities revealing up to $500 million in savings that could be achieved over five years. Three strategies emerged.

The first was to transform procurement into a strategic function. This meant more than just consolidating purchases; it also meant working with suppliers to innovate and improve end products, develop a strategic understanding of their supplier relationships, and identify opportunities to stay ahead of the commodities marketplace. Secondly, the company would need to build a hybrid centralized procurement division. They had no chief procurement officer (CPO), so there was no direct input on the topic when executive-level strategic decisions were being made. Procurement would need to be part of the firm's strategy to recognize risks and seize opportunities. Finally, sourcing pilots were set up to demonstrate the savings, and build momentum for the cultural change needed for the success of the new sourcing strategy.

They hired a CPO and brought the executives of their business units on board with the initiative, holding workshops to train key personnel in each business unit to define their sourcing strategy, develop their organizational structure, and identify key sourcing projects and savings targets.

Results

Well into the second phase of its procurement transformation, the client has created a hybrid centralized procurement department, a chief procurement officer has been hired, and a steering committee has been assembled to serve as a strategic sourcing advisory board. Now, all the business units use strategic sourcing to achieve savings and create innovation.

So far, the pilot tests on several commodities have yielded over $50 million in savings with an overall annualized savings rate of $80 million and a pipeline of more projects to save another $150 million. Tools, templates, and processes have been developed to continue to identify opportunities for savings across the organization, with a culture change from where procurement had been a cost of doing business, to the realization that it can be a strategic weapon to achieve product innovation and long-term growth for the company (www.pwc.com, 2014).

While strategic sourcing is important for the long-term success of a business, the actual procurement process is where the results can pay off; this is the topic of our next chapter.

8

Procurement

As stated in Chapter 1, procurement involves the process of selecting vendors, strategic vetting, establishing payment terms, the negotiation of contracts, and the actual purchasing of goods, and is concerned with acquiring the goods, services, and work vital to an organization.

It is essentially the overarching or umbrella term within which purchasing (the topic of our next chapter) can be found, and is a defined set of processes that, depending on execution, can be the difference between the success or failure of an organization.

In this chapter, we will go into some depth to understand the process, and then look at some case studies where Lean philosophies have been successfully applied.

THE PROCUREMENT PROCESS

The procurement process typically includes the functions of determining the purchasing specifications, selecting the supplier, negotiating terms and conditions, and issuing and administrating purchase orders.

There are some general steps involved in the procurement process, previously shown in Chapter 6, most of which we will now review in some detail (Figure 8.1). The steps to be reviewed are:

1. Identify and review requirements.
2. Establish specifications.
3. Select suppliers, issue quotations.
4. Determine the right price.
5. Issue purchase orders.

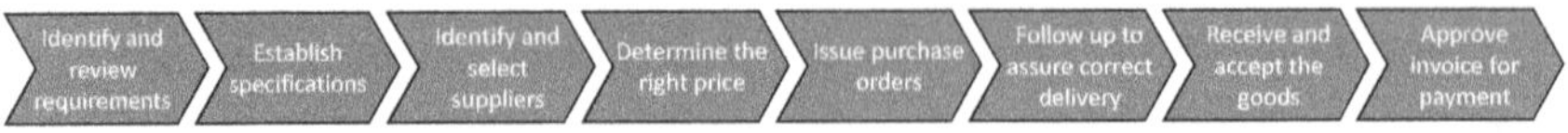

FIGURE 8.1
The Procurement Process.

6. Follow up to assure correct delivery.
7. Receive and accept the goods.
8. Approve invoice for payment.

Step 1: Identify and Review Requirements

When discussing requirements, it should be understood that procurement activities are often split into two categories, direct and indirect, depending upon the consumption purposes of the acquired goods and services (Table 8.1).

The first category, direct procurement, is production-related procurement and the second, indirect procurement, is non-production-related procurement.

Direct Procurement

Direct procurement is generally referred to in manufacturing settings only. It encompasses all items that are part of finished products, such as raw

TABLE 8.1

Direct vs. Indirect Procurement

		Types		
		Direct Procurement	**Indirect Procurement**	
		Raw Material and Production Goods	**Maintenance, Repair, and Operating Supplies**	**Capital Goods and Services**
Features	**Quantity**	Large	Low	Low
	Frequency	High	Relatively high	Low
	Value	Industry specific	Low	High
	Nature	Operational	Tactical	Strategic
	Examples	Resin in plastics industry	Lubricants, spare parts	Resin and plastic product storage facilities

materials, components, and parts. Direct procurement, which is a major focus in supply chain management, directly affects the production process of manufacturing firms. It also occurs in retail where "direct spend" may refer to what is spent on the merchandise being resold.

Indirect Procurement

In contrast, indirect procurement activities concern operating resources that a company purchases to enable its operations (i.e. maintenance, repair and operating or MRO inventory, as well as capital spent on plant and equipment). It comprises a wide variety of goods and services, from standardized low-value items, like office supplies and machine lubricants, to complex and costly products and services, like heavy equipment and consulting services.

The source for purchasing requirements can come from MRP systems via planners and purchase requisitions from other users in the organization. A purchase or material requisition is a document generated by an organization to notify the purchasing department of items it needs to order, the quantity, and the time-frame in which it will be needed in the future).

During this step, purchasing will review paperwork for proper approvals, check material specifications, verify quantity, unit of measurement, delivery date, and location, and review all supplemental information.

The topic of MRP and indirect procurement will be discussed in detail in Chapter 10.

Step 2: Establish Specifications

To establish specifications, one must identify quantity, pricing, and functional requirements as described below.

 Quantity: In the case of small volume requirements, you need to find a standard item. If you are dealing with larger volumes, then it must be designed for economies of scale to both reduce cost and satisfy functional needs.
 Price: This relates to the use of the item and the selling price of the finished product.

Functional: There is a fundamental need to understand what the item is expected to do per the user(s). This includes performance and aesthetic expectations (e.g. for a hand can opener: how smoothly it removes the tops of cans as well as how ergonomically appealing the design is).

In general, the description of the item may be by brand or specification. One would use brand if the quantity is too small, the item is patented, or is requested by a customer. It would be by specification if you are looking for very specific physical or chemical make-up, material, or performance specifications.

The source of the specifications themselves can be based upon buyer requirements or standards that may be set independently.

If the buyer sets the specifications, it can become a long and expensive process requiring detailed description of parts, finishes, tolerances, and materials used resulting in the item being expensive to produce.

Standards, on the other hand, set by government and non-governmental agencies, can be much more straightforward to use, as they tend to be widely known and accepted, lower in price, and more adaptable to customer needs.

Step 3: Identify and Select Suppliers

The next step in the procurement process is to identify and select suppliers. Typically, this process involves coming up with a "long-list" of supplier who meet your requirements in general, then whittling the list down to final candidates, before selecting the ultimate vendor.

Identification of potential suppliers can come from a variety of sources including the internet, catalogues, salespeople, and trade magazine and directories.

Once you have identified potential vendors, a "request for information" or RFI is issued to them that states some information about your company and its requirements, as well as requesting background on the vendor. It is usually not too difficult to refine the vendors that respond down to a smaller list of candidates (usually 5–10), and from there it is best to include a multi-functional team of employees to determine the finalist(s).

Once you have it down to a short-list, a "request for quotation" (RFQ), or "request for proposal" (RFP) is issued. An RFQ is an invitation to selected suppliers to bid or quote on delivering specific products or services, and will include the specifications of the items/service. The suppliers are requested to return their bids by a set date and time to be considered for selection. Discussions may be held on the bids, in many cases to clarify technical capabilities, or to note errors in a proposal. The initial bid does not have to mean the end of the bidding, as there may be more than one round.

Vendor Evaluation

I've found what is known as the "factor rating method" (see Figure 8.2) to be useful in the task of vendor evaluation.

The factor rating method identifies criteria that need to be considered as part of what you will be buying and assigns weights to the relative importance of each of these factors. You then score how well each supplier compares on each factor and give them a score which is weighted times the rating.

While this may not be the only decision-making tool used, it can get you close enough to help you make a final decision. There are also "intangible" factors that can come into play, such as personal opinions of executives, prior experience with a vendor, etc.

There are many factors or criteria besides price—and it is not always the lowest price that is selected—that are important when selecting a supplier such as:

Technical ability: As their product will become part of your product, can the potential vendor help you to develop and make improvements to your product?

Manufacturing capability: Can they consistently meet your stated quality and specifications?

Reliability: To the best of your ability, you need to determine if they are reputable and financially stable.

Criteria	Weights	Scores (1-5)	Weight x Score
Engineering and research capabilities	0.1	4.0	0.4
Production process capability (flexibility/agile)	0.2	5.0	0.8
Delivery capability	0.1	3.5	0.2
Quality and performance	0.2	3.0	0.6
Location	0.1	1.0	0.1
Financial and managerial strength (stability and cost structure)	0.2	5.0	0.8
Information systems capability (e-procurement, ERP)	0.1	2.0	0.2
Reputation (sustainability/ethics)	0.1	5.0	0.5
Total	1.00		3.4

FIGURE 8.2
Factor Rating Method for Vendor Evaluation.

After-sales service: Do they have a solid service organization that offers technical support?

Location: Are they close enough to support fast and consistent delivery and support service when needed?

Step 4: Determine the Right Price

As was pointed out before, while price may not be the only determinant, it certainly contributes greatly to the bottom-line, as it can be upwards of 50% of the cost of goods sold.

There are three basic models that are used as a basis for pricing. They are:

Cost-based: The supplier makes their financials available to purchaser.

Market-based: The price based on published, auction, or indexed price.

Competitive bidding: This is typically used for infrequent purchases, but can make establishing a long-term relationship more difficult.

When preparing to negotiate price, preparation is the key. On a personal level, if you are buying a house or car, the more research you do, the better idea you have of what is available, and what is a "fair" price in the market area (at least to you). Thanks to the internet, there are many sources available to get a good idea as to what is available, and a range of pricing based upon recent history. The same goes for business negotiations, where the buyer should have knowledge of the seller's costs to some extent.

Negotiation

For the most part, negotiations are based upon the type of product. General categories of products include:

Commodities: The price is usually determined by the market.

Standard products: The price is set by catalog listings and there is usually little room for negotiation (other than volume).

Small value items: Companies should try to reduce ordering costs or increase volume where possible.

Made-to-order items: Prices are based upon quotations from a number of sources, and as a result, prices are negotiated where possible.

Distributed and Integrative Negotiations

Where negotiations are possible, there are two general types of negotiation that can be used: distributive, and integrative.

In distributive bargaining, the goals of one party are in fundamental, direct conflict with another party, resources are fixed and limited, and maximizing one's own share of the resources is the goal for both parties. So, in this case, there is usually a "winner" and a "loser."

One needs to set a target point and a walk-away point to negotiate a final price that is satisfactory to the buyer. To determine these may take a good amount of research and judgment. The seller may have a listing or asking price, and you will submit an initial offer or counter offer. This type of negotiating usually requires sufficient "clout" to justify lower pricing. Larger companies with multiple locations or business units may have sufficient volume to justify this.

When I was a member of General Electric's corporate sourcing, we were able to leverage over $1 billion/year spent annually on transportation corporation-wide by collecting freight volumes by mode for the 100+ GE units to negotiate significant savings. This was accomplished not only by collecting and analyzing the annual spend, but also by reducing the number of carriers within each mode to a company-wide group of "core" carriers to maximize negotiation power.

Integrative negotiation on the other hand, is more collaborative with a goal for a "win–win" conclusion by the creation of a free flow of information, and an attempt to understand the other negotiator's real needs and objectives. This process emphasizes commonalities between the parties and minimizes the differences through a search for solutions that meet the goals and objectives of both sides.

At this point in the listed steps, we move from procurement to the "day-to-day" supplier scheduling and follow-up which go more under the heading of purchasing activities; these will be discussed in Chapter 9.

KEY METRICS

Price is only one measure of cost and only one element of assessing the attractiveness of a supplier, but it is the most common way most companies view and manage interactions with their suppliers.

Besides price (which is benchmarked against industry standards in many cases), most companies also spend a lot of time and attention on operational dimensions of measurement, which can include quality measures such as parts per million defect rates, and service level measures such as time to respond to inquiries, on-time delivery, etc.

Some of the most important key performance indicators (KPIs) to keep an eye on are:

Procurement cycle time: This begins when a company decides to order items and ends when the goods are delivered to the warehouse. If handled properly, the company can benefit from the opportunity to sell its inventory more quickly or take advantage of discounts by paying suppliers sooner. If cycle time lags, time must be spent correcting mistakes or streamlining workflow for faster results.

Quality: One common measurement is the number of defects per thousand or million to measure the quality of purchases. High rates of defective merchandise will, of course, limit the amount of quality merchandise in inventory, but also can increase the procurement cycle if items constantly have to be returned.

Procurement return on investment (ROI): This is measured by comparing department costs with the savings it generates. It involves detailed examination of your procurement operations, from the amount of labor and wages involved, to the supplies and technology being utilized, and even the amount of company space occupied.

Spend under management: Compares strategic sourcing expenditures on products and services against overall expenditures in a given fiscal period. The greater the percentage, the more influence procurement has for savings and optimization. A general rule of thumb is that top-performing companies are around 85%, average 55%, and weaker teams at 35% or less.

Implemented cost savings: Measures actual cost savings realized after implementation. Traditionally, procurement teams have credited savings at the time of negotiation while this calculation can help to drive organizations to improve the effectiveness of procurement activities.

Contract compliance: Looks at how well suppliers are meeting contract terms and conditions, and is usually the ratio of the number of contracts not meeting specifications compared to total number of contracts, or the dollar value of spend in noncompliant contracts versus total contracted spending.

Delivery: Measures whether procurement is obtaining what the organization needs when it needs it, such as the percentage of on-time deliveries, percentage of shipments arriving in usable condition, and quoted delivery time compared to actual delivery time.

Some forward-thinking companies share information about their strategic business strategies with their key suppliers, and have joint discussions about how they can contribute, and what metrics can be used to evaluate those contributions. These metrics can be designed to highlight areas for supplier improvement or development, provide early warning of potential problems at suppliers, and to ensure the ongoing financial health and sustainability of key suppliers.

LEAN PROCUREMENT

A Lean philosophy when applied to procurement can:

- Improve the procurement process, workflows, and other activities that add value to the company while reducing time and eliminating waste.
- Reduce costs while simultaneously improving the quality of products and services.
- Increase the performance and response time of suppliers.
- Shift procurement's focus to being more strategic in nature.

It is now apparent that Lean has moved beyond the shop floor to include elements of the supply chain, such as procurement, which includes the supply base. Lean procurement can be applied in all industries, in manufacturing and in service sectors, resulting in impressive operational and financial results.

Lean procurement questions why activities are being done and how to increase procurement's total value. While cost reduction is important in procurement, there needs to be a focus on how it adds value.

Basic Lean principles such as value steam, pull, and flow are extremely relevant to procurement. Many Lean tools such as value stream mapping

(VSM), 5S-workplace organization, visual, kaizen, and standard work can be applied to procurement processes.

Supplier proliferation is a major reason for increased transactions and waste in procurement, and companies that go through a supply base rationalization process end up with fewer, higher-performing suppliers.

By focusing on your current supplier base using performance management tools, it helps to ensure a higher-performing supply base that requires less expediting, resulting in higher quality, improved responsiveness, lower cost, and more value from suppliers, which means a more efficient and cost-effective procurement operation.

In addition, the adoption of supply chain technologies, such as strategic sourcing software and spend analysis, can help make procurement more Lean, as pointed out in the next section.

However, to be truly successful for the long term, focus should be on leadership, overall strategy, people, and culture, rather than primarily on the tools. Lean tools are a means to an end, not an end in themselves (www.ivalua.com, 2016).

Core Principles of Lean Procurement

So, with that in mind, there are some general guiding Lean procurement core principles derived from demand-driven manufacturing and supply chain initiatives to consider when embarking on this type of strategy:

1. Migrate from "push" to "pull": Strengthen and improve your "pull" supply chain processes by deploying supply chain event management solutions that enhance collaboration with your suppliers. By connecting people (i.e. buyers, suppliers, and partners) directly to their "pull" business processes, it allows buyers and their suppliers to communicate supply chain "exception-based" signals in real-time.
2. Develop a flexible and responsive supply chain: Help your procurement professionals eliminate long material lead times by utilizing postponement strategies for a more responsive supply chain. When customer demand unexpectedly goes up, your supply chain can meet that increase, and when forecasts go down, you are not left with excessive levels of inventory. This type of strategy will also help to reduce long lead-times normally associated with offshore

procurement, and can help to proactively manage potential shortages through automated forecast collaboration solutions, and proactive alerts when suppliers cannot support requirements.

3. Eliminate all waste in the procurement cycle: Without Lean procurement, buyers spend a lot of their time on non-strategic processes like tracking order status, purchase order entry, and maintaining individual spreadsheets for analysis. As a result, they miss opportunities for mutually beneficial supplier negotiations and process efficiencies. Being connected with suppliers to respond electronically with critical business process information, automate their purchase order acknowledgement approval processes, companies can end over-reliance on phone, fax, and e-mail, and spend more time on more strategic activities (Oracle, 2006).

PROCUREMENT TECHNOLOGY

Most ERP and accounting systems have at least some purchasing features, perhaps simply to create purchase orders directly or from an MRP system.

There are also internet applications such as e-commerce sites, exchanges, and auctions for e-procurement.

Web-based applications such as Ariba software, for example, enable companies to facilitate and improve the procurement process by providing solutions which help companies analyze, understand, and manage their corporate spending to achieve cost savings and business process efficiency. Ariba started off with the idea of purchasing staff buying items from vendors who provided their catalogs online, as the typical procurement process can be labor-intensive and often costly for large corporations. Customers are offered a large number of supplier catalogs to purchase from.

Today, Ariba software allows a company to automate, monitor, and control the complete purchasing life-cycle from requisition to payment. Users can create requisitions that are approved according to pre-configured business rules that each company decides upon. Purchase orders can be automatically generated and sent directly to suppliers, while order acknowledgements and shipping notices are sent back to the original requestor.

The invoicing process is relatively easy for the suppliers using a tool such as Ariba, as they can create an invoice directly from the requestor's purchase order. Invoices are then pre-matched with the purchase order line items, as well as any receiving information, so that the requestor can reconcile and pay without any delays.

Technology to Enhance Lean Procurement

New technologies can make your various procurement process Leaner and more efficient, especially in what has now become known as "e-procurement." For our purposes, we will define e-procurement as: business-to-business purchase and sale of supplies and services over the internet which can be integrated with internal computerized procurement processes and systems, as identified in Figure 8.1.

In procurement, which may sometimes include e-procurement functionality, there are two types of software vendors: (1) enterprise resource planning (ERP) providers offering both internal procurement and e-procurement as one or part of their modules; and (2) services or vendors focused specifically on e-procurement.

Procurement software itself is a computer program, or suite of products, that helps to automate (and thereby improve) the processes of purchasing materials and inventory maintenance of goods. Following the typical procurement process, it can generate purchase orders, execute the ordering process online, match invoices to materials received, and pay bills electronically.

Again, more often than not, systems today include e-procurement functionality, as well leveraging the benefits of the internet. As a result, the benefits of using procurement software include ease of administration and potential cost savings, as well as having a single interface for procurement to monitor a company's spending.

Procurement software helps to efficiently manage a variety of activities. Specifically, they include the ability to:

- Create a purchase order based on need.
- Verify a purchase order.
- Submit a pending purchase order for approval or rejection.
- Automate an electronic purchase order transmission.
- Confirmation or cancellations of purchase orders.

- Help to execute financial and inventory transactions when ordered materials arrive.
- Gather and analyze data to improve profitability.
- Streamline and standardize administration. For example, procurement systems generally offer multi-currency support, as well as tools that can automate purchases and purchasing approvals.

These systems can also connect users with large networks of qualified suppliers, which a critical capability for supply chain professionals who are trying to identify the most reliable raw materials suppliers at the best price, wherever they might be sourced from.

As opposed to procurement modules internal to ERP systems such as SAP and Oracle, there are also "standalone" procurement solutions available in a variety of forms. Dominick identified ten types of standalone procurement software systems:

1. Spend analysis: Allows you to find purchasing patterns within categories, by suppliers, etc., that might offer cost savings, performance improvements, and overall efficiencies. Most spend analysis vendors have been acquired by other types of procurement software vendors.
2. Supplier discovery: Allows you to search for suppliers that meet specific criteria, such as capabilities, location, supplier diversity, etc. Examples: ThomasNet, Ariba.
3. Supplier information management: Allows you to efficiently collect and maintain accurate supplier information, including contact information and certification status directly from suppliers. Examples: HICX Solutions, Hiperos.
4. eSourcing: Allows you to get quotes and proposals electronically from suppliers quickly. This can be done privately or can let suppliers see their rank among bidders to increase competitive pressure. Examples: WhyAbe, K2Sourcing, Trade Extensions.
5. Contract management: Enables you to prepare contracts using various templates. It can electronically route contracts for approval, track revisions, give notification of contract expirations, and store executed contracts. Examples: Selectica, Prodagio.
6. eProcurement: Allows end-users to search catalogs of pre-approved products and services from contracted suppliers, create requisitions,

and have some requisitions turned into purchase orders (either manually by buyers or automatically). Example: ePlus, eBid.

7. e-Invoicing (also known as "ePayment"): Enables you to efficiently receive accurate supplier invoices electronically. May include "dynamic discounting," allowing suppliers to reduce the amount your organization owes in exchange for faster payment. Examples: Taulia, Tradeshift.

8. Supplier management: Enables you to track and/or rate supplier performance using manual or scorecard-style ratings. Also integrates with other systems to gather actual performance. May include risk assessment capabilities. Examples: Aravo, BravoSolution.

9. Combination solutions: A type of eProcurement system allowing for direct payment to suppliers, commonly referred to as "procure-to-pay," or P2P. Ones that offer the option of soliciting quotes from suppliers are called "source-to-pay solutions." Examples: Coupa, Puridiom.

10. Complete suites: There are some software vendors that have many, or even all, of the solutions listed above. They are referred to as "suites." Examples: GEP, Zycus, SciQuest, iValua (Domonick, 2015).

Lean procurement when aided with the appropriate technology can:

- Remove the obstacles to the free flow of information to a supply chain.
- Create real-time visibility into inventory.
- Transition your supply chain from "push" to "pull" consumption-based replenishment models.
- Manage by exception by providing your buyers and planners with proactive real-time, exception messages that strengthen replenishment processes.
- Eliminate the long lead-times for critical materials and assemblies.
- Make sure you are covered for the upside of your material forecast.

There will be a more detailed discussion of the use of technology to enable Lean supply management in Chapter 13.

What follows are some applications of a Lean philosophy in a procurement process.

ERSKINE LEAN REVIEW OF PROCUREMENT–CASE STUDY #1

Challenge

Erskine Hospital Limited is the leading care organization in Scotland. Erskine provides nursing, rehabilitation and dementia care for residents in care homes throughout Scotland.

They have a dedicated procurement function responsible for negotiating contracts with suppliers, ordering, receiving, and issuing goods and products for the west coast care homes, and maintaining the stock room.

In 2014, Erskine's procurement manager left the organization giving it an opportunity to review their existing processes, and determine if there were opportunities for savings and/or improvements. Erskine asked consultant Scott-Moncrieff to carry out a Lean review of their procurement function.

Approach

After careful observation and analysis, the consultant identified that the existing procurement function was not adequate for the size of Erskine—the function had been designed and developed for a much larger organization—or the skills mix and level of staff required. The existing process was designed to identify and procure the required products and services, receive them in the stockroom, and process purchase invoices. In a larger organization, these activities are split across teams within the procurement function where no one person is responsible for purchasing, receiving and paying for all the goods received. In Erskine, the small procurement function was required to perform all these activities.

Erskine's procurement IT system did not effectively satisfy the needs of the procurement function, and staff found themselves often identifying ways in which they could make the system work better by putting in place "workaround" arrangements.

It was found that the existing stock control systems were not sufficiently robust, and did not represent an effective use of resources. Stockroom staff time was wasted due to the inability to find goods, and the systems in place for distributing goods between the main hospital and other sites were not consistent. In addition, as the stockroom held goods for multiple sites, there was limited room for deliveries to be received and processed, resulting in large deliveries being left outside until they could be unpackaged and processed, risking damage from possible adverse weather conditions.

Results

By applying Lean tools and techniques, the review identified the following recommendations for Erskine.

- Realigned responsibilities for procurement functions: Procurement staff would now be responsible for ordering the necessary goods, the stock controller for logging receipt of the goods, and finance staff for processing the payments, bringing them in line with procurement "best practices." By transferring an existing temporary procurement post to the current finance function, the recommendations had no resource implications for Erskine.
- Identified the need for the current software provider to deliver specific training sessions to Erskine's procurement and finance staff on the new finance system being introduced. This training was intended to prevent staff developing "workaround" options as they had done under the previous system, and would also remove the need to enter the data twice (i.e. once into their "workaround" arrangement and once into the IT system), freeing up staff time that could be better utilized on other duties.
- Stock should be delivered directly to the care homes, reducing the level of items to be held at the main hospital stockroom, and enabling Erskine to reorganize its stockroom to deal with the weekly deliveries. Goods are no longer required to be left outside, reducing the amount of money lost re-ordering items that were damaged.
- The Lean review has empowered Erskine staff to take greater ownership for the use of stock and the delivery of the procurement function, and delivered a more efficient procurement process, and the organization has made annual savings of at least $52,000 per annum from a review that cost the organization less than a tenth of this (Thomson, 2015).

 **SCAPA–CASE STUDY #2**

Challenge

The Scapa Group is a global supplier of bonding solutions and manufacturer of adhesive-based products for the healthcare and industrial markets.

Too much time was being spent on managing small, low-value items such as janitorial, packaging, safety, and office supplies. Scapa was ordering these products (313 items in total) from multiple suppliers and receiving multiple deliveries and invoices. The overload of ordering put pressure on the buyers and receiving, and the excessive number of invoices resulted in the accounts payable department spending a lot of time on relatively low-value items with frequent stock-outs ultimately becoming a problem.

Approach

The Consumers Interstate Consulting (CIC) group implemented a Lean procurement strategy. CIC did a full audit of the products currently used throughout the facility. CIC then organized all 313 items and created the unique list of products for all eight departments where they could place their orders using the CIC website (www.supersupplies.com), with a CIC manager taking charge of ordering and consolidating deliveries.

Results

As a result, the ordering process became streamlined, spending was controlled, and a large amount of time was given back to the procurement team and accounts payable. Scapa now receives one invoice a month instead of 25, and has much more time to spend on more value-added activities (www.Leanprocurement.com, 2017).

Next we will look in some detail at the more transactional purchasing process and how Lean concepts can be applied there.

9

Purchasing

Purchasing is a basic function in most organizations, and for the purposes of this book will be defined as the transactional function of buying products and services. In a business setting, this commonly involves the placement and processing of a purchase order through the receipt of and payment for goods (Steps 5–8 in the procurement process shown in Figure 9.1; steps 1–4 were previously discussed in Chapter 8).

THE PURCHASING PROCESS

In this chapter, we will discuss the purchasing process steps in terms of their basic mechanics, as well as how and where Lean thinking concepts can be applied.

STEP 5: ISSUE PURCHASE ORDERS

Issuing purchase orders involves the execution of the master schedule and materials requirements planning (MRP) recommended purchasing requirements to ensure good use of resources, minimize work in process (WIP) inventory and provide the desired level of customer service. This usually falls under the auspices of what is known as a buyer/planner who works hand in hand with the master scheduler. Buyers/planners are responsible for the control of production activity and the flow of work through the plant, and can be also be responsible for purchasing, materials

FIGURE 9.1
The Procurement Process.

requirements planning, supplier relationship management, product life cycle and service design, and more. They also coordinate the flow of goods from suppliers.

The purchase order is used to buy materials from a supplier. It clearly defines the price, specifications, and terms and conditions of the product or service, and any additional obligations for either party. The purchase order must be delivered by fax, mail, email or other electronic means, or in person.

Types of purchase orders may include:

Discrete Orders: Used for a single transaction with a supplier, with no assumption that further transactions will occur.

Pre-negotiated blanket order: A purchase order made with a supplier containing multiple delivery dates over a period of time, usually with predetermined pricing, which often has lower costs because of greater volumes (possibly through centralized purchasing and/or the consolidation of suppliers) on a longer-term contract. It is typically used when there is an ongoing need for consumable goods.

Pre-negotiated, vendor-managed inventory (VMI): The supplier maintains an inventory of items at the customer's plant and the customer pays for the inventory when it is consumed (or in some cases, when delivered). Usually for standard, small-value items, like maintenance, repair, and operating supplies (MRO), such as fasteners and electrical parts.

Bid and auction ("e-procurement"): This involves the use of online catalogs, exchanges and auctions to speed up purchasing, reduce costs, and integrate the supply chain. There are many e-commerce sites for industrial equipment and MRO inventory auctions which vary in format from catalog (e.g. www.grainger.com, www.chempoint.com) to auction (e.g. www.biditup.com). Websites can be for standard items or industry-specific.

Corporate purchase card (pCard): This is a company charge card that allows goods and services to be procured without using a traditional purchasing process; sometimes referred to as procurement or "p" cards. There is always some kind of control for each pCard, such as a single purchase dollar limit, a monthly limit, and so on. A pCard holder's activity should periodically be independently reviewed.

To further enhance the speed and accuracy of transactions, many companies use what is known as "EDI" (electronic data interchange), which is the computer-to-computer exchange of business documents in a standard electronic format between business partners. In the past, EDI transactions either went directly from business to business (in the case of large companies) or through third parties known as value-added networks (VANs). Today, a large portion of EDI transactions flow through the internet.

Sometimes included in the category of EDI is the use of electronic funds transfer (EFT), which is the electronic transfer of money from one account to another, within a single financial institution or across multiple institutions, through computer systems. This also includes e-commerce payment systems which facilitate the acceptance of electronic payment for online transactions, which has become increasingly popular from the widespread use of internet-based shopping and banking.

STEP 6: FOLLOW-UP TO ASSURE CORRECT DELIVERY

ERP software modules assume that scheduled dates will be received on time. However, a scheduled delivery date must be monitored and managed to identify and avoid possible missed dates, in advance where possible. In some cases, delays may be inevitable, and as a result, recovery plans must be developed and managed to minimize the negative effects of delays.

It is also critical to understand the supplier's production process, capacity, and constraints to resolve problems collaboratively in a timely and efficient manner.

On occasion, expediting is necessary, but should be on an exception basis. However, supplier performance should be monitored on an ongoing basis, and if an individual supplier is consistently being expedited, then corrective action should occur.

In many organizations, purchasing may work hand-in-hand with either their traffic or transportation department, or that of the vendors (this depends on shipping terms which, among many things, determine when ownership transfer takes place, and who arranges and pays for transportation).

STEP 7: RECEIVE AND ACCEPT GOODS

The key objective at receipt of goods is to ensure that proper physical condition, quantity, documentation, and quality parameters are met. To accomplish this requires cross-functional activity among purchasing, receiving, quality control, and finance.

Receiving is technically a "non-value-added" activity from a customer perspective, as it is designed to ensure that everything up to that point has been done properly. The goal is to ensure quality throughout, and reduce or eliminate the need for inspection. In many cases, technology such as barcode scanners and hand-held computers can automate the process. Some of the inspection processes can also be reduced or eliminated by various inspection and certification processes being performed by the vendor.

STEP 8: APPROVE INVOICE FOR PAYMENT

The final step in the procurement process is approving an invoice for payment (see Figure 9.2), according to the terms and conditions of the purchase order (PO).

The purchase requisition and purchase order forms are compared to make sure the order that was requested by a department was actually ordered by the purchasing department. Then the data in the request and PO is matched with that found on the packing slip that was received and checked when the product arrived, and is invoiced.

FIGURE 9.2
Document Flow.

If all three of these documents agree, the invoice price, date, and payment terms are compared with the prior three documents. This shows that the amount billed by the vendor is the same amount that was ordered by the company. After all the forms have been reviewed and compared, the accounting department can approve the payment to the vendor, and authorize the cashier to issue a payment check to the vendor.

Any discrepancies must be reconciled before payment is issued to the vendor. In some cases, small levels of discrepancies can be ignored (e.g. +/- 3% or +/- $20).

Freight bills are the carrier's invoice for charges for a given shipment, and special attention should be paid to them, as there tend to be large changes to fuel costs, low visibility of the future freight costs, and a relatively high complexity of freight quotes. Therefore, freight invoices are susceptible to human and process errors, and require auditing to ensure that the organization does not overpay for services it did not request or receive.

These audits can be performed internally or externally, both pre-payment and, in some cases, post-payment, and can lower a shipper's overall transportation costs by as much as 2%.

Discounts for early invoice payment should be taken whenever possible, although in a sluggish economy, many customers try to extend payment as long as possible due to cashflow issues.

LEAN PURCHASING

Five main principles of Lean can be applied to the purchasing function as a logical process to identify and eliminate waste in this support process (Torvatn et al, 2016). The principles are: specify value, identify the value stream, flow, pull, and seek perfection.

Specify Value

Vendors and the materials they supply are critical to quality and cost of a manufacturers end-product and the purchasing department is critical to maximizing value from the suppliers. As a result, purchasing personnel contact with customers is important to understanding customer needs. By raising the level of importance of purchasing to the organization, senior purchasing managers will come into contact with other senior managers more often, and gain more insight into customers and their concerns.

For lower level purchasing personnel, participating in cross-function teams (e.g. new product introduction, quality, S&OP, etc.) can bring customer concerns and requirements to their departments. They can also visit customers in this capacity to gain further insights.

Purchasing's main internal customer is production, and therefore it is important to understand their requirements for materials and how they are used in the end-product.

Value Stream

Purchasing processes such as ordering (including follow-up, expediting, and invoicing), supplier selection, supplier evaluation, supplier development, strategic decisions, and other internal activities need to be analyzed to identify and eliminate non-value-added activities and to focus on adding more value. Value-stream mapping (VSM), a Lean technique used to document, analyze, and improve the flow of information or materials required to produce a product or service for a customer, is a key Lean tool to accomplish this task.

The use of VSM will ensure a common understanding of the purchasing department's activities, and help that department to understand other department's value-added activities. It will ensure that the purchasing department understands customers' preferences, and those of other internal functions, to maximize value.

Flow

The Lean concept of one-piece-flow is important internally and externally when dealing with suppliers. The value stream mapping exercise just mentioned can allow the department to minimize various forms of waste such as waiting, overproduction, over-processing, and defects to help information and inbound flow to support production efficiently.

Even when the company uses the fourth principle of demand "pull" (see next section), there can still be waste, as purchasing has to coordinate delivery, storage, and handoff to production as close to just-in-time (JIT) as possible. The purchasing department also needs to be constantly updated on production plans and schedules to ensure adequate flow.

Waste also can occur from documentation and money-flow related to ordering materials and supplies. Purchasing should make sure that ordering and payment routines are simplified to use minimal resources.

VSM can also be used in terms of human resources to make sure that skills and competencies match requirements, and to enhance training and recruiting plans.

In the end, a majority of waste reduction activities focus on supplier interactions.

Pull

In a pull-based supply chain, procurement, production and distribution are demand-driven rather than to forecast-driven. However, a pull strategy does not always require make-to-order production, as in many cases limited inventory is kept on hand and is replenished as it is consumed. Kanban cards can be used to signal the need to replenish inventory factoring in supplier lead times, estimated demand, and safety stock.

A supply chain is usually a combination of both push and pull, where the interface between the push-based stages and the pull-based stages is sometimes known as the push–pull boundary and the further "upstream" (towards suppliers) the boundary, the Leaner the supply chain.

As a result, purchasing usually places orders based upon some combination of forecast and actual demand driven by the production requirements of the end item being made and sold (these purchased items are known as "dependent demand" items). In some cases, they purchase end items for products sold directly to customers by sales.

To execute a pull strategy, the company must have some combination of excellent forecasts, and short production and delivery cycles. When a supplier needs more time than requested by the manufacturer who is using a pull strategy, the purchasing department needs to work with the supplier to improve their cycle times, reduce the purchasing department's order cycle times to give the supplier more advanced warning or come up with other creative solutions, such as postponement and modularization.

If no solution can be found to support the pull strategy, as a last resort, a form of short-term scheduling (versus pure JIT) and prognosis-based purchasing should be used.

Seek Perfection

Perfection, in this context, means that purchasing people, processes, and systems need to continuously improve. To do this, value-added activities found during VSM need to be measured to track performance. This would include activity, process, quality, price, and cycle time measurements.

The measurements should be communicated both within the department and to other interested parties, such as production.

As part of continuous improvement, at some point, the "future state" VSM becomes the "current state" and the process begins again, as Lean is a long-term journey.

With that in mind, we will now look at some cases with Lean principles applied to the purchasing process.

EPA LEAN REVIEW OF PURCHASING–CASE STUDY #1

Challenge

The region one office of environmental measurement and evaluation (OEME) makes 600 small purchases to acquire necessary laboratory and field supplies, equipment, and services. In 2014, the environmental protection agency (EPA) region one held a value stream mapping event to examine and improve the OEME process from identification of the need for an item through completion of the purchase transaction. The region initiated the project to increase efficiency, as the process team was being reduced from three people to one person, as well as to prevent errors created by handwritten orders.

Approach

Participants in the event mapped the current purchasing process in region one and analyzed the process map to develop streamlined procedures.

The event team identified the following process changes that the region one lab would implement that included:

- Automating the order form so that information is standardized and submitted to purchasing correctly.

- Setting up a visual inventory system for commonly ordered supplies.
- Providing the purchasing agent with a list of employees who work in the same lab area so that their purchases can be combined.
- Reducing review steps for items that are ordered on a regular basis.

The team held regular monthly meetings to coordinate on implementation of the process improvements that the team identified during the event, as well as an all-hands meeting at the lab to train everyone affected by the new process. Over the summer of 2014, the team implemented all the identified improvements, and shifted responsibility for certain tasks, such as verifying that purchases of electronic equipment complied with relevant regulations, from the purchasing agent to the purchaser, thereby reducing review time and unnecessary steps.

Results

The team created a new process that will reduce the number of days to complete an order by 60%, combined similar purchases into fewer, larger purchases, and transferred all orders to an electronic system.

Errors in lab purchase forms have been reduced by 50% and improvements in the new process are expected to reduce lead time in permit review by 72%. The new process will also create new opportunities for staff learning and feedback (www.epa.gov, 2014).

CREATING A LEAN OFFICE–CASE STUDY #2

Challenge

The company is a small electrical manufacturer located in the Midwest. They have a wide variety of customers located all over the world, and their major products are industrial switchgears and switchboards made to their customers' exact specifications.

Through previous Lean initiatives, their manufacturing process has been reduced to one week, but their current design process (or "blue book"), had a lead time of 4 weeks, and consisted of engineering drawings, bill of material (BOM), and manufacturing process plan for a given customer order. They wanted to transform their office processes by applying a Lean strategy to increase the efficiency of the design department.

Approach

Employees were selected from the purchasing, electrical design, and structural design departments to participate in a value stream mapping (VSM) event.

The process documented started when the customer sent the order to purchasing who created a quote and a rough bill of materials (BOM). They then notified the president that they received the quote and the president generated the order that tells the project manager (PM) to create the BOM (note that the PM oversees customer communication and reviewing any design corrections).

The BOM was then sent to the customer for review (up to 10 days), after which the PM reviewed the BOM again, and forwarded it to purchasing for their review of things such as correct item numbers and material availability (the BOM was simultaneously sent to the customer again with corrections for their review).

After the PM approved everything, the structural and electrical departments started the design process. All designs were then checked by the PM before being sent to the customer for approval.

It was determined that the design correction process was repeated three times. Communications with the customer was done via email, and internally between the PM and design was done manually.

Results

Kaizen Event 1: Reduce the defect rate in the electrical design process.

As the defect rate in the electrical design process was found to be 100%, it was suggested that the company ask the electrical designers to cross-check each other's designs for accuracy.

It was also suggested that the purchasing process be completed before the design phase begins, since by waiting for a final BOM and cross-checking each other's work, the electrical design team can ensure that the PM is approving the final design, rather than a continuous cycle of corrections.

Kaizen Event 2: Reducing waiting time in the purchasing process.

There was a repeated cycle that occurs when purchasing contacts the supplier for clarification. The waste of waiting takes place when the supplier sent the order back because they did not recognize the part number indicated on the bill of materials. As a result, there was a lengthy correction cycle between the material supplier and purchasing.

The team proposed a work cell where purchasing and quoting were combined into one process to eliminate waste. The BOM will then be finalized and material ordered before the PM starts a design, and corrections will no longer need to be passed to the PM. As a result, the company can save approximately 20 hours ($340) of labor per job for an annual labor savings of $61,200.

Kaizen Event 3: Reducing transportation in the design process.

During the design creation process, unnecessary steps occurred that required manual transportation of design documents to several areas in the office.

The Lean team proposed a kanban post and card process where the kanban post visually shows the PM and designers each task and which department it is in. To track the tasks efficiently, each task is accompanied by a kanban card where a slip is torn off the kanban card and then placed on the board once a process is completed and the PM can then sign off on the kanban slips. During the purchasing or design process, any corrections are written on the slip, which is returned to the responsible person (Chen and Cox, 2012).

As mentioned in Chapter 8, there are two major types of items that are procured, direct and indirect items. In the next chapter, we will examine the processes for both and how Lean thinking can improve them.

10

Material Requirements Planning (MRP) and Indirect Procurement

In this chapter, we will look a little more closely at an operational aspect of purchasing known as material requirements planning (MRP), which is a production planning, scheduling, and inventory control process and system used to manage manufacturing processes and generate direct goods requirements (i.e. raw materials and production goods).

We will also look at the procurement process for indirect goods referred to as "maintenance, repair and operating" (MRO) goods which, for our purposes, will include machinery, tooling, parts, and consumables used to create a product as well as fluids, lubricants, office supplies, shop supplies, furniture, light fixtures, toolboxes, safety protection, and other consumables.

MRO items are often given a lower priority, but without them, businesses wouldn't be able to operate in an effective fashion. In fact, indirect procurement can range from 15–25% of a company's total revenue.

In both cases, we will discuss using Lean tools and techniques to improve the processes.

MATERIALS REQUIREMENTS PLANNING (MRP)

Once a master production schedule (MPS) has been solidified for independent demand or end items, it can be "exploded" through a bill of materials or "BOM" file to determine raw material and component (i.e. dependent demand) requirements.

The information needed to run an MRP model includes the MPS, a bill of materials (a list of the raw materials, sub-assemblies, intermediate assemblies, sub-components, parts, and the quantities of each needed to manufacture an end product), inventory balances, lead-times, and scheduled receipts (i.e. purchase orders and production work orders). These inputs need to be accurate and up-to-date, otherwise, it leads to a "garbage in, garbage out" situation, resulting in poor execution, and, ultimately, customer dissatisfaction.

MPS and MRP Calculations

The internal mechanics of the MPS and MRP systems are basically the same, with the time phased net requirements from the MPS (independent demand) driving MRP gross requirements (dependent demand) via the bill of material file.

In both cases, information (forecasts, inventory balances, outstanding production work orders, purchase orders, etc.) is netted to create new, future-planned receipts, usually in time-phased weekly or monthly time buckets well into the future, with lead-times offset to create replenishment requirements known as planned orders.

In a bicycle manufacturing example, Figure 10.1 illustrates the basic calculation where we have gross requirements (in MPS, "gross" would be the forecast "consumed" by open customer orders" in each time period before netting any on-hand or scheduled receipts) for the production of 75 bikes of a specific model in week 8. Typically, safety stock or safety time targets would be in place for independent demand items, but for sake of simplicity, there is none in the example.

As we have 50 bikes in inventory, we will deduct that from the gross requirement of 75 bikes and will need to produce an additional 25 units by week 8 (i.e. the net requirement). To do so, we will need to have 50 wheels and 25 frames available in week 6, after offsetting the components' lead-time, for the bike production. Through the BOM "explosion," these requirements show up as gross requirements for the wheels and frames in MRP. The same calculations are then performed to create net (of on-hand inventory) requirements, with resulting planned receipts and planned orders for the wheels and frames (and then level 2, level 3, etc., items).

MPS for 26" Boys Blue Bicycle:

	Week:							
	1	2	3	4	5	6	7	8
Gross Requirements								75
Scheduled Receipts								
Projected On-Hand	50	50	50	50	50	50	50	50
Net Requirements								25
Planned Receipts								25
Planned Orders						25		

Item	26" Boys Blue Bicycle
Lot Size	10
Lead Time (weeks)	2
Beginning On-Hand	50
Safety Stock	0
Level Code	0
ABC Code	A

MRP for 26" Boys Blue Bicycle:

	Week:							
	1	2	3	4	5	6	7	8
Gross Requirements						50		
Scheduled Receipts								
Projected On-Hand	20	20	20	20	20	20		
Net Requirements						30		
Planned Receipts						30		
Planned Orders					30			

Item	Wheel
Lot Size	10
Lead Time (weeks)	1
Beginning On-Hand	20
Safety Stock	0
Level Code	1
ABC Code	B

	Week:							
	1	2	3	4	5	6	7	8
Gross Requirements						25		
Scheduled Receipts								
Projected On-Hand	15	15	15	15	15	15		
Net Requirements				10				
Planned Receipts						10		
Planned Orders				10				

Item	Frame
Lot Size	10
Lead Time (weeks)	2
Beginning On-Hand	15
Safety Stock	0
Level Code	1
ABC Code	B

FIGURE 10.1
MPS and MRP Mechanics.

Although it has been said that no safety stock or safety time are required for raw or components since it is factored into finished goods requirements, the reality is that quality and other issues may arise, as well as vendor minimum order quantities, that may call for safety stock as a prudent thing to have.

Lot-Sizing Techniques

The actual quantity required is typically rounded up based upon various lot sizing techniques. They range from lot for lot (L4L; the exact requirement no matter how small), which is appropriate for JIT operations, to an economic order quantity (EOQ) calculation, described in the next section of this chapter, and beyond. Somewhere in between L4L and EOQ is the periodic order quantity (POQ) technique that orders the quantity needed during a predetermined time between orders. The POQ interval is usually defined as the EOQ divided by the "near-term" (user-defined) average demand per period. This technique takes a shorter-term view of demand trends, and tends to produce a balance between holding and ordering costs, and is therefore useful where item seasonality exists.

A form of the POQ for slow-moving items, an order time (OT) may be used which basically states that the planned orders will be grouped together so that one larger order versus many frequent small orders will be placed. In the case of purchased material or parts, vendors may set order minimums (which can always be negotiated). While this may result in greater holding costs, in the case of slower-moving items, it may be the right thing to do.

It should be noted that in the case of MRP, there are also "Resource" as opposed to "Requirement" versions that look beyond material requirements and consider other resources impacted such as labor, facilities, and equipment. Some are known as "closed loop" systems which allow for the planners to schedule work based upon period capacity constraints using smoothing tools that allow the system (manually or automatically) to move requirements around to meet capacity based upon priority rules set by the planner, such as order-splitting (running parts of a work order at two different times) and overlapping (part of a work order can move to a second operation while the rest is still on the first operation).

Some of these closed loop systems include capacity requirement planning (CRP) functionality. CRP is only performed after each MRP run, after planned and actual manufacturing orders from the shop floor control system have been considered. This generates a detailed view of what capacity is needed for each work center. The capacity required is compared to the available capacity and identifies over/under load conditions at the work center level.

For the most part, CRP isn't really used for interactive planning but more as a verification tool, and requirements are unconstrained or infinite as they don't take capacity constraints of each machine or work center into account.

It should be noted that by using CPP, much unnecessary waste can be avoided in terms of planning man hours, and issues created by creating unrealistic plans that then require "firefighting," resulting in expediting, shortages, unplanned overtime, etc.

In the end, planned orders for both independent and dependent demand are then used—either manually or sent electronically to either an ERP or accounting system—to create production work orders and purchase orders in what is known as short-term scheduling.

TOTAL COST MINIMIZED–HOW MUCH AND WHEN TO ORDER

A couple of concepts need to be understood and utilized by the procurement professional to help minimize costs and efficiently coordinate timing, whether using MRP or other methods. They are the economic order quantity (EOQ) model, which helps to determine how much is ordered, and the reorder point (ROP) model, which answers the question of when to place an order.

Economic Order Quantity Model

EOQ's goal is to minimize total costs. Graphically, as shown in Figure 10.2, that occurs at the intersection of holding costs, which go up as lot size quantities increase, and set-up costs, which go down as the number of orders/set-ups decrease. So, in effect, holding and set-up costs are inverses, resulting in a trade-off between the two of them. The point at which those costs intersect is where total costs are minimized, and is calculated by the simple economic order quantity inventory (EOQ) model.

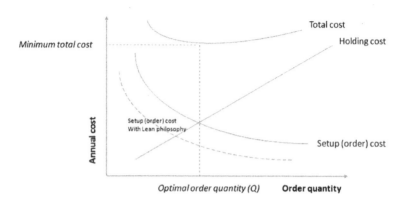

FIGURE 10.2
Holding vs. Set-Up Cost Trade-Off.

As has been mentioned, there is a lot of pressure to lower inventory costs in an organization. As a result, this pressure ends up falling to a great degree on the shoulders of the procurement organization. Ultimately, process improvement techniques like Lean (Chapter 6, and throughout this book), need to be utilized to effectively create a "paradigm shift" of sorts as shown on Figure 10.2.

The order quantity that minimizes total inventory costs by optimizing the trade-offs between holding and ordering costs is known as the economic order quantity (EOQ). It is one of the most common inventory techniques used to answer the "how much" question.

The EOQ contains some assumptions. They are that:

1. The ordering cost is constant.
2. The rate of demand is known and spread evenly.
3. The lead time is known and fixed.
4. The purchase price of the item is constant.
5. The replenishment is made instantaneously, and the entire order is delivered at one time.

These assumptions can be visualized in terms of inventory usage over time in Figure 10.3, which has become known as the "saw tooth model," for obvious reasons.

There are three basic EOQ models. We will mainly discuss the first of these, which is known as the basic or simple economic order quantity (EOQ) model.

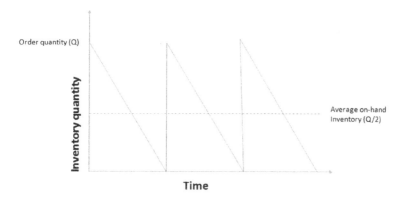

FIGURE 10.3
Sawtooth Model.

The other two are the:

1. Production order quantity model: As distinct from the basic EOQ model, the production quantity model assumes that materials produced are used immediately, and as a result lowers holding costs (i.e. no instant receipt, as in the basic model). As a result, this model also takes into account daily production and demand rates.
2. Quantity discount model: This is a version of the simple EOQ where pricing discounts are factored into the model based upon reaching certain minimum purchase quantities. This then compares the effect of buying more than perhaps is needed, but with a lower price, which may offset the impact on holding costs, which in part are based upon the price of the product, as we shall see in the basic EOQ model.

Basic EOQ Calculation

In order to calculate the EOQ as well as annual set-up, holding, and total inventory costs, we need the following information:

Q = Optimal number of pieces per order (EOQ).
D = Annual demand in units for the inventory item.
S = Set-up or ordering cost for each order.
H = Holding or carrying cost per unit per year.

Once we have that information we can solve for:

Annual set-up costs = (number of orders placed per year) * (set-up or order cost per order) or (D/Q)*S.

Annual holding cost = (average inventory level) * (holding cost per unit per year) or (Q/2)*H.

Total annual cost = set-up cost + holding cost or (D/Q)*S + (Q/2)*H

Economic Order Quantity (EOQ) = $\sqrt{\dfrac{2DS}{H}}$

Reorder Point (ROP) Models

Now that we've used the EOQ to determine how much we need, the next question is when to replenish, also referred to as the "reorder point."

Basically, there are two primary types of models that are used in this regard: fixed quantity (Q) models and fixed period (P) models.

Fixed Quantity (Q) Model

The fixed quantity or Q model has a reorder point (ROP) that is based upon inventory reaching a specific quantity (Q), at which point inventory is replenished based upon the calculated EOQ (Figure 10.4).

The calculation for the ROP = demand per day x lead time for a new order (in days) or D × L.

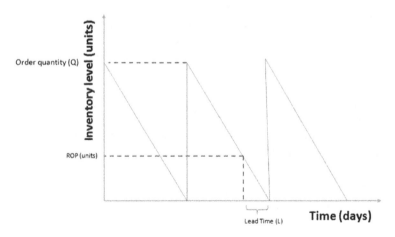

FIGURE 10.4
Fixed Quantity (Q) ROP Model.

In a simple example, if our demand is 10 units per day and our replenishment lead time is 3 days, our ROP would be 30 units (i.e. 10 units × 3 days).

This simplistic model assumes that demand and lead time are constant, which does not reflect reality. So typically, extra "buffer" inventory is included in this calculation to compensate for this variability which is known as "safety stock" (SS).

Safety Stock

There are a variety of ways to calculate required safety stock. Many are "rules of thumb" and some are statistically based.

In general, the safety stock quantity that is arrived at is additive in nature and thus the ROP calculation becomes: D × L + SS

Probabilistic Safety Stock

The idea behind a probabilistic safety stock calculation is that we would like to keep a certain quantity of safety stock to meet a desired service level to compensate for demand variability. If we assume a normal distribution, we can assign a service (or confidence) level as meeting X% of demand during the lead time (Figure 10.5).

To calculate this we can associate the number of standard deviations around the mean to a confidence level—defined as the number of standard deviations extending from the mean of a normal distribution required to

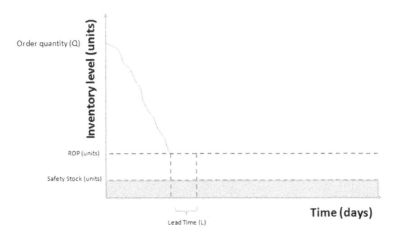

FIGURE 10.5
ROP with Probabilistic Safety Stock Model.

contain x% of the area—which are contained in a commonly available Standard Normal (Z) table (see some commonly used samples below):

Z	Confidence Level
1.0	85%
1.3	90%
1.6	95%
3.0	99%

To use this method, we also need to calculate the mean and standard deviation of demand for our item, as demand is variable in this case.

Let's take an example where we have a mean demand of 100 units per day, a one-day lead time, a standard deviation during lead time of 15 units and a desired service level of 99% ($Z = 3.0$).

In this type of calculation, the reorder point is the expected demand during lead time plus safety stock.

So, in our example, the ROP with safety stock calculation would then be: $100 + (3.0 \times 15)$ or 145 units.

While this model only considers demand variability during lead time only, there are also other models that compensate for:

- Variable demand with constant lead time
- Variable lead time with constant demand
- Variable lead time and demand

Rules of Thumb Safety Stock Calculations

Besides probabilistic safety stock models, some in industry prefer to use "rules of thumb" instead (which are sometimes referred to as "safety time," as they are expressed in days of supply), which, while perhaps not as scientific, are easier to understand and calculate. Some "rules of thumb" examples include:

1. ½ lead time: If demand is 10 units per day and replenishment lead time is 3 days, then the calculated safety stock would be 15 units (i.e. $(10*3)/2$).
2. Maximum sales less average sales: Provides coverage on the "upside" for the occasional large oversell.
3. Statistical safety stock converted to days: Uses the safety stock probabilistic models' unit calculation above converted to days of supply inventory target.

Fixed Period (P) Model

The use of periods of supply targets, such as in the third example above, can be advantageous when you tend to have seasonality with your products, which is one of the main features of fixed period or P models (Figure 10.6).

In this type of model, inventory is continuously monitored. Typically, faster moving items are reviewed more often, with slower movers being reviewed less often.

As opposed to a ROP quantity, individual SKU inventory targets (usually in terms of periods of supply) are the trigger point for replenishment.

Fixed period models work well where vendors make routine visits to customers and take orders for their complete line of products, or when it is beneficial to combine orders to save on transportation costs, such as shipments to a distribution center. A tool known as distribution requirements planning (DRP), which enables the user to set inventory control parameters such as safety stock, and calculate the time-phased inventory requirements, is commonly used in the case of managing a network of finished goods distribution centers.

Single Period Model

A single period model is used by companies that order seasonal or one-time items. The product typically has no value after the time it is needed,

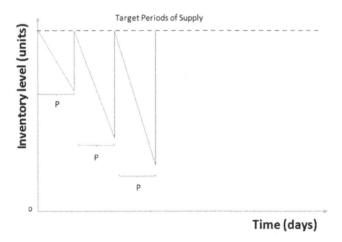

FIGURE 10.6
Fixed Period (P) ROP Model.

such as a newspaper or baked goods. There are costs to both ordering too much or too little, and the company's managers must try to get the order right the first time to minimize the chance of loss.

A probabilistic way of looking at this is most helpful. We do this by estimating both the cost of a shortage (sales price/unit – cost/unit) and of an overage (cost/unit – scrap value/unit).

We can then determine a service level (i.e. probability of not stocking out) by dividing the cost of shortage by the combined cost of shortage and overage.

The calculated service level percentage can then determine a reorder quantity using the same method as was outlined for the "Q" ROP model.

LEAN AND MATERIAL REQUIREMENTS PLANNING

As mentioned in Chapter 6, and bears repeating in this chapter, MRP has been around since the 1970s and was created by Joseph Orlicky of IBM as a concept for planning and time-phasing the procurement of parts, components, and materials (dependent demand) tied to the forecast (independent) demand requirements from the master production schedule. It was the first use of computers to generate the supply orders, which can be quite a task, as many finished goods items can be made from hundreds, if not thousands, of parts, components, sub-assemblies, and raw materials. This was great for large manufacturing companies, saving a lot of time spent on manual order point systems. MRP was developed at a time when most companies used a demand "push" mentality well before today's customers began demanding shorter lead-times and smaller quantities.

Lean-type thinking became prevalent in the 1980s, and focused operational management on timing production rates to actual market consumption. It uses replenishment signals known as kanbans that summarize customer demand up the supply chain (known as a demand "pull" system).

Lean processes can have trouble dealing with extreme variability and can be difficult to use in mixed-mode manufacturing environments with resources shared across multiple products with unique demand rates. Lean can also lack visibility into the actual flow of materials through the supply chain, especially if it is focused only on the manufacturing operation.

As a result, typical thinking on MRP vs. JIT is that MRP is usually best for companies with many product options, frequent engineering changes, and a variable product system, and JIT is best used in environments with fewer product options, engineering, and product mix changes, and less variability in demand levels.

The reason for this type of thinking is that MRP and Lean view inventory a little differently. MRP typically uses finished goods inventory to meet future customer orders, while Lean attempts to produce as needed, "just-in-time," meaning producing to order, not to stock.

Not surprisingly, MRP and Lean also look at the production process differently. Companies using MRP try to steer clear, to some degree, of small lots of a finished product because of cost inefficiencies (i.e. they don't have Lean processes). Manufacturers using Lean concepts, however, are more open to small order batches as they have minimal machine set-up times.

LEANING OUT MRO INVENTORY

Indirect procurement activities can encompass a wide variety of goods and services, from standardized low-value items like office supplies, to maintenance, repair and operating (MRO), where indirect items tend to be hoarded "just in case." While many companies have strategic sourcing initiatives, they typically do not extend to the indirect purchasing categories such as MRO.

MRO supplies tend to be lower volume and higher variety compared to the raw materials, sub-assemblies and parts that go directly into a product. Despite accounting for up to 40% of procurement costs, purchasing and storage of MRO supplies is usually highly decentralized.

Buying processes and vendor and inventory management practices for the same type of supplies may differ between departments and facilities, which, from a Lean management perspective, can present opportunities for waste and cost reduction and productivity improvements.

A white paper by MH&L and Penton, entitled "Leaning Out the MRO Supply Chain" (www.mscdirect.com, 2017) described how several basic Lean tools can be applied to MRO items. They included:

One-Piece-Flow and Layout

During the MRO ordering and replenishment process, the focus should be on eliminating unnecessary paperwork and other activities that provide little internal or external value. Where possible, you should attempt to simplify and automate procedures and transactions as this can both improve productivity and reduce opportunities for error.

5S: Workplace Organization

5S is a basic Lean tool used to make a work area organized, safe, and free of clutter. This is a great application for supply and parts storage areas, which tend to be poorly organized and cluttered. Its goal is to help employees do their job more efficiently and effectively by improving organization, order, and cleanliness. It includes the steps of sort out, set in order, shine, standardize, and sustain.

- Sort out: Large amounts of space are freed up by removing unused equipment and getting rid of excess or unneeded material.
- Set in order: The next step is to assign and mark storage locations so the work space remains orderly, using visual indicators where possible.
- Shine: During the shine process, we clean trash, filth, dust, and other foreign matter. Contamination can include debris, oil, documents, water, dust and dirt, food and drink, poor work habits, and materials left by other people, such as maintenance. As a group, you need to determine what needs to be cleaned, who is responsible, how it is done, and what tools are needed.
- Standardize: Means creating a consistent way to carry out tasks and procedures ... everyone does it the same (documented) way.
- Sustain: The final S, and perhaps the hardest one to accomplish, is sustain. Sustain refers to making a habit of maintaining correct procedures over the long-term.

By applying 5S to storage areas where MRO materials are found like tool cribs and shadow boards, productivity is improved because tools, parts, and supplies can be found, and if necessary replenished, quickly.

Value Stream Mapping

Value stream mapping (VSM), discussed in Chapter 6, is a great tool to gain a common understanding across an organization for a set of activities, as well as to identify where waste occurs. When applied to a supply chain, activities may include transportation links, delivery steps, shipping, and receiving processes.

Mapping MRO ordering and replenishment processes can result in benefits such as centralizing inventory management, whether it is accomplished internally, or as part of a vendor management agreement.

Standardized Work

The more variability in a process or activity, the better chance for waste through errors, quality, and processing time. Thus the need for standardized work which is easy to understand and visual (an important step in 5S as mentioned above).

For areas that impact MRO materials such as scheduled maintenance, standard work can improve scheduling and budgeting accuracy, resulting in less waste, and better inventory management of consumables.

Just-in-Time

Pull/kanban-type systems using a variety of signals to inform upstream activities when additional supply is needed can be used in a JIT environment, once other Lean tools such as quick changeover, batch size reduction, etc., have been implemented. It is important for all participants to have visibility downstream and upstream to reduce inventory buffers and improve service levels.

The same goes for MRO materials to improve availability and reduce costs. There are a variety of options here which include vending machines and other types of vendor-managed inventory, including the use of a handheld scanner to send replenishment signals to MRO suppliers, to provide clear visibility of usage.

These type of VMI processes, when combined with paperless order processing not requiring purchase orders, and other manual processes, can eliminate significant waste from MRO supply chains.

Now let's look at some actual examples of improvements made in MRP and indirect procurement.

 GABLES ENGINEERING MOVES TO A "REAL" MRP SYSTEM–CASE STUDY #1

The Challenge

Gables Engineering is an avionics manufacturer in a business that builds custom cockpit controls, including the design and building of the switches, housings, and LCD display modules for the airline and airframe industry.

Gables had a pseudo-material requirements planning (MRP) system based on reorder points which used current customer demand, as well as historical demand, to determine what they needed to buy. It was basically moving forward by looking backward (which assumes the past will repeat itself, which as we know, isn't always the case). The company wanted a product using the Oracle® database that had a Windows® front end, that would seamlessly interface with other third party systems.

Approach

Gables formed a team to look at its business processes to see if they needed a new enterprise application system. A request for quotation (RFQ) was sent to a number of software vendors.

Gables selected IFS enterprise resources planning (ERP)/e-business that includes a true MRP module with a better understanding of actual demand. Previously at Gables, demand was determined by customer orders as well as historical demand causing them to buy and build unnecessary parts, loading shops with unnecessary work and inflated purchased inventories.

Results

Once Gables implemented the new IFS system, it was able to calculate demand using actual customer orders and forecasts, enabling them to order and build parts by looking at forecasts, not at history. This reduced work-in-process and overall inventory by 50% and 30% respectively. It used to take two days to get a spare part shipped out, from time of order to time of shipment; now same-day shipping is possible.

The software also tracks the history of changes made to a product down to serial number, including the parts removed from inventory to manufacture it. During a customer audit, Gables was able to show the traceability of a component using the audited part's sub-assembly, which they could never have done previously.

Gables has also reduced kitting time to less than one month before assembly, kitting almost 99% of the entire product right before assembling it. They also now have notebooks, allowing stock room personnel to review pick lists online, and pick and update inventory instantly (www.top10erp.com, 2008–16).

ACCURATE GAUGE GAINS A STRATEGIC BUSINESS ADVANTAGE FROM MSC CONTROLPOINT INVENTORY MANAGEMENT–CASE STUDY #2

Challenge

Founded in 1966, Accurate Gauge is one of the premier manufacturers of carrier housings for the Class 5–7 and Class 8 heavy-duty truck market, and supports daily production requirements for the major truck axle suppliers in North America.

When the company started looking at vending solutions, they were interested in the traditional benefits of reducing inventory carrying costs, tooling/MRO waste and tooling consumption.

Approach

The company selected MSC, a North American distributor of metalworking and MRO products and services, to install its first vending solutions, three drawer units and three cabinets, on a trial basis.

MSC's vending machines provide both visibility and traceability to all items used by Accurate Gauge and help them prepare weekly by keeping their supply chain information up to date. On Sunday night, stock reports are shared with key manufacturers to ensure they are reviewed Monday morning, avoiding stock-outs.

During the trial, Accurate Gauge had a tooling inventory reduction of roughly 50%, and continued to further implement the program.

Results

Today, between the drawers, carousel, and cabinets, the company has more than 20 units in place, or scheduled for installation, across three locations, as well as a new VMI (vendor-managed inventory) program for coolant, safety, and maintenance products.

The new system has resulted in:

- A 50% reduction in tooling inventory.
- A rate of 3% or less spent on perishable tooling, versus an industry standard of 5%.
- The ability to support their quality control process by detecting tool failures when replacing critical tooling. When a critical tool fails and a new tool is withdrawn from vending, it triggers an automated alert which is then emailed both to engineering and quality where they check the product machined when the tool failure occurred. This ensures that tool failure is contained, not affecting the customer (www.mscdirect.com, 2006).

In the next section, we will look at various ways to make the entire procurement process more Lean, through a focus on cost management, contracts and supplier performance management, technology, and thorough data analysis.

Part III

Tools and Techniques for a Leaner Supply Management Process

11

Cost Management

As we know, the concept of Lean is about identifying and eliminating waste by reducing non-value-added activities through continuous improvement.

To the customer, value can mean many things, such as a lower price, greater benefits such as quality, performance, reliability, etc. While the primary focus of Lean isn't really cost, many of the end results, such as increased throughput, better quality, fewer errors, etc., can certainly result in lower costs to the manufacturer, distributor, and retailer, not to mention the ultimate consumer. As a result, cost considerations have a significant impact on the "Lean-ness" of an organization, especially through the efforts of the procurement organization, since purchases can account for a significant percentage of a company's costs.

PROCUREMENT PRACTICES THAT CAN RESULT IN ANNUAL COST SAVINGS

In today's competitive global marketplace, managing an organization's spend is an important step to realizing profit objectives, and with that in mind, companies are increasingly relying on procurement and supply management functions to deliver the cost savings.

Below are six practices that can realize significant annual cost savings (Barve, 2002):

1. Centralized supply management organization.

   Centralizing purchases across business units can achieve cost savings through volume-based discounts, gain a better understanding of user requirements across the company, and address them more effectively. By having access to upper management, corporate expertise, and the power to influence standards, a centralized supply organization structure guides strategic management of corporate-wide supply activities, with a higher level of control over outside spending.

For example, before centralizing purchasing, IBM had 60–70 disconnected procurement organizations around the world, and kept its suppliers at arms-length. After going to a centralized purchasing organization, with commodity councils to leverage worldwide purchasing, and leveraging the internet, IBM saved over $5 billion during a five year period. They went from about 4,900 production suppliers in 1993 to having about 85% of IBM's $17.0 billion in production purchases consolidated with 50 suppliers by 1999.

Additionally, about $43 billion of the $46 billion that IBM spent on purchases was spent on purchasing conducted electronically, saving $377 million in costs through its e-procurement program in 2000, primarily due to a decrease in administrative tasks.

2. Implementing a strategic sourcing process.

While this is a great example of successfully implementing supply management technology, a robust sourcing strategy aligned to the company's business needs and a solid sourcing process provides direction and structure to a company's sourcing efforts.

3. Talented supply management professionals.

The need for talented and experienced people to lead supply management operations is another important aspect of achieving long-term cost savings.

Similar to IBM, John Deere Corporation also established best practices in supplier development, strategic sourcing, and cost management, but also established a group of programs to recruit and train purchasing and logistics talent internally. In 2000, Deere had about 80 interns in the supply department (as well as an on-site MBA program in conjunction with Arizona State University), costing them $1.25 million and resulting in direct savings of $15 million.

4. Strict processes for determining real cost savings.

One should never forget about the need to effectively measure performance. As a purchasing magazine poll pointed out, companies that consistently achieve cost savings on the supply side of their operations create strict processes and definitions for identifying cost savings (Barve, 2002).

AT&T South (formerly known as BellSouth), for example, has established a formal process of review, where the supply manager justifies the cost saving to a review committee made up of CFOs from different business units, showing the starting point, the sourcing process, and the resulting projected budget savings.

5. Executive compensation linked to cost reduction goals.

There is no greater motivator than tying one's compensation to goals that help increase the value of an organization, and this was never more true than in the sourcing function.

This also helps to minimize what is known as the "principal–agent problem," where agents (i.e. employees) are motivated to act in their own best interests, which are contrary to those of their principals (i.e. owners).

6. Active investment in supply management technology.

There is no doubt that companies can significantly benefit by successfully implementing supply management technology. As has been mentioned though, implementing technology solutions without analyzing the underlying sourcing processes won't necessarily bring you the intended results. You must first make sure that you have processes that align with your overall sourcing strategy that are Lean and Agile.

SEGMENT MAJOR PURCHASING CATEGORIES FOR BETTER COST MANAGEMENT

As the purchasing organization controls much of the organization's expenditures, they need to think about creative ways to strategically manage the supply base to better manage costs.

In Chapter 4, the idea of developing procurement categories was discussed. Here we will discuss focusing on the use of four major categories of segmentation to control costs: non-critical purchases, leverage purchases, strategic purchases, and bottleneck purchases, along with developing effective relationship and cost management strategies (Tate, 2011).

It is important to keep in mind that the cost (and price) strategies and analysis techniques applied need to support the relative importance of the item being purchased, and the type of relationship with the supplier that the organization wants (Figure 11.1).

FIGURE 11.1
Four Major Cost Categories.

Non-Critical Purchases

These are generic purchases of relatively low importance to the organization, with the focus on obtaining the lowest possible purchase price from a field of many suppliers. Supplier relationships are generally transactional and arms-length in nature.

As a result, the focus in this category is on price analysis with a goal of getting the best possible price while still maintaining customer value. In this segment, competitive bidding or publicly posted price lists are typically used to compare the price being paid by your company with the market value (e.g. producers price index or PPI, published by the Bureau of Labor Statistics, is compared with actual historical prices paid).

In the case of non-critical purchases, staying abreast of market trends is an important metric to ensure that the organization receives the lowest price.

Leveraging Purchases

The leveraged category of items procured are typically ordered in large quantities, often made-to-stock, with many available sources, and often are often found on the commodity exchanges. As a result, there is usually a relatively low amount of complexity involved in these purchases. However, these products and services have a large impact, and are of great importance to the organization in terms of volume and cost. So, in this category, it is not surprising that the focus is on cost analysis.

Many organizations use a technique called "white-sheeting," which is a combination of price benchmarking and cost analysis. This process starts with a blank page where all the cost elements of an item are identified using industry knowledge and averages, price indices, and other benchmarking techniques. By understanding what the item **should** cost (factoring in a reasonable profit for the seller), you gain a better understanding of what the final price should be.

Benchmarking proposed price increases against market changes also helps purchasers avoid paying too much.

Strategic Purchases

Strategic purchases represent items that are important to an organization's competency, and are complex and risky, because of limited availability of supply or fewer capable suppliers. Relationships with suppliers of these items tend to be longer-term and strategic.

The cost techniques used in this area are generally the most detailed and time-consuming, with a focus on continuous improvement.

The primary tool used here is a total cost of ownership analysis, which seeks to identify costs associated with the entire acquisition process over the life of the product or service, including service costs, failure costs, administrative costs, special handling costs, transportation costs, and other elements.

A total cost of ownership analysis can also help to compare the purchase from differing locations (e.g. offshore suppliers versus domestic suppliers).

After the cost elements are identified and estimated, a total cost model can also help develop different "what if" scenarios, and negotiation strategies, after which the buyer and the targeted supplier can work together to continuously improve the process and reduce the cost.

Bottleneck Purchases

Items that may require long-term capital investment and are often project-oriented are referred to as bottleneck purchases. While the relationship with the supplier is not always strategic, the supply market itself is highly complex. In general, a bottleneck purchase is a one-time (or infrequent) large expenditure with capital equipment, information systems, and other long-term assets falling into this category. Total cost models can also be used here, but they will tend to focus more on cost components across the total life-cycle of the item, such as extended service, warranty costs, replacement parts, and disposal costs.

COST AND PRICE ANALYSIS

The general sources of price information discussed in some of the strategies just mentioned are price lists, quotations, other buyers in the market, trade journals, negotiations, competitive bidding. In some cases, the specific supplier may be the best source of price information, as the buyer can require the supplier to furnish cost information, or, at the least, to supply a basic cost breakdown.

Pricing Strategies

The most popular pricing methods used are standard price lists, competitive bidding, and negotiations.

In any case, it is imperative that purchasing professionals understand the strategies used by suppliers to price their products to optimize their market position. These strategies include:

- Market penetration pricing: Where a low price is used to win a large share of the market.
- Market-skimming: When pricing a new product high to make a large profit from the purchases by initial customers. This is an effective strategy when there is no competition (the price is usually dropped when competition appears)
- Cost-plus pricing: A cost-based method for setting the prices of goods and services. Under this approach, you add together the direct material cost, direct labor cost, and overhead costs for a product, and add to it a mark-up percentage (to create a profit margin) to derive the price of the product.
- Marginal pricing: When a company sells a product at a price that covers its manufacturing costs, but not its overhead. The benefit of marginal pricing is that the lower price point increases customer demand.
- Going rate pricing: Pricing a product at a similar level to the competition (usually the market leaders).
- Premium pricing: Higher pricing where the market is prepared to pay extra for the features, quality, reputation, or functionality associated with the product.

- Buyer-based pricing: This strategy sets prices primarily according to the estimated value of a product or service to the customer rather than according to the cost of the product or historical prices.
- Discriminating pricing: Charges customers different prices for the same product or service. Examples are off-peak prices, special rates for children, senior citizens, etc.
- Captive pricing: Used to maximize revenue by pricing high when the buyer has no choice but to buy from the supplier. This strategy attracts customers to a core product with a low price, but allows sellers to make a profit off the captive products, which are necessary to use the product.
- Relationship pricing: Pricing aimed at maintaining a long-term relationship with a buyer. The price is determined based on a customer's overall purchases and circumstances, rather than being delivered on a product-by-product basis.

Price may also be characterized as the supplier-stated value of a product or service. However, the customer may have a different value for the product or service, based largely on the utility level assumed to be achieved from ownership of that product or service.

Maximizing Customer Value

While price and value are closely related, value takes into account the optimum combination of full-life cost and quality needed to meet the customer's requirement.

Techniques available to the purchaser to maximize value are:

- Value analysis: An approach to improving the value of an item or process by understanding its components and their associated costs, and then seeking to make improvements to the components, by either reducing their cost or increasing the value of the functions.
- Process re-engineering/improvement: To focus on waste identification and elimination in the manufacturing, distribution, and storage processes, including the reduction or elimination of inventory.

- Standardization: To minimize variation which causes a variety of wastes to occur related to quality, inventory, and efficiency, among other things.
- Whole-life methodology: Rather than simply focusing on initial price, this refers to the total cost of ownership over the life of an item.
- Post-tender negotiation: A contact between the buyer and the bidder(s) to refine and improve the bid(s), to ensure that prices, delivery, or associated terms of the contract are competitive.
- Global proactive sourcing: Casting a wider net by, for example, encouraging competition by avoiding repeated use of established suppliers.
- Re-purposing and re-use: Giving consideration to refurbishment of existing equipment rather than buying new.

Buyers understand the importance of price, and as a result, should have a number of key factors in mind for determining the reasonableness of the price being asked. This would include the price paid by competitors, what is considered a fair price, length and quantities involved, and the level of risk involved in the purchase.

Once this is settled, the buyer will enter into a price agreement with the supplier. Most commonly, this will be either on a firm price basis, or on a cost-plus basis, as previously mentioned.

While price is the most visible part of the purchase costs, there is a tendency to focus on it too much. Buyers should keep in mind that there are other costs associated with a purchase, as pointed out before when discussing the total cost of ownership (www.cips.org, 2013).

A key requirement to securing the best price and terms is having a solid negotiation process.

NEGOTIATIONS

Procuring a product or service always involves negotiation with the supplier, whether that be price, terms, quality, service, support, etc. Negotiation is one of those activities that is a true blend of art and science, so the more thorough and efficient this process, the better the results.

Stages of Negotiation

While there are many approaches to the negotiation process, it should always include the following stages (Figure 11.2):

1. **Prepare**: This is perhaps the most important phase, since, as the saying goes, "to be forewarned is to be forearmed." With the advent of the internet, there is even more information available making costs and prices more transparent. Even though it is the first stage of negotiations, people often don't give it the time it deserves, as they often go quickly (or even directly) to the information exchange stage, or in some cases directly to bargaining.

   Preparation starts with determining if the situation is collaborative or competitive, so that you can select the appropriate strategy. After that, time is spent researching information, analyzing data and leverage, and identifying interests and positions, all the while considering the type of relationship you want to build with the negotiation partner.

 **Lean link**: *This stage identifies potential value.*

FIGURE 11.2
Stages of the Negotiation Process.

2. Information **exchange** and validation: This stage starts when you begin to engage the other side, share information, and explore options that address interests (i.e. what you each need, as opposed to positions established in the bargaining stage).

   During this stage there is an emphasis on building rapport and trust, which helps support sharing interests. It helps to find out and show interest in the other party's business culture, personality, outside interests, and values at this point.

   It is important to gauge your negotiating partner's trustworthiness, competency, ability to work well with you, and alignment of both parties' interests during this phase.

   If your assessment in this stage of the negotiation process is negative based upon your reservation price—the least favorable point at which one will accept a negotiated agreement—you can make adjustments, or implement your best alternative to a negotiated agreement (BATNA), which is the most advantageous alternative course of action a party can take, if negotiations fail and an agreement cannot be reached.

   If your assessment in this stage of the negotiation process is within the bargaining zone (i.e. the overlap area between walk-away positions in a negotiation where potential agreement is satisfactory to both negotiating parties), you move forward. With trust developed, you explore for creative solutions that address interests and see the potential to create real value.

Lean link: *There is the discovery and creation of value while building rapport and trust during this phase.*

3. **Bargain**: This is where give-and-take occurs. You make and manage your concessions in bargaining, trying to satisfy both parties' interests, so you can build a lasting relationship and capture real value.

   The negotiator's tools and behavioral skills matter greatly here. Communication skills are critical at this point as you try to create value and execute trades to capture value. Successful agreements happen when solutions satisfy everyone's needs (also known as a "win–win" negotiation).

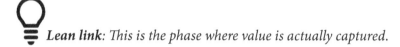

Lean link: The creation and distribution of value while simultaneously making and managing concessions can occur in this phase.

4. **Conclude**: This is the stage where you reach agreement and produce a comprehensive summary of the agreement, while considering next steps.

Lean link: This is the phase where value is actually captured.

5. **Execute**: This is the implementation of the agreement and can also be viewed as preparation for the next negotiation opportunity. It is a good idea to follow through on promises made, to strengthen the relationship and to build trust. You will learn during this stage, leading to easier negotiations next time around, and you will likely apply best negotiating practices to unexpected events, failures in performance, and changes.

Lean link: Value is expanded and relationships are strengthened in this phase (Watershed Associates, 2017).

Effective and Efficient Negotiations

There are variety of ways to make sure a supplier negotiation session produces favorable results, such as:

1. Renegotiate contracts annually: It seems that most U.S. businesses assume that all multiple-year contracts will result in lower costs. By considering annual contracts, it forces annual bidding, or at least renewal discussions with the current suppliers which usually results in lower cost of goods, while a multi-year contract will usually favor the vendor.
2. Conduct regular spend assessments: It is important to look at exactly how much you're spending, what you're getting in return, and what other suppliers in the marketplace are charging for similar goods, to gain insight into where potential negotiating points are.

3. Aggregate volume buys across the organization: After conducting regular spend assessments, procurement agents can more effectively aggregate volume purchases across various organizations and divisions. Bundling purchases under the same supplier can enable some economies of scale and better negotiating power.

4. Help suppliers work more efficiently: By working with the vendor of a product with a major component whose price tends to fluctuate, and perhaps suggesting another material option, for example, buyers can help to reduce fluctuations, as well as their own costs, in the process gaining a better negotiating position for their purchases.

5. Explore the alternatives: There is always room to look at other products or materials versus ones that you've been using, and may have been satisfied with for years, that are being made for half the price of an existing item.

6. Have a "win–win" integrative negotiation: Demanding price decreases across the board will not help to solidify positive supplier relationships. Think about how you can make it into a win–win situation through an "expanded pie" negotiation, versus a "win–lose" or distributive "fixed pie" negotiation, where one party's gain is another party's loss, by suggesting more affordable manufacturing processes, transportation options, or material choices.

Always consider what you can do to help your suppliers give you a better deal by asking yourself "what will satisfy you and what do you need to do to satisfy the needs and interests of the other party" and "do they value the process of expanding the pie or are they fixed on a single outcome"? (McCrea, 2013)

We will now look at some real-life examples of focusing on cost management in creative ways, instead of the old style "hammer in search of a nail" cost reduction and "win–lose" negotiation approaches.

GLOBAL ENERGY SUPPLIER SEES MAJOR INCREASE IN PRICE OF PARTS–CASE STUDY #1

Challenge

The world's largest supplier of power generation and service technologies in the energy industry saw an increase in purchase prices of its parts, thereby reducing its margins. This was due to a number of reasons:

- Lack of knowledge of cost drivers in different market regions.
- Lack of visibility into the manufacturing processes by the suppliers who were manufacturing the parts.
- Use of a more traditional approach in acquiring parts by selecting the lowest cost bids.
- Unable to fight supplier price increase requests due to poor negotiations and lack of knowledge of cost drivers.
- No decision support system in finalizing costs for new parts, and prices for these parts were based on similar existing parts.

Approach

With the help of the consulting firm Genpact, a study was conducted on the client's direct spend, and it identified part families and suppliers that had recent, significant cost increases. The part families were prioritized and selected for a "should cost" program, utilizing a toll-gating procedure (i.e. defined barriers that allow the prospect to move to the next step in a process) to identify the potential parts candidates based on monthly planned orders, purchase orders, and forecasts of parts. Genpact set up data and document requirements, as well as operational definitions, after which an analysis was conducted to define roles, responsibilities, and procedures for stakeholders at different levels.

The project was approached using three phases:

Phase 1: Toll-gating of parts

- The potential parts from the selected family were prioritized based on annual volume of spend.
- Prioritized high-impact parts were selected for a "should cost" analysis.

Phase 2: Analysis of part costs through "should cost" models

- Studied bill of material (BOM) and engineering drawings of assemblies, sub-assemblies, and child parts.
- Collected details on material specification, material costs, annual usage, source, and destination.
- Developed a manufacturing process plan and testing procedures.
- Development of "should cost" model identifying the material, processing, and logistics cost drivers.
- Recommended cost reduction opportunities.

Phase 3: Negotiation support

- Identified negotiation levers.
- Re-modeled "should cost" models basis for discussions with suppliers.
- Supported client's negotiations with suppliers and drove cost reductions.

Results

- 17% reduction in part costs.
- Savings of $0.7 million in the first year of the program.
- Gained visibility into supplier's manufacturing processes.
- Collaborated with client's supply chain partners.
- Increased visibility into various drivers of part costs.

This case illustrated that using "should cost" models can be a very effective tool when negotiating with a new supplier on repeatable parts with limited variations and tight margins (Genpact, 2011).

WIN–WIN NEGOTIATION FOR A MANUFACTURER OF ELECTRONIC COMPONENTS–CASE STUDY #2

Challenge

A manufacturer of electronic components wanted to stop its cycle of "win-lose" negotiating sessions with a major supplier, which had led to broken promises, delivery delays, and lack of transparency.

Approach

The company asked a consultant to facilitate a strategy and skill development training for its negotiating team in anticipation of an upcoming $350 million contract.

The goal was to transfer negotiation skills and processes to the team, set a negotiation strategy and tactics, and specify the behaviors and outcomes needed to avoid previous results.

The consultant interviewed participants on the company team to conduct a situation appraisal.

The next step in the process was helping the team take a deep dive into tactics by delving into topics such as how issues would be negotiated, timing, pressures, kinds of information needed, and existing power relationships.

Results

As a result of the preparation, team members gained a better understanding of the negotiating process, especially the need to set clear goals, and to understand the objectives and constraints of the other side, along with power relationships, pressures, timing, and information requirements.

During the negotiations, the team felt it could be more flexible and creative because it had a clear understanding of the other side's needs, and therefore the negotiating sessions went smoothly, with both sides satisfied and fully committed (Guttman, 2017).

After a deal has been struck, it is just the beginning, not the end, as contract and performance management can have a huge impact on delivering anticipated value to internal and external customers. This is the subject of our next chapter.

12

Contract and Performance Management and Ethics

Contract management is a critical part of the procurement cycle and a good contract management plan can assist the procurement staff to manage contracts by addressing transition management, and performance monitoring and help to ensure that both parties fulfill their commercial and contractual commitments.

Performance monitoring, also referred to here as supplier performance management (SPM), directly affects the quality of the whole supply chain, as companies rely on timely delivery, price reduction, and service quality offered from their suppliers. It is therefore essential to establish an efficient mechanism to enhance and accelerate its improvement and ensure the quality of services and/or products. Through the evaluation and comparison of supplier performance, companies can ensure and maintain the best service, and eliminate suppliers who fail to comply with performance requirements.

In this chapter, we will discuss how contract management focusing on supplier performance can minimize waste and improve efficiency in a supply chain.

DEVELOPING AND MANAGING CONTRACTS

There is great pressure on businesses today to reduce costs and improve financial and operational performance. On top of that, new regulatory requirements, globalization, and increases in contract volumes and complexity make businesses realize the importance and benefits of effective contract management.

The contract development process therefore allows both parties to fully understand their obligations and key success criteria as part of the agreement, forming the foundation to manage the contract and relationship effectively.

On an ongoing basis, contract life-cycle management is the process of systematically and efficiently managing contract creation, execution and analysis to maximize operational and financial performance and minimize risk.

To manage this entire process, the Chartered Institute of Procurement & Supply (www.cips.org) contract handbook (Elsey, 2007) identifies all activities associated with contract management, from the establishment of the business case and the confirmation of need, through contract administration and relationship management, to the review of contract performance. These activities are divided into two distinct, but interdependent, phases upstream and downstream of the award of the contract.

The CIPS methodology is applicable to all contracts from a simple order through longer-term contracts and to complex construction or service contracts. We will now use that methodology to review best practices and how they can help create a Lean and efficient contract management process. The first upstream activity involves preparing the business case and securing management approval.

Upstream or Pre-Award Activities

Preparing the Business Case and Securing Management Approval

Any contract requires management commitment and approval. This requires a legitimate business case that is aligned with the company's corporate and functional strategies.

Therefore, the contract should address outcome(s) of the contract, critical success factors, possible alternatives including existing contracts, risk identification and potential impact, and a mitigation plan for those risks with the greatest impact and likelihood of occurring.

The business case is a working document and should form the basis of the post-implementation review. It is a management tool, ensuring that the original outcomes and benefits have been achieved.

Assembling the Project Team

The need for a procurement team depends on the scale, nature, complexity, and significance of what is being procured, and the necessary skills and experience required. The project team may have members from a variety of functions within the organization including design, research and development, production, quality control, logistics, marketing and sales, legal, finance, and human resources.

To assemble a team, you need to identify the necessary technical skills, knowledge and experience, as well as the ability of selected team members, to work together effectively and the significance of the role of the leader in the procurement project's success.

Developing a Contract Strategy

The strategy relating to a contract should align with the organization's overall procurement strategy ensuring that:

1. Strategic priorities agreed at the outset are delivered in a timely and cost-effective manner.
2. Issues of non-compliance or variation are identified early, and dealt with or escalated for resolution.
3. Costs and risk are managed appropriately.
4. Reviews are undertaken, and any lessons learned are brought back to the procurement process for continuous improvement.

Lean link: This activity sets the stage for a Lean contract management and performance process.

Risk Assessment

Risk assessment includes analysis, assessment, and mitigation.

Risk analysis identifies potential issues that can go wrong with an activity, with an estimate of the probability of each happening. It is a fundamental part of formulating contract strategy. The process can range from a simple listing of risks on an informal basis, to a formal process involving set procedures that include brainstorming, and technically and financially evaluating potential risks with other functions.

Risk assessment looks at the likely impact of a risk on the organization. Some risks may have a low impact, and it may not be worth taking action to control or avoid such risks; on the other hand, low probability risks may have a significant impact requiring action to be taken to mitigate the risk. To deal with this systematically, it is common for many companies to use a vulnerability map, or risk-matrix, to visualize unforeseen and unwanted events, as shown in Figure 12.1 (Sheffield and Rice Jr., 2005).

This type of analysis has two dimensions: disruption probability and consequences. Obviously, risks with a high disruption probability and severe consequences should be given a great deal of attention.

One problem with this method is that it relies heavily on risk perception, which can vary depending on recent events, a person's experience and knowledge, their appetite for risk, and their position in the organization among other things.

Having assessed the risks and identified those requiring action, plans for mitigating them should be implemented based upon the assessment of the likelihood and consequence of the risk.

The risk mitigation process should include identifying the most appropriate body to manage or control the risk in terms of expertise, time and/or resources, establishing a fair and reasonable reimbursement mechanism, insurance, and possible risk transfer to suppliers.

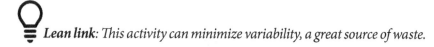

Lean link: *This activity can minimize variability, a great source of waste.*

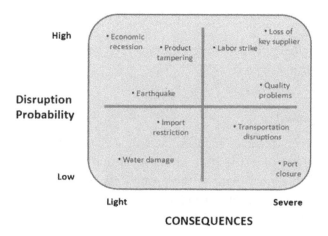

FIGURE 12.1
Vulnerability Map.

Developing a Contract Exit Strategy

A contract will conclude when both parties have satisfactorily fulfilled their responsibilities under the terms of the contract, such as when the goods or services have been supplied, and payment made at the end of a pre-agreed period.

However, there is still a need to develop a contract exit strategy as part of the risk identification and reduction process.

While standard terms and conditions are included in most contracts, there remains a need to address potential circumstances, and rights and responsibilities of the parties, and how any damages or costs may be mitigated.

Developing a Contract Management Plan

Time and effort must be spent on determining how the contract will work once it has been awarded, to identify the obligations of all the parties so they can be carried out effectively and efficiently.

The foundations of successful contract management may include:

- Flexibility by the contracting parties, such as the ability to adapt the terms of the contract to reflect change and unforeseen problems.
- The buying organization should have clear business objectives, including understanding of what the contract will contribute to them, as well as an understanding of the provider's business objectives and drivers.
- People with the right skills to manage these relationships.
- Processes for managing the contract which provide the level of control.
- How to share common quality management systems and escalation procedures.
- Timing and methods to increase suppliers' level of knowledge and understanding of your business.

Drafting Specifications and Requirements

A specification is a statement of needs used to present the organization's needs to potential suppliers so that they can propose solutions to those needs. It should also enable the organization to evaluate offers, measure supplier performance and help to settle any future disagreements.

The process starts with the development of the business case, which breaks down the overall scope into more detail and into schedules of detailed requirements.

Specifications should:

- Clearly state the organization's requirement(s).
- Focus on the deliverables and how they are to be achieved.
- Have sufficient information for potential suppliers to submit reasonable offers and for the proper evaluation of offers submitted against specific criteria stated by the organization.
- Enable all potential suppliers to submit offers without bias towards any one supplier.

Lean link: *If performed thoroughly, this activity can save a lot of time and effort **after** the contract is awarded and will greatly benefit both parties through the elimination of unnecessary waste.*

Establishing the Form of Contract

While it is beyond the scope of this book to discuss the specific form of a contract, as there are many varieties and variations, it is important that the contract not only reflects the nature, value, and complexity of the need, but also the desired type of relationship with the potential supplier(s).

This will have a major impact during the post-contract award process, especially in terms of clarity and comprehensiveness, to help determine the form and content of the final contract document.

Establishing the Pre-Qualification, Qualification, and Tendering Procedures

At this point, it is typical to have some kind of "pre-qualification system" to evaluate potential suppliers as to whether they meet the commercial requirements of the organization.

These potential suppliers will typically be sent an RFI (request for information), which is used to gather information to help decide on what steps to take next.

The goal of the pre-qualification activity is to both develop a large enough list of potential suppliers to be able to proceed to the tender invitation stage where a shortlist of qualified suppliers goes through a more in-depth evaluation.

This activity typically looks for the following general information:

- Table of contents.
- Introduction and purpose of the RFI.
- Explanation of scope.
- Abbreviations and terminology.
- Template to complete.
- Details of next steps–RFP or RFQ (request for proposal or quote).

The RFI should also make it clear that references may be sought from selected current customers of the supplier.

Lean link: *A lot of time and effort should be put into this activity, as while it casts a wide net, it also ensures that there is a common understanding of the needs of the two parties, as well as at least a general fit between them.*

Appraising Suppliers

Supplier appraisal is a key activity in strategic sourcing, supplier management, and achieving competitive advantage in procuring goods or services. As such, the activity looks at a potential supplier's capability of delivering goods and services to your organization, and capacity to control quality, delivery, quantity, price, and all the other factors in the contract.

Appraisal should include finance, production capacity, production, human resources, quality, performance, corporate social responsibility (CSR) issues, and information technology.

Following a successful appraisal, the supplier is placed on an approved list of suppliers, and/or is moved from a longlist to a shortlist of potential suppliers.

It is especially important to conduct an extra-thorough appraisal during certain types of procurement situations requiring:

- Strategic, high-risk, non-standard requirements.
- Capital intensive and construction projects.
- Supplier development.

- Just-in-time (JIT), long-term partnerships.
- Global sourcing.
- e-Procurement arrangements with long-term strategic suppliers.
- Strict quality requirements for high profit or high-risk items.
- Outsourcing including third party logistics (3PL) providers.
- Service level agreements (SLAs), which are agreements between a service provider and a client.

Drafting Tender (i.e. Call for Bids or RFP) Documents

The RFP or RFQ draft should clearly and comprehensively state the obligations of the parties to the agreement, and should generally include the following sections:

- Form of tender (i.e. contract period, signatures, etc.).
- Specifications of requirements.
- Terms and conditions of contract.
- Scope of work or technical specifications including drawings.
- Administrative and offer submission instructions.
- Pricing and invoicing schedules, terms, and methods.
- Testing and award procedure and criteria.
- Contract management, communications, dispute, and exit procedures.

Evaluating Offers

Supplier bids need to be looked at both commercially and technically, and evaluated not only in terms of price, delivery, quality, methodology, but also by the quality of the bidder's offer.

The evaluation should include a clarification process where the buying organization can ask for additional information useful in the decision-making process.

Factor Rating Method

One time-tested tool worth mentioning in this context (and previously discussed in Chapter 8) is the "factor-rating method" (Table 12.1) which, while it is traditionally used for evaluating location alternatives, can also be used in comparing competitive bids.

In this case, it is used to identify criteria that need to be considered as part of what you will be buying, and to assign weights to the relative importance

TABLE 12.1

Factor Rating Method for Vendor Evaluation

Criteria	Weights	Scores (1–5)	Weight x Score
Engineering and research capabilities	0.1	4.0	0.4
Production process capability (flexibility/Agile)	0.2	5.0	0.8
Delivery capability	0.1	3.5	0.2
Quality and performance	0.2	3.0	0.6
Location	0.1	1.0	0.1
Financial and managerial strength (stability and cost structure)	0.2	5.0	0.8
Information systems capability (e-procurement, ERP)	0.1	2.0	0.2
Reputation (sustainability/ethics)	0.1	5.0	0.5
Total	1.00		3.4

of each of these factors. You then score how well each supplier compares on each factor and give them a score which is weighted times the rating.

Negotiation

While this topic was covered in the previous chapter(s), it is important to spend some more time on it, as it is the goal of every purchasing professional to get the best deal possible for their organization, and it is the last step before awarding, and then managing the contract.

Things to consider when developing your negotiation strategy include:

- Whether the approach will be adversarial or cooperative (i.e. a "win–lose" versus "win–win" situation). Adversarial tactics may be the right course where no ongoing relationship is required, and a cooperative negotiation tactic may be appropriate where a long-term, stable relationship is more appropriate.
- The fallback or best alternative to a negotiated agreement (BATNA) positions of both parties.
- The personalities, authority levels and responsibilities of negotiators needed.
- The buyer's and the supplier's respective negotiation situations, strengths, and weaknesses.

There are also issues to be considered during each stage of the negotiating process:

Pre-negotiation stage: A team or individual approach may be appropriate. If the team approach is used, consideration must be given to roles and expertise, the venue, information-gathering, determining the strategy, objectives, and tactics used.

Negotiation stage: Thought needs to be given to procedural rules, the agenda, issues to be resolved, common goals, and barriers to achieving those goals. Consideration should also be given to any behavioral tactics needed.

Post-negotiation stage: Issues to consider include drafting final agreement statements, and then communicating, implementing, and monitoring the final agreement to all participants.

Finally, there are some general principles of negotiations, which are especially useful in negotiating large, high value contracts. They are:

- Avoid treating each negotiation as a separate event, as this can come at the expense of the long-term relationship with the supplier.
- To arrive at a better, overall result, avoid negotiating each component of a single negotiation individually
- Look beyond price and quality, and consider measuring innovation and creative alternative solutions.
- Know the difference between deals and relationships, as concessions granted during deals can damage long-term relationships.
- Know when to walk away from a negotiation.

Lean link: *Preparation during the pre-negotiation stage is key to getting the best results for your organization from a negotiation process. As the saying goes, "to be forewarned is to be forearmed."*

Awarding the Contract

The contract award stage is comprised of some important activities: communicating the award to the successful tenderer, and notifying and debriefing the unsuccessful (as well as the successful) tenderers.

While one might think you need only debrief unsuccessful bidders, debriefing the winning bidder can help your organization to understand their view of the procurement process, gain a better understanding of that market, improve communications, and help establish a good working relationship with the new supplier from the start.

Downstream or Post-Award Activities

Changes within the Contract

Changes should not necessarily be a cause for concern, but are to be managed to improve upon the contract deliverables.

Change can be instigated by modifications to strategies and objectives of both parties, changing business needs, market changes, improvements in technology, economic trends, and legislative change, any of which can lead to changes in service required, metrics, infrastructure, and resource requirements.

Service Delivery Management

The intention of this activity is to make sure that the actual service provided by the supplier matches the agreed standards and prices. Therefore, it is important to measure the performance of the supplier, and to provide feedback to ensure effective contract management and supplier development.

The general performance measurements need to cover issues such as:

- Actual cost and value delivered.
- Supplier delivery capability and performance.
- Customer satisfaction.
- Anticipated benefits that have been gained.
- Relationship strength and responsiveness.

The performance measures should help to identify the information needs, as well as the contract management teams, skills, and processes required to successfully work with the supplier.

While the actual measurements will vary by industry and organization, in general, they should focus on the attributes that are most important to your organization.

Some attributes are easy to measure, while others are not. In general, it is best practice to consider the total costs associated with a purchased product or service, not just the purchase price.

Some of the metrics that can be considered are:

- Quality and service level.
- Cycle or lead-time.
- Correct and complete order and line item.
- Accurate documentation including accurate price/cost of product.
- On-time, complete delivery in desired condition.
- Willingness to share sensitive information.
- Presence of certification or other documentation.
- Flexibility to respond to unexpected demand changes.
- Communication skills/systems (phone, fax, e-mail, EDI, internet).
- Quick response time in case of emergency, problem, or special request.
- Willingness to change their products and services to meet your changing needs.
- Participation in your firm's new product development and value analysis.

Relationship Management

There should be mutual trust and understanding to create an open and constructive environment so that the relationship can work effectively.

The supplier needs to gain an understanding of the organization's business needs and style, so they can be proactive and innovative in helping with improvements and savings, and more willing to share problems and concerns for the longer-term benefit of both parties.

On the other hand, the buying organization needs to gain a better understanding of the strengths and weaknesses of the supplier, so that it can focus its management and development support in those areas.

Contract Administration

While it may seem that the awarding of a contract may be the end, in many ways, it's just the beginning. So, post-award contract management should not be underestimated and should be resourced correctly.

The change control procedures set up in the original contract documentation are designed to be used during administration activities to avoid misunderstanding, and communicate responsibilities and any actions that may need to be taken.

Furthermore, other actions during contract administration can include charges and cost-monitoring, ordering and payment procedures, budget procedures, and resource management and planning.

Assessment of Risk

It is important to conduct continuous risk analysis and assessment **throughout the period of the contract**, not just pre-award, to manage the risks that may arise.

Examples of risks to the contract include lack of capacity of the supplier, reduction in demand leading to higher unit costs, an increase in the total of the price to the purchaser, deterioration in the supplier's financial standing, deterioration of quality, and force majeure issues.

Issues to consider to better manage risk include:

- Having a process for early warning of issues just mentioned, as soon as either a supplier or the purchaser becomes aware of them.
- Identifying who can best control the situation, and the risk itself, leading to the risk occurring.
- Determining who should be responsible if the risk cannot be controlled.
- Deciding if a given risk is transferred to the supplier, will the cost to the buying organization be reduced.

Purchasing Organization's Performance and Effectiveness Review

Besides measuring a specific supplier's performance, it is also important to measure your purchasing organization's performance effectiveness and efficiency.

The goals of performance measurement of the purchasing department are to:

- Make sure that individual, functional and corporate aims are aligned.
- Compare planned and actual results and where applicable, identify reasons for poor performance and create a basis for improvement.

- Improve both future decision making, and the contribution purchasing can make to the organization.
- Motivate and develop staff.

Some of the metrics are the same as those used in supplier performance measurement, such as on-time delivery, vendor cycle times, and quality. However, there are also other more internally focused metrics used, such as:

- Savings on the purchase price.
- Reduced inventory levels.
- Procurement cycle time.
- Cost of change.
- Cost of placing orders.

More strategically, the measurement of the purchasing organization should help to better manage internal and external relationships, contracts and performance, change, customer support, infrastructure issues, business continuity, and transition.

Contract Closure

Contract closure includes activities associated with closing the project down, which may be due to the terms of the contract, or because of early termination.

There is typically a requirement to show evidence that the contract has been completed to the satisfaction of all parties (usually signatures of the parties certifying acceptance of the product, work, or service), to determine internally that there are no outstanding matters, and, externally, to secure agreement from the supplier that, apart from any ongoing liabilities, the contract has ended.

The terms and procedures for renewal or extension should be part of the original contract.

In some cases, a contract may not be completed to the satisfaction of both parties. In this case, there will be recourse to adjudication, mediation, conciliation, arbitration, and possibly litigation.

ETHICS IN PROCUREMENT, INCLUDING CONTRACT MANAGEMENT

The procurement of goods and services deals with interactions with all external suppliers and outsourced partners. As procurement spend can be significant, there are lots of opportunities for unethical employee behavior. So it is not hard to see why it is extremely important for an organization to encourage its procurement associates to act with integrity, avoid conflicts of interest and personal enrichment, treat suppliers equally and fairly, and comply with legal and other obligations.

Poor ethics can cause more damage than just harm to a company's reputation, and adding to liabilities. Beyond ineptitude—or if intentional, corruption—it can also cause inefficiencies, resulting in waste in the procurement process by focusing on personal gain, instead of adding value to the organization and the customer.

As a result, many organizations create a procurement ethics manual, while others may have a code of conduct in a more wide-ranging employee handbook. A good example is the United Nations Procurement Practitioner's Handbook (www.ungm.org), which has two definitions of ethics:

1. "The moral principles governing or influencing conduct."
2. "The branch of knowledge concerned with moral principles (the Concise Oxford Dictionary of Current English)."

Ethics, in the form of fairness, integrity, and transparency is the foundation on which most procurement related principles are based.

In general, professional standards of ethical conduct, have typical characteristics, including to:

- Behave honorably regarding work and professional activity.
- Conduct oneself to maintain trust and confidence in the integrity of the procurement process.

- Avoid taking undue advantage of others or the system.
- Maintain the organization's standards and policies.
- Have no conflicts of interest.

Codes of Conduct

A code of conduct is a written collection of the rules, principles, values, and employee expectations, behavior, and relationships that an organization considers significant, and believes are fundamental to their successful operation.

The code of conduct is named by an organization to reflect the culture that is present in the organization, and to make a statement, and it serves as a framework for ethical decision-making within an organization.

It is important to understand that procurement professionals should be guided by the broader concept that a code of conduct is intended to express rather than just the letter of the law, as that may give the impression that anything not prohibited is permitted. Therefore, procurement officers need to understand what the law or rule is intended to accomplish.

Ethical Concepts, Principles, and Risks

Ethical concepts and principles that relate to the procurement process are loyalty and respect for rules and regulations, integrity, impartiality and fairness, transparency, confidentiality, avoidance of even the appearance of impropriety, and due diligence.

Some of the common ethical risks in the procurement process include conflict of interest, fraud, corruption, coercion, and collusion.

In summary, an organization can't assume that doing the right thing in terms of procurement ethics will just happen automatically; there must be a clear ethical model for everyone to follow. This will result in greater efficiency and value from procurement activities, a better brand image for the organization, and increased loyalty from customers.

Today, contract and performance management, and in fact every aspect of the procurement process (including ethics to some degree), are enabled by technology, which will be explored in the next chapter.

13

e-Procurement and Other Supply Management Technologies

THE PROCUREMENT PROCESS AND TECHNOLOGY

Today, technology is heavily used not only in the short- to medium-term purchasing process in a variety of sources, such as an MPS (master production scheduling), procurement plan, MRP, etc., but also for the broader, longer-term needs of an entire procurement/sourcing process (see Figure 13.1).

As described earlier in this book, procurement (also known as sourcing and supply management), is the process of managing a broad range of processes associated with a firm's need to acquire goods and services in a legal and ethical manner that are required to manufacture a product (direct items), or to operate the organization (indirect items), the foundation of which is provided by the purchasing function. Per Figure 13.1, the procurement process typically includes the functions of determining purchasing specifications, selecting the supplier, negotiating terms and conditions, and issuing and administrating purchase orders.

Automation of Procurement Documents and Processes

Preparing and managing purchasing documents involved in this process has always been a time-consuming process. Many firms have streamlined the document flow process using Lean and other process improvement techniques to reduce the paperwork and handling required for each purchase.

FIGURE 13.1
The Procurement Process.

The types of purchase orders generated because of the procurement process may include:

Discrete Orders: Used for a single transaction with a supplier, with no assumption that further transactions will occur.

Pre-negotiated blanket: A purchase order made with a supplier containing multiple delivery dates over a period, usually with predetermined pricing which often has lower costs because of greater volumes—possibly through centralized purchasing and/or the consolidation of suppliers—on a longer-term contract. It is typically used when there is an ongoing need for consumable goods.

Pre-negotiated, vendor-managed inventory (VMI): The supplier maintains an inventory of items at the customer's plant and the customer pays for the inventory when it is consumed. Usually for standard, small-value items like maintenance, repair, and operating supplies (MRO), e.g. fasteners and electrical parts.

Bid and auction (e-procurement): This involves the use of online catalogs, exchanges and auctions to speed up purchasing, reduce costs, and integrate the supply chain. There are many e-commerce sites for industrial equipment and MRO inventory auctions which vary in format from catalog (e.g. www.grainger.com, www.chempoint.com) to auction (e.g. www.biditup.com). Websites can be for standard items, or be industry-specific.

Corporate purchase card (pCard): This is a company charge card that allows goods and services to be procured without using a traditional purchasing process; sometimes referred to as procurement or "p" cards. There is always some kind of control for each pCard, such as a single purchase dollar limit, a monthly limit, and so on. A pCard holder's activity should be reviewed periodically independently.

To further enhance the speed and accuracy of transactions, many companies use what is known as EDI (electronic data interchange), which is the computer-to-computer exchange of business documents in a standard electronic format between business partners. In the past, EDI transactions either went directly from business to business (in the case of large companies) or through third parties known as value-added networks (VANs). Today, a large portion of EDI transactions flow through the internet.

Sometimes included in the category of EDI is the use of electronic funds transfer (EFT), which is the electronic exchange or transfer of money from one account to another, within a single financial institution or across multiple institutions, through computer systems. This also includes e-commerce payment systems which facilitate the acceptance of electronic payment for online transactions and which have become increasingly popular because of the widespread use of internet-based shopping and banking.

There are numerous other documents and/or information requirements which can be automated and integrated in an e-procurement process including:

- Identifying and reviewing requirements, establishing specifications: specification sheet, statement of work, product requirement, customer order/MRP requirement, and purchase requisition.
- Selecting suppliers (approved): purchasing card, e-catalog, EDI, stock check, and reorder point.
- Selecting suppliers (unapproved): request for quote/information (RFQ/RFI) and request for proposal (RFP).
- Issuing purchase orders (PO): purchase order approval and release/acknowledgement and blanket order.
- Delivery and receipt: bill of lading (B/L), packing slip, discrepancy report, kanban, receipt acknowledgement.
- Payment: supplier invoice, match PO and invoice, pay invoice, and update supplier scoreboard.

It should come as no surprise then, that procurement is an area where technology has been heavily applied over the past 25 years. In fact, every one of the steps involved in the procurement process typically utilizes technology to one degree or another.

In its totality, the suite of tools used to achieve efficiency in purchasing transactions are broadly defined as "e-procurement." Companies are using e-procurement tools to manage the flow of documents by: (1) automating the document generation process, and (2) electronically transmitting purchase documents to suppliers.

PROCUREMENT TECHNOLOGY

There is a variety of technology available today to help an organization automate and improve their various procurement processes. For our purposes, we will define e-procurement as the business-to-business purchase and sale of supplies and services over the internet which can be integrated with internal computerized procurement processes and systems as identified in Figure 13.1.

In procurement, which may sometimes include e-procurement functionality, there are two types of software vendors: (1) enterprise resource planning (ERP) providers offering both internal procurement (including individual MRP vendors such as shown in Figure 13.2) and e-procurement as one or part of their modules, and (2) services or vendors focused specifically on e-procurement.

Procurement software itself is a computer program or suite of products that helps to automate (and thereby improve) the processes of purchasing materials and maintaining an inventory of goods. Following the typical procurement process, these systems can generate purchase orders, execute the ordering process online, match invoices to materials received, and pay bills electronically.

Again, systems today may include e-procurement functionality, as well as leveraging the benefits of the internet. As a result, the benefits of using procurement software include ease of administration and potential cost

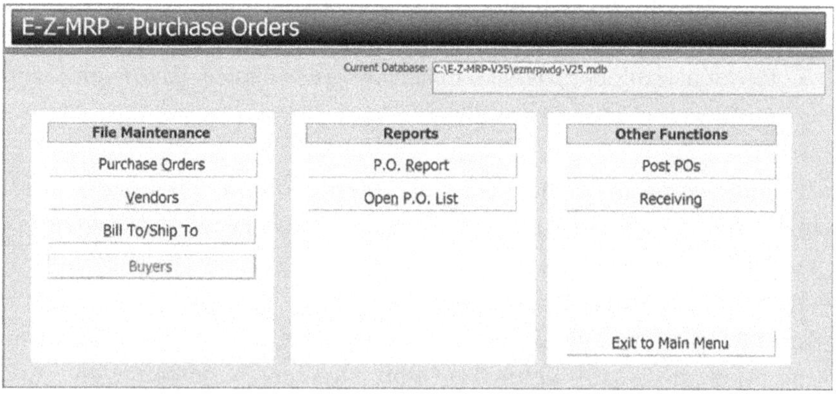

FIGURE 13.2
MRP Material Planning–Purchase Order Main Screen (Printed with Permission from Weeks Software Solutions, LLC).

savings, as well as having a single interface for procurement to monitor their company's spending.

Procurement software helps to efficiently manage a variety of activities. Specifically, they include the ability to:

- Create a purchase order based on need.
- Verify a purchase order.
- Submit a pending purchase order for approval or rejection.
- Automate an electronic purchase order transmission.
- Confirm or cancel purchase orders.
- Help to execute financial and inventory transactions when ordered materials arrive.
- Gather data and analyze to improve profitability.
- Streamline and standardize administration. For example, procurement systems generally offer multi-currency support as well as tools that can automate purchases and purchasing approvals.

These systems can also connect users with large networks of qualified suppliers, which is a critical capability for supply chain professionals who are trying to identify the most reliable raw material suppliers at the best price, wherever they might be sourced from.

Source to Pay Example

One example of technology in this area is known as a "procure-to-pay" solution that enables a cross-functional workflow to streamline and improve the process from the act of purchasing to accounts payable. Source-to-pay takes this a step further, expanding the scope to include the process of sourcing the products or services to be purchased.

Applying Lean principles to a source to pay (S2P) process can reduce low (or non-) value-added activity, and relieve stress on your employees by shifting focus to higher value tasks.

Standalone Procurement Solutions

As opposed to procurement modules internal to ERP systems, such as SAP and Oracle, there are also standalone procurement solutions coming in a variety of forms. Dominick identified ten types of standalone procurement software systems:

1. Spend analysis: Allows you to find purchasing patterns within categories, by suppliers, etc., that might offer cost savings, performance improvements, and overall efficiencies. Most spend analysis vendors have been acquired by other types of procurement software vendors.

2. Supplier discovery: Allows you to search for suppliers that meet specific criteria, such as capabilities, location, supplier diversity, etc. Examples: ThomasNet, Ariba.

3. Supplier information management: Allows you to efficiently collect and maintain accurate supplier information, including contact information and certification status directly from suppliers. Examples: HICX Solutions, Hiperos.

4. eSourcing: Allows you to get quotes and proposals electronically from suppliers quickly. This can be done privately or suppliers can be allowed to see their rank among bidders, to increase competitive pressure. Examples: WhyAbe, K2Sourcing, Trade Extensions.

5. Contract management: Enables you to prepare contracts using various templates. It can electronically route contracts for approval, track revisions, notify of contract expirations, and store executed contracts. Examples: Selectica, Prodagio.

6. eProcurement: Allows end users to search catalogs of pre-approved products and services from contracted suppliers, create requisitions, and have some requisitions turned into purchase orders (either manually by buyers or automatically). Example: ePlus, eBid.

7. e-Invoicing (also known as ePayment): Enables you to efficiently receive accurate supplier invoices electronically. May include dynamic discounting, allowing suppliers to reduce the amount your organization owes in exchange for faster payment. Examples: Taulia, Tradeshift.

8. Supplier management: Enables you to track and/or rate supplier performance using manual or scorecard-style ratings. Also integrates with other systems to gather actual performance. May include risk assessment capabilities. Examples: Aravo, BravoSolution.

9. Combination solutions: A type of eProcurement system allowing for direct payment to suppliers, commonly referred to as procure-to-pay, or P2P. Ones that offer the option of soliciting quotes from suppliers, are called source-to-pay solutions. Examples: Coupa, Puridiom.

10. Complete suites: There are some software vendors that have many or even all the solutions listed above. They are referred to as suites. Examples: GEP, Zycus, SciQuest, iValua (Dominick, 2015).

Now let's look at some examples where technology has enabled a Leaner procurement process.

LEAN PROCUREMENT AND TECHNOLOGY CASE STUDIES

Enabling Online Supplier Collaboration at Toshiba Semiconductor Company–Case Study #1

Challenge

Toshiba Semiconductor Company wanted real-time information for its global operations to stay a global leader in the industry, with the lack of this information limiting the company's success in the future.

At the time, purchasing employees bought products locally with no sharing of information among buyers, factories, or headquarters, as these activities were being conducted separately, primarily because no central database existed.

Approach

Toshiba selected JDA software for spend optimization to help manage its supplier relationships using a web interface with their customers and suppliers. This would allow Toshiba to operate on a real-time basis using accurate information enabling them and their suppliers to collaborate on sourcing and procurement for supply management. In this way, they could integrate product development, sourcing, supply planning, and procurement across the entire supply chain.

Toshiba decided to implement JDA Negotiate and Strategic Sourcing for direct materials, information-gathering, and decision-making processes.

This would enable them to send out RFQs to suppliers via the internet and help the company to create a supplier database shared by all their purchasing staff, to assist in the selection of the best suppliers in future negotiations, and to make balanced scorecards for each supplier.

Results

Because of its successful implementation, JDA solutions helped Toshiba to gain a competitive advantage by refining its supplier base, and adding speed, efficiency, and reliability to purchasing.

Toshiba can now handle between 7,000 and 8,000 RFQs per site at six of their major factories in Japan.

The company feels that it has achieved a competitive edge due to the increased level of speed and intelligent decision-making from using JDA software.

Toshiba firmly believes that this improvement will help the company reduce its number of preferred suppliers, using a balanced scorecard from information contained in the new database, and that purchasing agents will become more strategic by enabling them to collaborate with product designers in the design stage, where 80% of a product's cost is determined (www.jda.com, 2016).

Clariant: Increasing Interenterprise Productivity and Extending Its SAP Software Investment Value–Case Study #2

Challenge

Clariant, a global leader in specialty chemicals, markets innovative chemicals in a variety of business areas. They wanted to improve the accuracy of their catalogs for their global supply base, and to develop more collaborative supplier relationships. Additionally, they wanted to improve invoice cycle times.

Approach

By deploying Ariba Procurement Content, PO Automation, and Invoice Automation solutions, they determined that they would be able to purchase all indirect goods and services through their existing SAP ERP software system.

Results

Clariant eventually deployed the Ariba Procurement Content solution to manage more than 300 catalogs, deployed the Ariba PO Automation solution in 21 countries, and rolled out the Ariba Invoice Automation solution in Germany and Switzerland.

This integrated smoothly with the existing SAP Supplier Relationship Management application for order initiation.

It enabled a consumer-like shopping experience, covering all countries with one user-friendly solution. To accomplish this, they utilized Ariba services, which incorporated catalogs and suppliers on the Ariba Network.

Clariant reached their goal of purchasing all their indirect goods and services through the integration of Ariba PO and Invoice Automation with their SAP ERP application, thereby increasing order accuracy, reducing non-catalog orders, and streamlining invoice processing in Germany and Switzerland. It allowed procurement personnel to focus on higher-value activities and improved collaboration internally and with suppliers (www. sap.com, 2016).

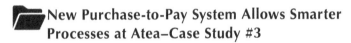

New Purchase-to-Pay System Allows Smarter Processes at Atea–Case Study #3

Challenge

Atea is a leading supplier of IT infrastructure in Europe which helps enable their customers' IT purchasing, delivery, and service processes to run smoothly by delivering the necessary hardware and software solutions.

Other than their hardware purchases which are the majority of items purchased and are handled by central purchasing, Atea lets employees do their own purchasing for indirect items.

Currently department heads must provide authorization twice: once to authorize a purchase, and later to authorize the invoice after delivery was made.

Approach

Atea looked for a combined technology solution that included purchasing, automated invoice processing, and travel and expense management. It had to support their decentralized (indirect item) purchasing strategy and integrate with their existing ERP and payroll systems, all the while being user-friendly.

They needed the solution to help optimize their purchasing, invoice, and expense handling processes, as well as integrate their invoice-processing and travel and expense management systems. The solution would need to enable department heads to deal with purchases just once.

Results

Atea licensed a purchasing system from Basware where employees can now create a purchase requisition and get it approved electronically by their department head. When the invoice arrives, it's already been approved and can be sent for payment automatically, thereby reducing the work of two people by 50%.

They no longer search for invoice documents, ownership of invoices, or approvals, ensuring the right purchases are made.

The purchasing system integrates with invoice and travel and expense processing, as well as with the entire payables side, enabling many approvals to be granted automatically.

The responsibility for invoice posting has now been delegated to individual departments with decentralized invoice posting.

There is no need to send invoices from one department to another anymore and departments have a better idea of what they are actually spending.

Atea also chose to shut down expensive manual advances and is switching as many staff as possible to personal liability credit cards (www. basware.com, 2016).

Modern technology has exponentially increased the amount of data available, which needs to be turned into useful information for it to be truly beneficial in the decision-making process, the topic of our next chapter.

14

Procurement Analysis, Tools, and Techniques

As has been discussed throughout this book, procurement has evolved from a transactional function to one which can give an organization a competitive advantage by adopting a more strategic approach.

DATA ANALYTICS

To accomplish this takes not only access to an ever-growing amount of data, but to actual information and knowledge. Thus, the boom in data analytics, which is the discovery, interpretation, and communication of meaningful patterns in data.

When applied to procurement, analytics is the use of data to gain insight into what has happened, and what may happen, to better manage spend, contracts, vendors, and internal customers.

Categories of Data Analytics

In general, data analytics can be broken into four categories:

1. Descriptive analytics: Uses historical data to describe a business. Also described as business intelligence (BI) systems. In supply chain, descriptive analytics help to better understand historical demand patterns, to understand how product flows through your supply chain, and to understand when a shipment might be late.

2. Diagnostic analytics: Once problems occur in the supply chain, an analysis needs to be made of the source of the problem. Often this can involve analysis of the data in the systems to see why the company was missing certain components, or what went wrong that caused the problem.
3. Predictive analytics: Uses data to predict trends and patterns; often associated with statistics. In the supply chain, predictive analytics could be used to forecast future demand, or to forecast the price of a product.
4. Prescriptive analytics: Using data to select an optimal solution. In the supply chain, you might use prescriptive analytics to determine the optimal number and location of distribution centers, set your inventory levels, or schedule production.

Analytics Applications in Procurement

While analytics tools have improved significantly, their usage within procurement are still fairly limited, with their purpose not being clearly understood.

However, if the data and tools are available and properly applied, procurement analytics can provide an opportunity to:

- "Reduce costs by consolidating expenditures on fewer providers, thereby exerting greater leverage in purchasing negotiations.
- Avoid wasteful expenditure through over-specification—where materials are ordered to a higher standard or specification than is actually required—and the use of non-preferred suppliers.
- Improve buying efficiencies by enforcing compliance with pre-agreed pricing, discount, and volume-based price break structures" (Wheatley, 2013).

As total spend can be significant, then why isn't this tool used more often? Some explanations can be:

- Organizational: Purchasing is always involved in sourcing decisions (e.g. other functions), and does not always capture spending data.
- Coding and classification: Similar items may be classified and coded in different ways depending on which designers and engineers are involved.

- Mergers and acquisitions: Various MRP, procurement, and ERP systems used over multiple organizations can lead to situations where enterprises spread spend over multiple suppliers, missing the opportunity to consolidate spend onto one product code and one supplier.

Proponents of procurement analytics point to three separate areas where better insights into procurement practice can determine ways to achieve lower prices and/or better payment terms.

1. **How *well* do we buy?**: Purchasing doesn't take place in isolation. Included in vast numbers of transactions are price agreements, contracts, internal guidelines, and service standards.

   A combination of aggregating individual transactions and reviewing individual purchases comparing actual buys with contracted terms and conditions, procurement analytics applications can identify non-complaint behavior.

2. ***What* do we buy?**: Having accurate detailed information can help buyers to reduce costs such as by consolidating volumes of similar materials or services onto fewer suppliers, or bundling together different items into "packages" of materials or services.

3. **How *well* do our suppliers perform?**: Sourcing agreements state prices to be paid, quantities to be bought, expected levels of quality, invoicing and payment terms, discount levels, volume-based price breaks, and many other stipulations to which suppliers should adhere. But do the suppliers adhere to them, and if not, is that costing you money?

Without procurement analytics, it can be difficult to measure supplier performance, compounded by the fact that these days, companies increasingly want to better understand the environmental impact of their supply chains, leading to specialist environmental-centric reporting products.

In best in class companies, procurement analytics delivers real procurement intelligence by identifying where the supply base needs to go to support the business and add value to the basic sourcing decision (Wheatley, 2013).

Identifying Data Gaps

One place to start is by looking at the data needs versus the available data, to determine the data gap to be filled (see Figure 14.1). Once the business needs are clear, and the data gap identified, the next step is to align your procurement analytics program to them.

Specific areas where gaps may be found and analytics used in procurement include:

Vendor evaluation: Factoring in complete and timely deliveries, quality of materials, and the time and effort taken to resolve problematic orders, in addition to lowest cost.

Spend analytics: Examine multiple types of data sets (e.g. accounts payable data, supplier-provided invoice data, tax data). This can result in an entirely different look at data elements, decrease "maverick" spend, and find economies of scale in spending.

Demand forecasting: Identify average cycle volume and maximum demand peaks to better manage spend.

Contract management: Optimize discount levels and forecast financial liabilities.

Supplier relationship management: Calculate vendor score, purchase order value, and purchase order volume.

Process data: Evaluate cycle times and visibility.

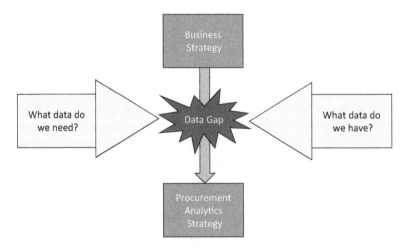

FIGURE 14.1

Business and Procurement Analytics Strategies.

Market data: Identify industry and competitor activity, merger and acquisition activity, and new products and services.

Other examples: Find opportunities for vendor consolidation, reducing duplicate orders, and increasing contract orders, while reducing open market transactions.

After a procurement analytics system is in place, it needs to link to key applications where improved visibility provides valuable inputs across the procurement value chain. This would include applications such as P2P, inventory, finance, risk, category management, sourcing, contracts, and supplier relationship management.

Focus on Category Management

Category management, which organizes procurement resources to focus on specific areas of spending, links strategic sourcing to the business, and as a result, it is in this area that the application of procurement analytics can have the biggest effect on a business.

During a category management analytics process – and in fact during the entire analytics process – questions are raised such as:

- How do we access and transform data?
- What is the best data structure?
- What types and forms of outputs will help us to best interpret the information?

When applied correctly, procurement analytics can provide the capability to extract, transform, load, and analyze an organization's data. This can then be used to create actionable intelligence throughout the category management and sourcing processes. Category analytics improves the category management process by focusing on strategies that benefit their category while helping to achieve business goals.

In summary, analytics helps procurement to see potential improvements and develop an implementation roadmap by leveraging previously unknown data, such as buying behaviors and marketplace activities, that may directly impact your organization. It can be used as a key differentiator, giving your organization a competitive advantage, and helping it change to a more strategic function (Henshall, 2015).

STRATEGIC PROCUREMENT TOOLS AND TECHNIQUES

There are a variety of procurement tools, many of which have been touched on throughout this book, that, when applied, can help to move procurement from a more transactional to strategic process.

Your Lean procurement "toolkit" should include the use of:

Spend Analysis

When used at a strategic level, spend analysis is a great tool for identifying and massaging detailed spend data, such as by category, provider, cost unit, and time-period. This information can be the key foundation for other strategic procurement decisions, such as category management, supplier relationship management, and procurement strategy, and is an important part of resource mapping and planning, as it allows organizations and their partners to identify where financial resources are being allocated, now and in the future.

Collaborative Procurement

Collaboration on procurement activities, whether internal or external, local, regional, national, or worldwide can not only improve existing operations but also identify future ones.

Benefits will typically include improved value for money due to economies of scale, greater leverage in the market, and greater provider attention, access to resources and ideas from others working in the same functions, and sharing of procurement administration duties.

However, there is often a reluctance to collaborate on procurement, due to factors such as not wanting to spend extra time reaching agreement with all stakeholders, slightly differing requirements, multiple time zones, managing the contract with multiple parties, and some loss of control.

These concerns can be eased to some degree by pooling of procurement resource and/or budgets, senior management commitment, written agreements with partners on the split of roles and responsibilities, or service level agreements if necessary, and involving participants in the requirement.

Procurement Strategy and Plan

As discussed, organizations should have a corporate procurement strategy and plan, normally produced by their procurement department and should include procurement activities across the organization and business units.

The strategy should include elements such as the goals and priorities of the strategy, the resources and skills required, key suppliers, governance and sign-offs, use and extent of e-procurement, relationships with corporate procurement, and other functions and plans for monitoring and reacting to developments in the market.

The plan should support the strategy and provide timing for significant item procurement, as well as detailed targets with owners and timing. These targets should drive continuous improvement.

Category Management

Category management, discussed in detail in Chapter 7, is a corporate strategic approach which organizes procurement resources to focus on specific areas of spend. It comprises a wide number of tools and techniques, and should be repeated regularly to take account of changing priorities, demand, and markets.

A few of the major tools used are:

- Spend analysis: Previously described as the process of collecting, cleansing, classifying/categorizing, and analyzing expenditure data, with the purpose of decreasing procurement costs, improving efficiency, and monitoring compliance.
- Portfolio analysis: Allows procurements to be mapped against a cost/risk matrix (see Figure 14.2), and highlights categories where a more hands-on style of management may be appropriate (e.g. the strategic/critical quadrant), and the organization should have strong relationships with providers. It can also identify categories better suited for automated, streamlined management, by using e-catalogs, for example (i.e. the acquisition/routine quadrant).

Categorization can be impacted by collaboration with other organizations, changes to business requirements, market dynamics, and limited resources.

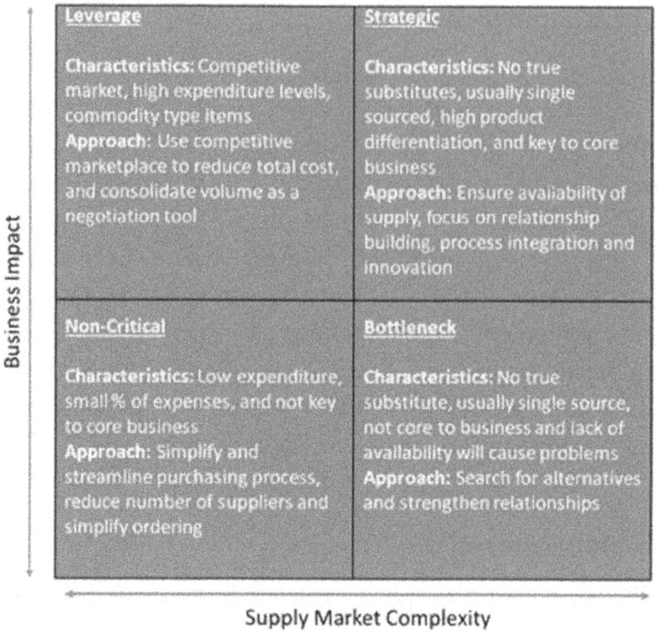

Leverage	Strategic
Characteristics: Competitive market, high expenditure levels, commodity type items **Approach:** Use competitive marketplace to reduce total cost, and consolidate volume as a negotiation tool	**Characteristics:** No true substitutes, usually single sourced, high product differentiation, and key to core business **Approach:** Ensure availability of supply, focus on relationship building, process integration and innovation
Non-Critical	Bottleneck
Characteristics: Low expenditure, small % of expenses, and not key to core business **Approach:** Simplify and streamline purchasing process, reduce number of suppliers and simplify ordering	**Characteristics:** No true substitute, usually single source, not core to business and lack of availability will cause problems **Approach:** Search for alternatives and strengthen relationships

Business Impact (vertical axis)

Supply Market Complexity (horizontal axis)

FIGURE 14.2
Portfolio Analysis (Kraljic Matrix).

Once the categorization has been agreed upon, you can analyze the data, and determine the best strategy for dealing with a specific category.

Challenging and managing procurement activities using category management tools and techniques will ensure that resources are focused where they will achieve the greatest value for the resources applied.

Supplier Relationship Management (SRM)

Supplier relationship management (SRM) is an important element of category management, and should be an ongoing activity with all critical suppliers.

SRM recognizes that different suppliers require different relationships, the type of which will depend largely on the importance and/or value of the goods or services they supply, as well as other factors, such as the number of suppliers in the market, and the global availability of an item.

SRM develops strategies to achieve value, and reduce the risk of poor performance, and allows procurement to focus effort on the right suppliers.

For many suppliers, it will not be necessary to expend significant resources building a relationship but for others, it may be necessary to enter full relationship management, requiring continuous improvement and ongoing communication management, cost management, and benchmarking.

The success of SRM, and of any management strategy, will depend on the supplier's cooperation, which to a great degree depends on how your supplier values your business.

Supplier Preferencing

In this vein, supplier preferencing, a concept introduced in 1996 by Steele and Court can help with understanding your perceived value provided to the supplier, at least from a tactical perspective (Figure 14.3). It plots account attractiveness to the supplier against the relative value of the customer or account to the supplier (e.g. percentage of supplier's revenue).

From the supplier's perspective, "core" accounts or customers are worth nurturing and supporting, and even defending from competitors, while "nuisance" customers are given minimal maintenance, standard terms, minimum order sizes, and dealt with relatively inflexibly. Customers in the "development" category, due to their attractiveness to the supplier, are at least given the opportunity to grow, and are given high amounts of attention and trials to show value. "Exploitable" customers are used more to seek a short-term advantage, primarily through cost pressures, and it is considered worth the risk of losing them as a result.

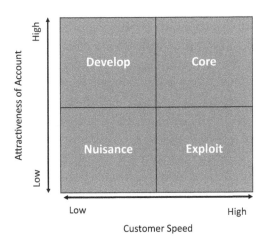

FIGURE 14.3
Supplier Perception of Clients.

The reason that this matrix is best used for tactical procurement, as opposed to strategic category management, is that it doesn't offer much insight into future development of relative value; for example, considering the future effect of competitive threats.

Supply Chain Value Analysis

Supply chain value analysis is the systematic mapping and analysis of the internal and external supply chain, and allows the identification of linkages which provide value, and those that pose a risk. It is an important element of category management and supplier relationship management, as complex supply chains can hide inefficiencies, financial problems, and poor processes.

This type of analysis should be started once the priority categories have been identified using category management. Progress against action plans, both internally and among suppliers, should be tracked afterwards.

Mapping the internal and external supply chain for a category to identify areas of wasted activity, delays, or unnecessary costs, as part of an SRM program, can increase value by reducing costs and improving performance. Value stream mapping (VSM) is a great tool for this.

Value Stream Mapping (VSM)

Value stream mapping (VSM), a handy Lean tool used to identify waste within a family of products or services, is ideal for analyzing priority categories (or possibly critical item families within a category) within your supply chain.

VSM is a team-based approach to mapping a "value stream" (i.e. specific activities, in this case within a supply chain, required to design, order, and provide a specific product or service) or process from beginning to end. It visually and quantitatively breaks the process down into value-added and non-value-added steps from the viewpoint of the customer.

Typically, you start at the customer end and work your way back through your internal processes all the way back to the supply end. When doing a VSM exercise, it is best to have a diverse team of employees (no more than 8–10) that are typically supervisory and management level—although front-line employees will be involved in the mapping process as well. It should typically take no longer than two days; one day for training and creating the current state map, and the second day (usually a week or so later) to create the future state map. The entire process including implementation should be completed in less than six months at most, if not sooner.

The team first maps the current state (e.g. Figure 14.4), while at the same time it gathers ideas and input for an improved, future state. The maps are drawn using standard symbols (easily found on the internet) showing the flow of materials (shown at the bottom of the map) and information (at the top of the map). It should typically take no more than one day to map a process' current state, and this is really a "10,000 foot" level view so it shouldn't be too detailed, although information should be validated.

The future state map (e.g. Figure 14.5), using data contained in the first map, is the same value stream with any waste, defects, and failures eliminated.

It is usually best to put some time in between doing the current and future state maps to give time for the ideas to germinate.

The two maps are used to create detailed strategic and implementation plans to enhance the value stream's performance.

Competition

Although not usually thought of as a tool, competition is an important way to gain value from a financial, efficiency, and quality sense.

In procurement, competition is the process of inviting more than one potential provider to put forward a proposal, versus single sourcing where only one proposal is considered—this usually is only used for very low-value procurements.

Competition incentivizes suppliers to submit a more attractive proposal than if they knew they were the only ones being considered.

One potential downside of competition is the possible collusion of providers. This can be minimized by inviting a wider number of potential suppliers to submit proposals, while encouraging innovation in their proposals, and checking for any unusual trends in pricing.

e-Procurement

Electronic or e-procurement, which we covered in the previous chapter, is increasingly being used as a strategy to streamline and improve the efficiency of the procurement process.

Some uses include systems to manage the process for receiving and evaluating quotations and tenders (e-tendering), those that assist with the management of contracts, the use of e-auctions to identify the best price offered by suppliers, and online e-marketplaces which allow buyers and sellers to interface and do business.

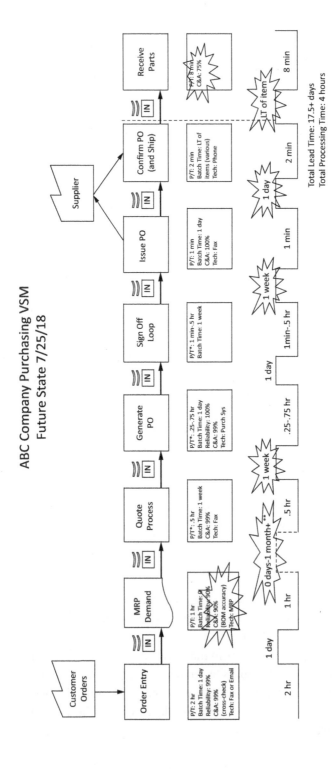

ABC Company Purchasing VSM
Future State 7/25/18

Order Entry
P/T: 2 hr
Batch Time: 1 day
Reliability: 99%
C&A: 99%
(cross-check)
Tech: Fax or Email

MRP Demand
P/T: 1 hr
Batch Time:
Reliability: 90%
C&A: 90%
(BOM accuracy)
Tech: MRP

Quote Process
P/T*: .5 hr
Batch Time: 1 week
C&A: 99%
Tech: Fax

Generate PO
P/T*: .25–.75 hr
Batch Time: 1 day
Reliability: 100%
C&A: 99%
Tech: Purch Sys

Sign Off Loop
P/T*: 1 min–.5 hr
Batch Time: 1 week

Issue PO
P/T: 1 min
Batch Time: 1 day
C&A: 100%
Tech: Fax

Confirm PO (and Ship)
P/T: 2 min
Batch Time: LT of items (various)
Tech: Phone

Receive Parts
P/T: 8 min
C&A: 75%

Supplier

Customer Orders

2 hr — 1 hr — .5 hr — .25–.75 hr — 1min–.5 hr — 1 min — 2 min — 8 min

1 day — 0 days–1 month+** — 1 week — 1 day — 1 week — 1 day — LT of item

Total Lead Time: 17.5+ days
Total Processing Time: 4 hours

* depends on $ value
** parts, electrical components, etc. MRP req not being consistently acted upon.
(maybe be due to quantity low and told to wait by O&R, wrong Lead Time which is too long, new product requirement told by Eng not to buy, but there are some legitimate ones as well)

FIGURE 14.4
Current State Value Stream Map.

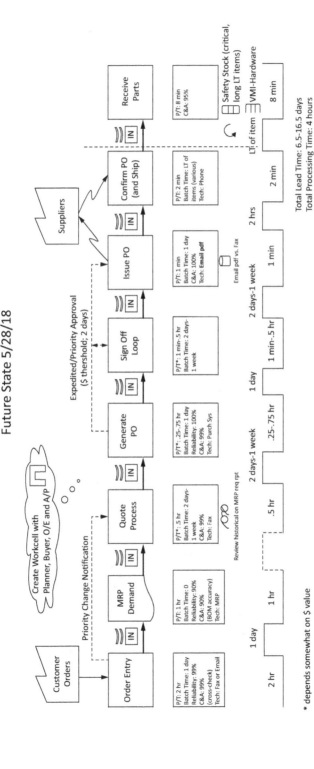

FIGURE 14.5
Future State Value Stream Map.

Standard Terms and Conditions of Contract

Most organizations have standard terms and conditions in their contracts for goods and services, which should be attached to invitations to tender offers, with shorter versions available for lower-value requirements where they can help to lower the barrier to market entry for small suppliers.

Standard terms and conditions reduce the risk of procurers missing out critical conditions, such as intellectual property rights, default, termination, and liquidated damages from the final contract, and are a helpful tool for the non-professional buyer.

It is also important that any specification for a requirement does not conflict with the standard terms and conditions.

Framework Contracts and Agreements

Framework agreements are agreements between two businesses or organizations that recognize that the parties have not come to a final agreement on all matters relevant to the relationship between them, but have come to agreement on enough matters to move forward with the relationship, with further details to be agreed to in the future. Specific to procurement, framework agreements are used to establish the terms governing contracts to be awarded during a given period, in particular regarding price, and, where appropriate, the quantity.

A framework agreement is the same arrangement as the framework contract (described in next paragraph), but without the up-front consideration. In this case, each time a buyer uses the agreement, a separate contract is formed by the consideration paid for the order in question.

A framework contract has the consideration of a monetary sum paid up-front by the buying organization to the supplier. This payment is made to create a contract on the terms and conditions offered by the supplier to the buying organization, so it is important to first ensure that the terms and conditions are correctly drafted, so that the supplier fully understands what has been agreed to.

Framework agreements and contracts are a very useful tool for aggregating demand and using economies of scale where there is a repeat requirement for a good or service, and are typically used for high-value items.

In most cases, frameworks restrict choice to only a small number of (potentially large) suppliers, and may discourage the entry of new suppliers to the market. If there is a high monetary value benefit to not restricting the market to a small group of providers, then a longer term may not be a viable solution.

Preferred Supplier Lists

When repeat requirements for relatively low-value supplies or services exist, it may be useful to set up a list of preferred providers for use across the organization. The list would be made up of potential suppliers suitable to be included in the competitive process.

To ensure equality when choosing which suppliers to compete for requirements, a system should be used that is open and transparent, with new suppliers who meet the criteria included.

Sustainable Procurement

Sustainable procurement is a process whereby organizations meet their needs for goods and services in a way that achieves value that produces financial and other benefits, not only to the organization, but also to society and the economy, while minimizing damage to the environment.

Procurement has historically been based largely on price and quality to maximize benefits for the procuring organization. Sustainable procurement broadens this, while also considering external consequences of procurement decisions, a triple baseline, if you will, of goals to be met.

Environmental impacts that can be calculated include consumption of finite resources, water quality, and pollution emitted. Social impacts include community health, worker safety, education quality, and diversity.

By factoring these impacts into the overall corporate strategy, a company can be more successful, as it can deliver increased efficiency, long-term savings, more efficient and effective use of natural resources, reducing the harmful impact of pollution and waste, and encouraging innovation (www.yor-ok.org.uk, 2018).

Total Quality Management (TQM)

Total quality management (TQM) led to methodologies like Six Sigma and Lean Six Sigma. It is directed at quality improvement and takes a customer-focused approach. While Lean Six Sigma focuses upon speed, flexibility, metrics, reducing variation, and waste elimination, TQM focuses on longer-term quality improvement.

The fundamental philosophy of TQM is to reduce production and service defects, increase customer satisfaction with the product and streamline supply chain management. In addition, it helps to ensure that equipment is well-maintained and current, and that employees are well-trained. Most companies who use TQM also utilize other Lean processes, such as kaizen, kanban, and 5S-workplace organization.

Features of TQM include:

- Having a consistent, constant, and stated purpose behind improving quality.
- Reducing dependence upon inspections (Lean Six Sigma is very data-intensive).
- Getting rid of fear and hierarchy in the company.
- Ensuring everyone in the company has undergone training and that they are working toward quality improvement.
- Ensuring that education is an ongoing process.

While this book is about applying a Lean philosophy to a procurement organization, improving quality is directly connected to waste elimination (e.g. smaller lot sizes affect fewer items when a quality issue occurs). Furthermore, many of the tools of TQM (e.g. Pareto diagrams, fishbone diagrams, etc.) are used in Lean, and both are forms of continuous improvement, just to name a few of the many similarities.

Utilizing the aforementioned tools and techniques and more is required to manage procurement in today's complex and ever-changing global supply chain; this is our next topic.

Part IV

Lean Ahead

15

Global Procurement and Its Impact on the Lean Supply Chain

In the late 1980s, a considerable number of companies began to integrate global sources into their core business, establishing global systems of supplier relationships and expansion of their supply chains across national boundaries and into other continents around the globe.

The globalization of supply chain management in organizations had the goals of increasing their competitive advantage, adding value to the customer, and reducing costs through global sourcing.

In addition to sourcing globally, many companies also sell globally and/or compete with other companies that do.

Ultimately, global supply chain management is about sourcing, manufacturing, transporting, and distributing products outside your native country. It ensures that customers get products and services that they need and want faster, better, and more cost-effectively, either locally or from around the world.

Thus, we can define global supply chains as worldwide networks of suppliers, manufacturers, warehouses, distribution centers, and retailers, through which raw materials are acquired, transformed, and delivered to customers.

GROWTH OF GLOBALIZATION

The growth of global sourcing has been enhanced by a number of things, primarily: information and communication technology development, reduction in logistic costs, together with the improvement of the transport infrastructures, and by the general improvement in quality and efficiency of global suppliers.

Additionally, we have seen a change in how firms organize their production into global supply chains, where companies are increasingly outsourcing some of their activities to third parties, and are locating parts of their supply chain outside their home country (known as "offshoring").

They are also increasingly partnering with other firms through strategic alliances and joint ventures, enabling not only large companies, but also smaller firms and suppliers to become global.

These types of global business strategies have allowed firms to specialize in core competencies to sustain their competitive advantage.

This is not limited to just outsourcing manufacturing and supply chain operations, but also includes business process outsourcing (BPO), and information technology (IT) services that are supplied from a variety of locations, as well as other knowledge-intensive activities, such as R&D.

Factors Influencing Globalization

There are some key factors influencing the growth of globalization that one should be aware of when considering a global procurement strategy. They are:

Improvements in transportation: In general, larger container ships mean that the cost of transporting goods between countries has decreased. Economies of scale are found as the cost per item can be reduced when operating on a larger scale. Transportation improvements also mean that both goods and people can travel more quickly.

Containers have made the supply chain more efficient in a variety of ways. This includes the ability to put cargo into standardized modules to be much more efficient with space. Containers can be stacked into rows and columns that maximize the surface area of a cargo ship.

Containers have also made intermodal shipping much more feasible, as instead of having to unload break bulk cargo from a ship into a warehouse and load it again onto a truck, a container can go seamlessly from ship to truck or train. Furthermore, shipment tracking has become much more reliable and precise, as containers are labeled with unique codes, making it easier to know where a specific piece of cargo is at any given time.

Freedom of trade: There are organizations like the World Trade Organization (WTO) that promote free trade between countries, helping to remove barriers between them. Most countries are also members of regional free trade areas, such as NAFTA, that lower trade barriers among participating countries.

However, most governments still impose some protectionist policies that are intended to support local employment, such as applying tariffs to imports or subsidies to exports (e.g. the current effort by the Trump administration to impose steel and aluminum tariffs on imports).

Improvements of communications: The internet and mobile technology has allowed greater communication between people in different countries.

Labor availability and skills: Less developed nations in Asia and elsewhere have lower labor costs and, in some cases, also high skill levels. Labor-intensive industries such as clothing can take advantage of cheaper labor costs and reduced legal restrictions in these less developed countries.

Transnational corporations: Globalization has resulted in many businesses setting up, or buying operations, in other countries. When a foreign company invests in a country by building a factory or a shop, this is sometimes called "inward investment." Companies that operate in several countries are often referred to as multinational corporations (MNCs) or transnational corporations (TNCs). The US fast food chain McDonald's is an example of a large MNC, having nearly 30,000 restaurants in 119 countries.

Many multinational corporations not only invest in other economically developed countries, but also invest in less developed countries (e.g. Ford Motor Company makes large numbers of cars in the UK, as well as India).

Reasons for a Company to Globalize

The reasons a company may choose to globalize (or not) vary, but are usually affected by global market, technological, cost, and political and economic influences. Some reasons to globalize within each of these influences are:

Global market forces

- Foreign competition in local markets.
- Growth in foreign demand.
- Global presence as a defensive tool.
- Companies forced to develop and enhance cutting-edge technologies and products.

Technological forces

- Knowledge diffusion across national boundaries, hence the need for technology sharing to be competitive.
- Global location of R&D facilities.
- Close to production (as product cycles get shorter).
- Close to expertise (e.g. Indian programmers).

Global cost factors

- Availability of skilled or unskilled labor at lower cost.
- Integrated supplier infrastructure (as suppliers become more involved in design).
- Capital intensive facilities utilize incentives such as tax breaks, price breaks, etc., which can influence the "make versus buy" decision.

Political and economic factors

- Trade protection mechanisms such as tariffs, quotas, voluntary export restrictions, local content requirements, environmental regulations, and government procurement policies (e.g. discount for local).
- Customs duties which differ by commodity and the level of assembly.
- Exchange rate fluctuations and operating flexibility.

We don't have to look far to see the impact of some of recent political and economic factors, as by sticking to campaign promises, the Trump administration seems to be governing on a populist, nationalist, and protectionist platform to "Make America Great Again," with goals such as renegotiating and cancelling trade deals, and trying to bring the manufacturing of items like cars and air conditioners home again—if, in fact many items we now buy overseas could even be manufactured with any efficiency in the US again.

The potential impact of this can be trade wars, rising prices of supplies and consumer products, longer lead times, and higher manufacturing costs. The first potential example of this was the March 2018 Trump Administration announcement of steel and aluminum tariffs.

If trade deals such as NAFTA are in jeopardy—which may be the case as the U.S. withdrew from Trans-Pacific Partnership—not only may costs rise, but inventory could very well be stalled around the globe, lengthening lead times, as it takes longer to get products to the U.S. This will certainly raise risk in operating a global supply chain, since the global economy is still struggling somewhat from the 2007 financial meltdown and the resulting global recession, and the last thing it needs is another shock to the system like this. It will also most likely impact our exports as well, as protectionism will probably rise around the world to some degree.

Ultimately, this can lead to significant inflation as prices rise for goods (either imported or manufactured here), increased unemployment, and excess capacity, at the very least, in the international transportation industry (and possibly other industries, such as retail, as prices rise).

On a somewhat positive side, it may drive more nearshoring, or increased investments in U.S., and some regional supply chain capabilities.

Regardless, one thing is for sure: businesses will need to adjust their global supply chain strategies accordingly to deal with it as efficiently as possible, and there will be an even greater need for a flexible, Agile supply chain.

Lean Global Procurement

As we know, a Lean philosophy focuses on improving performance by eliminating non-value-added activities, while global procurement or sourcing looks to find an advantage from cost reductions in the purchase of raw materials, components, sub-assemblies, and products around the world.

As a result, the two approaches don't appear to be fully consistent, as global sourcing can require purchasing large quantities with long lead times, exposing companies to higher variability, quality issues, and other risks. All these factors combined imply increasing stock levels (both cycle stock and safety stock), and increasing dependency on forecasts.

A study entitled "Global Sourcing: Lessons from Lean Companies to Improve Supply Chain Performances" (Staudacher and Tantardini, 2009) looked to see how global procurement/sourcing could coexist.

Lean supply management and global sourcing are two distinct approaches to achieve competitive advantages, whose complete integration is difficult. However, the opportunity to exploit managerial countermeasures to reduce some of the negative impacts of global sourcing seems to be possible.

They concluded that it could be successful if a variety of countermeasures were enacted. They included:

Consolidation centers: The introduction of a consolidation center for deliveries near global suppliers to combine load units with products from multiple suppliers.

Use of a local supplier next to the global supplier: The local supplier can guarantee the supply's continuity in case of problems. This also makes the customer less dependent on the global supplier.

Quality control at supplier location: Aims to reduce non-quality costs, by avoiding useless long-distance transport of goods for defective products.

Milk runs: A company can enlarge its "milk runs" (i.e. delivery method for regular mixed loads from different suppliers) in order to include other countries.

Flexibility and frequency increase of the supplier: Increase the flexibility and frequency of deliveries from suppliers as a measure to reduce stock levels.

Delivery services: Reduce and focus on more reliable delivery companies.

What follows is an example of the practical application of a Lean philosophy in global procurement.

BECTON DICKINSON: LEAN GLOBAL PROCUREMENT EXAMPLE

Becton Dickinson (BD) is an American medical technology company that manufactures and sells medical devices, instrument systems and reagents. They have a global procurement strategy that is outlined at their website that can be considered a good example of a Lean global procurement strategy.

In it they state that

BD global procurement strives to continuously deliver the highest sustained value for our company by leveraging our full competitive supply base using highly effective and efficient systems and processes.

BD products and businesses require greatly diverse materials, supplies and services. To select the right supply strategy and supplier base for each need while accommodating continual global and industry changes, BD global procurement must analyze internal and external dynamics—from risk to pricing to innovation.

Our associates lead cross-functional stakeholder sourcing teams to review each business' needs, for each category of purchase, against the following critical sourcing factors:

- Assurance
- Quality
- Service
- Cost
- Innovation
- Regulatory

We align these factors with stakeholder and business requirements by applying our knowledge of the external supply market. Implementing them while considering rigorous testing and validation protocols required by government regulations, we enable significant annual savings throughout procurement and continuous improvements to purchased materials, supplies and services. These capabilities yield long-term impacts, maximizing value from the supply base.

(www.bd.com, 2018)

BD's strategy looks at their global procurement from multiple views of process efficiency, supplier relationship and risk management, functional capability and culture, and continuous improvement programs.

Process Efficiency

BD looks at entire processes using financial targets, as well as focusing on efficiency and customer satisfaction. They use a buying technology for indirect goods and services, to receive and process invoices, as well as provide visibility to their suppliers and stakeholders, allowing them to focus on value-added activities.

BD operates shared service centers around the world to streamline transactions for various processes with a single global SAP platform to further increase the efficiency of their various processes.

Supplier Relationship and Risk Management

BD uses a supplier relationship management (SRM) program with key suppliers, and actively manages supply base risk and compliance requirements to ensure reliable supply.

Furthermore, they have developed mitigation plans for key risk areas such as supply interruption, reputation, and compliance, to maintain a competitive advantage while meeting stakeholder and business needs.

Functional Capabilities and Culture

BD global procurement has a culture of curiosity, collaboration, and knowledge-sharing to help their employee and business performance.

BD employees are encouraged to participate in ongoing training and development programs which help them build their knowledge of the entire supply chain and interact with various stakeholders. They believe that this helps to make them more Agile, capable, and engaged.

Continuous Improvement Programs

As can be found in many Lean programs, BD global procurement focuses on continuously improving the reliability, quality, and cost-effectiveness of their procured products and services. They collaborate with strategic suppliers on continuous improvement projects, such as Lean waste reduction measures and Six Sigma programs, to create and maintain a competitive advantage.

GLOBAL SUPPLY CHAIN STRATEGY DEVELOPMENT

Today, in most industries, it is necessary to develop a global view of your organization's operations to survive and thrive. However, many companies find it difficult making the transition from domestic to international operations, despite the fact that there have been significant improvements in transportation and technology over the past 25 years.

To be successful in the global economy, a company must have an end-to-end supply chain strategy. This should include significant investments in ERP and other supply chain technology to prepare them to optimize global operations by linking systems across their businesses globally, helping them to better manage their global supply chains.

Earlier in this book we discussed organizational strategies and how the supply chain must support them. It is no different when discussing a global supply chain. In general, an organization should have their global supply chain set up to maximize customer service at the lowest possible cost.

Kauffman and Crimi in their paper "A Best-Practice Approach for Development of Global Supply Chains" (Kauffman et al, 2005) suggest that developing a global supply chain requires not only the same information as when developing one domestically, but also additional information on international logistics, law, customs, culture, ethics, language, politics, government, and currency. Cross-functional teams should be utilized that are supplied with detailed information including the "what, when, and where" of the global supply chain, as well as quantity demand forecasts. Supplier evaluations must include the ability for them to handle international operations and subsequent requirements.

To implement a global supply chain for your business, after identifying your supply chain partners, the team should document and test the required processes and procedures before implementation. All participants must be trained in the processes and procedures with metrics established to manage and control the global operations. The team must establish a project plan with responsibilities and milestones for the implementation.

The actual step-by-step approach for developing global supply chains recommended by Kauffman and Carmi is as follows:

1. "Form a cross-functional global supply chain development team.
   - Include all affected parties, internal and external.
   - The team composition may change as development and implementation proceeds.
2. Identify needs and opportunities for supply chain globalization.
   - Determine the requirements your supply chain must meet.
     - Commodities, materials, services required … dollar value of materials and services … importance of commodities, materials, and services …
     - Performance metrics for qualification and evaluation of suppliers.
   - Determine the current status of your supply chain "as is."
     - Existing suppliers of materials and services.
     - Customers …
     - Commodity markets …
     - Current performance, problem areas.
     - Competitiveness …
     - "Fit" of your current supply chain with your operational requirements.

The main components of this particular framework ... should include all operational dimensions of supply chains which must be identified, considered, and included in any determination of requirements and assessment of current status of supply chains.

3. Determine commodity/service priorities for globalization consideration based on needs and opportunities.
4. Identify potential markets and suppliers and compare to "as is" markets, suppliers, and supply chain arrangements, operations, and results.
5. Evaluate/qualify markets and suppliers, identify supplier pool (determine best ones based on likely total cost of ownership (TCO), and best potential to meet or exceed expectations and requirements).
6. Determine selection process for suppliers, e.g. request for proposal (RFP), negotiation, etc.
7. Select suppliers or confirm current suppliers.
8. Formalize agreements with suppliers.
9. Implement agreements.
10. Monitor, evaluate, review and revise as needed." (Kauffman et al, 2005).

Your company's global supply strategy must also consider risks and mitigation plans.

GLOBAL SUPPLY CHAIN RISKS AND CHALLENGES

The global supply chain is fraught with risks and challenges.

As operations become more complex, procurement and logistics becomes more challenging, lead times lengthen, costs increase, and customer service can suffer. With a global footprint, different products are directed to more diverse customers via different distribution channels, requiring different supply chains.

There are also many other additional issues to address, such as the identification of sources capable of producing the materials in the quality and quantity required, the protection of a firm's intellectual property, understanding import/export compliance issues, communication with suppliers and transportation companies, differences in time zones, language and technology, and product security while in transit.

Questions to Consider When Going Global

All of this raises some initial questions that companies need to consider as their operations globalize (www.pwc.com, 2013).

They are:

1. What are the drivers of supply chain complexity for a company with global operations?

   Supply chains are exposed to both domestic and international risks. The more complex the supply chain, the less predictable the likelihood and the impact of disruption. Over recent years, the size of the supply chain network has increased, dependencies between entities and between functions have shifted, the speed of change has accelerated, and the level of transparency has decreased.

   Overall, developing a product and getting it to the market requires more complex supply chains needing a higher degree of coordination.

2. What are the sources of supply chain risk?

   Risks to global supply chains vary from controllable to uncontrollable ones and include:
   - Raw material price fluctuation
   - Currency fluctuations
   - Market changes
   - Energy/fuel prices volatility
   - Environmental catastrophes
   - Raw material scarcity
   - Rising labor costs
   - Geopolitical instability

3. What parameters are supply chain operations most sensitive to?

   Respondents to a PWC and MIT forum for supply chain innovation survey replied that their supply chain operations were most sensitive to reliance on skill-set and expertise (31%), price of commodities (29%), and energy and oil (28%). For example, when U.S. diesel prices rose significantly in 2012, shippers rapidly adjust budgets to offset the increased costs higher fuel prices produce.

4. How do companies mitigate against disruptions?

   A great majority of respondents (82%) to the survey said they had business continuity plans ready. Nissan, for example, had a well-thought-out and exercised business continuity plan ready to kick into action to facilitate a quick recovery. Other major strategies by respondents included:

- Implement dual-sourcing strategy.
- Use both regional and global strategy.
- Pursue (1st and 2nd tier) supplier collaboration.
- Pursue demand collaboration with customers.

Key Global Supply Chain Challenges

According to a survey by PRTM consultants for Supply Chain Digest (www.scdigest.com, 2010), key global supply chain challenges include:

"Supply chain volatility and uncertainty have permanently increased - Market transparency and greater price sensitivity have led to lower customer loyalty. Product commoditization reduces true differentiation in both the consumer and business-to-business (b2b) environments …

Securing growth requires truly global customer and supplier networks - Future market growth depends on international customers and customized products. Increased supply chain globalization and complexity need to be managed effectively…

Market dynamics demand regional, cost-optimized supply chain configurations - Customer requirements and competitors necessitate regionally tailored supply chains and product offerings. End-to-end supply chain cost optimization will be critical…

Risk management involves the end-to-end supply chain - Risk and opportunity management should span the entire supply chain—from demand planning to expansion of manufacturing capacity—and should include the supply chains of key partners …

Existing supply chain organizations are not truly integrated and empowered - The supply chain organization needs to be treated as a single integrated organization. In order to be effective, significant improvements require support across all supply chain functions."

GLOBAL RISK MANAGEMENT

An organization's supply chain is greatly impacted by globalization and its inherent logistical complexity. This has resulted in having risk beyond just the demand and supply variability, limited capacity, and quality issues that domestic companies have traditionally faced, to now include other trends such as greater customer expectations, global competition, longer and more complex supply chains, increased product variety with shorter life cycles, security, and political and currency risks.

As a result, it is important for global supply chain managers to be aware of the relevant risk factors and build in suitable mitigation strategies.

Potential Risk Identification and Impact

Before planning for risks in your supply chain, you must first identify potential risks, as well as their impact.

To accomplish this, many companies use a vulnerability map or risk-matrix, described in Chapter 12 for use in contract and performance management, to visualize unforeseen and unwanted events, as shown in Figure 15.1 (Sheffield and Rice Jr., 2005).

This type of analysis has two dimensions: disruption probability and consequences. Obviously, risks with a high disruption probability and severe consequences should be given a great deal of attention.

One problem with this method is that it relies heavily on risk perception, which can vary depending on recent events, a person's experience and knowledge, their appetite for risk, and their position in the organization, among other things.

Sources of Risk

Before determining a global risk management strategy for your organization, it is important to consider the possible sources of risk. There are five sources of risk in a supply chain, some of which are internal, and others external to your organization (Figure 15.2; Christopher and Peck, 2004).

Internal Risks

Process risk refers to the value-adding and managerial activities undertaken by the firm, and to disruptions to these processes. These processes are usually dependent on internally owned or managed assets, and on the existing infrastructure, so the reliability of supporting transportation, communication, and infrastructure should be carefully considered.

Control risks are the rules, systems, and procedures that determine how organizations exert control over the processes, and are therefore the risks arising from the use (or mis-use) of these rules. For the supply chain, they

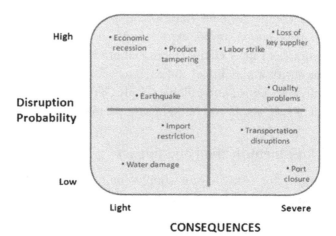

FIGURE 15.1
Vulnerability Map.

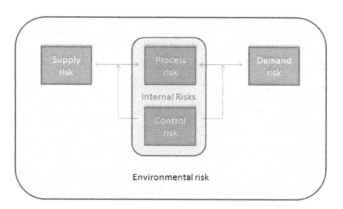

FIGURE 15.2
Sources of Risk in the Supply Chain.

include order quantities, batch sizes, safety stock policies, etc., and any policies and procedures that cover asset and transportation management.

External Risks

Demand and supply risk are external to the organization, but are internal to the networks through which materials, products, and information flow between companies. The organization should consider potential disruptions to the flow of product and information from within and between all parties in the extended supply chain network, and at least understand and monitor the potential risks that may affect other supply chain partners.

Supply risk is the upstream equivalent of demand risk, and relates to potential or actual disturbances to the flow of product or information from within the network, upstream of your organization.

Environmental risks are disruptions that are external to the network of organizations through which the products flow. This type of event can impact your organization directly, those upstream or downstream, or the marketplace itself.

Environmental-related events may affect a particular product (e.g. contamination) or place through which the supply chain passes (e.g. an accident, direct action, extreme weather, or natural disasters). They may also be the result of sociopolitical, economic, or technological events far removed from your firm's own supply chains, with the effects often reaching other industry networks. In some cases, the type or timing of these events may be predictable (e.g. regulatory changes), and many will not be, but their potential impact can still be evaluated (Christopher and Peck, 2004).

Supply Chain Disruptions

Supply chain disruptions are the actual occurrence of risks, including the categories mentioned above, and are unplanned and unanticipated events that disrupt the normal flow of goods and materials within a supply chain.

There is usually some triggering event, followed by the situation (with its consequences) that occurs afterwards.

Disruptions that a company must deal with come primarily, although not always as previously mentioned, from customers, suppliers, and/or the supply chain. The consequences can be immense to your company, and can include higher costs, poor performance, lost sales, lower profits, bankruptcy, and damage to your organization.

The actual characteristics of the supply chain structure you have may determine the drivers of your supply chain's vulnerability.

These characteristics may include:

- Complexity of the supply chain (e.g. global versus domestic sourcing).
- Density of the supply chain (using these high-density regions leads to higher vulnerability of supply chains).
- Single or sole sourcing versus multiple vendors for the same item.

- Lean and JIT production philosophies require precise timing.
- Centralization of warehouse/manufacturing locations results in lengthy lead times due to distance issues.
- Dependency on major suppliers/customers (i.e. the "all your eggs in one basket" syndrome).
- Dependency on IT infrastructure, electricity, etc.

Flexible, secure supply chains with a diversified supplier base are less vulnerable to disruptions than those that are not.

Therefore, to a great degree, potential disruptions are the result of "conscious" decisions regarding how you design the supply chain. Risk management is about using innovative planning to reduce potential disruptions by preparing responses for negative events.

Risk Mitigation

Depending on the type of global supply chain risk, what follows are some common supply chain risks and tactics for risk mitigation (Heizer and Render, 2013).

Supplier failure to deliver: Use multiple suppliers with contracts containing penalties. When possible, keep subcontractors on retainer.

Example: McDonald's planned its supply chain many years before opening stores in Russia. All plants are monitored closely to ensure strong links.

Supplier quality failure: Ensure that you have adequate supplier selection, training, certification, and monitoring processes.

Example: Darden Restaurants (i.e. Olive Garden restaurants) uses third-party audits and other controls on supplier processes and logistics for reduction of risk.

Logistics delays or damage: Have multiple or back-up transportation modes and warehouses. Make sure that you have secure packaging, and execute contracts with penalties for non-conformance.

Example: Walmart always plans for alternative origins and delivery routes bypassing problem areas when delivering from its distribution centers to its stores with its private fleet.

Distribution: Have a detailed selection and management process when using public warehouses. Make sure that your contracts have penalties for non-conformance.

Example: Toyota trains its dealers on improving customer service, logistics, and repair facilities.

Information loss or distortion: Always back up databases within secure information systems. Use established industry standards, and train supply chain partners on the understanding and use of information.

Example: Boeing utilizes a state-of-the-art international communication system that transmits engineering, scheduling, and logistics data to Boeing facilities and suppliers worldwide.

Political: Companies can purchase political risk insurance. In such a situation, you may decide to go the route of franchising and licensing with your business.

Example: Hard Rock Café restaurants try to reduce political risk by franchising and licensing in countries where they deem that the political and cultural barriers are great.

Economic: Hedging, the act of entering into a financial contract to protect against unexpected, expected, or anticipated changes in currency exchange rates, can be used to address exchange rate risk.

Example: Honda and Nissan have moved some of their manufacturing processes out of Japan since the exchange rate for the yen has made Japanese-made automobiles more expensive.

Natural catastrophes: In many cases, natural disasters can be planned for by taking out various forms of insurance (e.g. flood insurance). Companies may also consider alternate sourcing for example.

Example: After the 2011 earthquake and tsunami, Toyota established at least two suppliers in different geographical regions for each component.

Theft, vandalism, and terrorism: Again, in some cases, there is insurance available for these types of risk. Companies also enforce patent protection, and use security measures such as RFID and GPS.

Example: Domestic Port Radiation Initiative: The U.S. government has established radiation monitors at all major U.S. ports that scan imported containers for radiation.

This discussion leads us directly to our final chapter, which looks at the future direction of Lean procurement.

16

The Future of Lean Procurement

As the reader should now understand, the principles of Lean and Agile procurement are based on those of Lean production, with the focus being on the customer, and the efficiency of the operation. Lean supply is part of continuous improvement, and aims to streamline processes within the supply chain to eliminate waste and non-value-added activities. Waste can be defined as time, costs, or inventory.

For an organization to be Lean, it must have had all non-essential resources removed. This is efficient and cost-effective, in that the value/ supply chain can theoretically do exactly what is needed of it and no more, but to do so requires sound forecasting and planning of demand and supply. While it is most suitable for industries with stable product specifications, long lead times, and few impulse purchases, Lean procurement, to varying degrees, can be applied anytime and anywhere in procurement.

Organizations which are Agile react as quickly as is practical to provide a cost-effective response to customer demand. This is based on flexibility in design, supply, production, and distribution. It is most appropriate for products such as fast fashion and foodstuffs which must be on display and available when wanted by the customer.

Throughout this book, much has been discussed as to how to understand and apply these concepts in today's procurement organization. With that in mind, I will try to predict where things are headed.

A good way to look at it, I believe, is from the perspective of people, process, and technology (Figure 16.1), the three elements necessary for successful business transformation.

Far too often, business transformation efforts concentrate on process improvement strategies and business process reengineering,

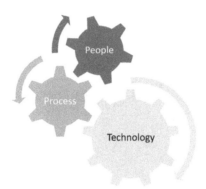

FIGURE 16.1
The Interaction of People, Process, and Technology.

while essentially ignoring the people aspect of the change initiative. Subsequently, these transformation initiatives do not achieve their desired results as studies have shown that approximately three-quarters of business re-engineering efforts do not achieve their objectives, and subsequently do not sustain themselves long-term. One of the most commonly cited reasons for their failure is due to a lack of focus on the organization's culture. That being said, let's start with people.

PEOPLE

According to the US Bureau of Labor Statistics, millennials (a person reaching young adulthood in the early 21st century) will represent over half of America's workforce by the end of 2020. They are known for their familiarity with emerging technologies, collaboration, and innovative spirit. Their success in bringing new life to procurement will depend on successful collaboration with the input of senior resources.

As procurement's role evolves within leading organizations, the skillsets of its top professionals will likewise need to evolve, requiring hiring managers to look beyond traditional supply management position descriptions, and hire with a more open mind. They will need to balance analytical skills with people skills, and leverage strategic sourcing more than just cost savings. This requires employees that go beyond the numbers to develop and implement strategies, manage stakeholder relationships, and predict future trends.

Furthermore, the very perception of procurement throughout many organizations needs to change, as procurement needs to present itself as an ally, rather than an adversary.

Procurement professionals will also need to gain a better understanding of other departments' processes, goals, and metrics for success to be able to collaborate and communicate more effectively. They need to emphasize their shared goals, and stress the ways in which their value goes beyond traditional cost savings. As a result, hiring managers should look for applicants with broad ranges of experience.

Furthermore, it's not only important to hire great talent, but to retain it. As part of this effort, organizations need to develop new models for providing feedback and rewarding success. Procurement groups need to apply a proactive, strategic method to employee management. Constructive feedback, recognition, and professional advancement must become part of an ongoing dialogue.

Employees lacking a clear career path may leave, so managers need to take the time to learn the personal interests and aspirations of their team members. Actionable paths for accepting new roles and responsibilities promote a more engaged, motivated workforce.

Externally, porous national borders and inconsistent policing make global procurement riskier than ever. A lack of due diligence can lead organizations to break international laws and incur serious penalties (e.g. use of child labor or forced labor by a contractor).

Consumers are committed to supporting businesses that hold themselves to high moral and ethical standards. The transparency afforded by the internet and social media makes it easier than ever to dig deeply into a company's dealings and determine which ones measure up.

Procurement should take the lead in ensuring ethical practices across supply chains to protect corporate reputations (Source One Management Services, LLC, 2018).

Next, let's look at possible trends in procurement processes in the coming years.

PROCESS

To help reach the goal of Lean procurement, the following trends stand out as most likely to take hold for this to happen:

Procurement and supply chain collaboration: Collaboration as a procurement trend is gaining prominence across all business sectors. As a part of their strategic move, organizations are collaborating on business functions, including procurement and supply chain. For instance, e-procurement systems allow stakeholders across the company and suppliers to share and manage valuable data online.

Transparency and visibility: There has been an explosion of demand from consumers to know where their products are originating, and the required information can be extremely detailed.

Innovation: Companies must rely on innovation to try to gain an edge against the competition. Companies will have to be less risk-averse, and seize opportunities to embrace innovations to implement the latest procurement trends. Although it may incur significant cost or pose challenges at the start, it can pay off and help improve profits for business in the long run.

Simplicity: Although the majority of procurement trends call for complex technologies and complex benchmarks, there is still room for simplicity and easy-to-understand goals. For instance, cost advantages and cashflow improvements are still the driving force of procurement and supply chain functions.

Nearshoring: Over the past few years, many companies from developed nations were jumping on the bandwagon for outsourcing their business processes in a bid to reduce costs. However, nearshoring is amongst the new procurement trends recently as companies try to exploit country-based opportunity and shared laws, and to have closer control of procurement and supply chain functions.

Corporate social responsibility (CSR): Another procurement trend gaining traction is the increased pressure for businesses to become involved in sustainability practices as a part of their CSR activity. The need for sustainability is heightened by the fact that consumers now prefer brands that are doing good environmentally or socially.

TECHNOLOGY

According to a report released in 2018 by Accenture entitled "The Next Generation Digital Procurement," many supply managers are seeking to modernize this function, but the digital revolution has largely overlooked procurement.

Still a Long Way to Go for Procurement

The Accenture report found that many companies are using digital technology to transform key areas of their businesses, including customer-facing functions such as marketing, sales, and service, and have implemented eProcurement systems, and some cloud-based procurement tools.

However, leading companies have gone further and have begun to create a true digital procurement organization which automates repeatable tasks to increase efficiency and drive down costs. These systems include real-time access to online tools, with new and smarter ways to create data models which enhance operations and decision-making.

So, while supply chain visibility is not new, the ability to gain visibility with embedded predictive analytics is, especially when dealing with thousands of suppliers and carriers.

Current procurement policies and tools are designed to drive a process having a lot of rigor and controls, instead of an experience or outcome.

According to Accenture, most companies today have a focus on using technology to automate processes and record what has happened (e.g. a transaction executed, an invoice paid, an item purchased, a contract signed, etc.), whereas leading company procurement organizations are making strides in using technologies to dig deeper to get much more contextual information about what happened and why (Burnson, 2018).

The Potential Is Out There

There seems to be never-ending, constantly changing array of technologies impacting all areas of business, including procurement. They include:

Cognitive procurement: In recent years, there has been a lot of big data hype and this has been raised up a notch with procurement professionals now turning towards cognitive procurement. It goes far beyond automation of manual and repetitive tasks, and assists supply chain managers in decision-making in a complex and dynamic environment.

Additionally, it is now possible to automate spend analysis, supplier management, and contract life-cycle management. Its true power can be unearthed when natural language processing (NLP) comes into play, where it can go through texts in the contract and policies to help professionals in spot buying, identifying the best value, and performing contract analysis.

Cyber-security: As the whole world adopts digital technologies, the procurement trends slowly shift towards cyber-security more than physical security. In recent times, there have been numerous cyber-attacks with malware and ransomware troubling procurement professionals seeking to keep their data safe. Cyber-attacks such as Shadow Brokers, WannaCry, Petya, and Cloudbleed caused a lot of problems to businesses all around the world.

Blockchain: The procurement function is highly dependent on decentralized coordination and transaction history. Since supply chain and procurement decision are all based on data, blockchain, a continuously growing list of records, called blocks, which are linked and secured using cryptography, is one of the top procurement trends.

Cloud technology and IoT (Internet of Things): Cloud-based technologies, along with IoT, are expected to remove physical boundaries and create a centralized system, thereby increasing the efficiency and productivity of the supply chain and procurement function. This procurement trend is expected to give rise to the popularity of software-as-a-service (SaaS) applications, and encourage even the small businesses to reap the benefits of such services.

Big data: Big data and predictive analytics are still an untapped resource that can potentially provide insights which help anticipate or respond to events or disruptions. Unpredictable consumer behavior, traffic or weather patterns, and labor unrest are all external events that can disrupt a supply chain and lead to increased costs and customer service challenges. Big data can help organizations become better trading partners for their customers and suppliers. But before insights and analytics can be leveraged for a better supply chain, there is a huge task at hand for the many organizations that need to first collate data points from all sources and align them to their business operations (SpendEdge, 2018).

Continued technology evolution: Integrating sourcing, purchasing, and procurement technology, and its interface, into wider business applications, has been transformational for many organizations.

Technology will continue to evolve over the medium- to longer-term to a mode with a core "container" and a myriad of transactional apps. Companies will see the impact as they start to control a much larger percentage of indirect spend.

Next-gen analytics and artificial intelligence: Real-time, accurate information and insights enable enterprises to rapidly adapt to shifts in the business landscape. As procurement professionals focus on playing a more strategic role in the enterprise, they need the right information and insights to make effective decisions.

Today, artificial intelligence-based procurement technology is helping procurement professionals to strategize by providing insights, suggestions, and recommendations based on the study of market trends and automated forecasts.

Consumer app-like features: One of the biggest challenges with procurement technology systems in the past was that they were complex to use and required a lot of training, which limited their adoption and utility. Traditional procurement tools and applications lack the intuitive interfaces and enhanced user experience available on today's mobile consumer apps.

Today, users expect the same experience and intuitive interfaces from their procurement technology system. Next-generation procurement apps enable functionalities like supplier catalogs, category rooms, and supplier networks that allow an intuitive shopping-style experience and provide procurement professionals with real-time supply/demand visibility and supplier performance ratings to better inform the buyer.

End-to-end solutions: A decade ago, when procurement technology was at an early stage, many enterprises had separate software or tools for various sourcing and procurement activities. Then came procurement technology suites that simply put all these different tools together. Many enterprises today prefer having a comprehensive spend management tool to automate and optimize all their source-to-pay activities.

LEAN AHEAD WITH PROCUREMENT

Lean thinking when applied to procurement can become a strategic weapon, by aligning the process more tightly to internal and external customers' real interests, helping leaders to rethink the end-to-end procurement process, and transforming the effectiveness of strategic procurement activities.

However, this requires that organizations make new demands on their personnel, improving their everyday tasks, and think and act in new ways in their interactions with customers and colleagues.

A large European industrial client of consultant McKinsey & Company adopted Lean as part of an organization-wide procurement transformation across all its business units. By applying a single set of standard methods, the client increased the efficiency of its direct sourcing activities by 20%, and its indirect sourcing activities by 25%. But instead of a typical reduction in procurement staffing, they assigned its newly freed people to a center of excellence responsible for driving the adoption of new tools, increased savings targets, and invested more time in negotiations than before. This enabled the company to reduce spend by double-digit percentages in a variety of categories (www.mckinsey.com, 2018).

This example illustrates the importance of integrating people and process in the Lean procurement journey. At the same time, while it may sound "sexy" to digitalize procurement processes, if not streamlined and improved first, it can generate problems. Processes must be mapped to highlight waste and low-quality first. Only after the process is improved, should the appropriate technology be implemented.

Companies that develop Lean procurement strategies, integrating people, process, and technology will surely benefit the most during their Lean journeys, and that's something that we can all buy into.

Appendix A: A Lean (Philosophy) for Life

As I have been on this journey of encouraging organizations to apply a Lean philosophy to their supply chain and logistics management processes, I've come to realize that many of the concepts and tools of Lean can be applied to one's personal, financial, and professional life and that it is actually a close fit to how I've lived my life (intentionally or not).

So I thought that this might be a good time to write down some thoughts on this idea for the reader to consider as they go through their journey of life. It may be a natural fit for some, like me, or there may be some particular aspects of it that interest others.

Let's start with some personal applications of Lean thinking in your everyday life.

PERSONAL EFFICIENCY AND HAPPINESS: ARE YOU A FELIX OR AN OSCAR?

In the classic movie "The Odd Couple" (1968), there were two roommates, Felix and Oscar. Felix was very neat and organized, and Oscar was basically a disorganized slob. While we don't all fit totally into one type or the other, it can be used to illustrate some of the characteristics and potential benefits of having a Lean philosophy in your personal life.

Personal Organization

An easy example of a personal application is to think of how one can apply 5S, or workplace organization, at home. I'm more of a natural Felix and my wife and son are more like Oscar. So needless to say, there is always a constant battle for me to keep the house neat and organized.

We know the old story about Spring cleaning—if you don't find a way to keep things organized, then each Spring you are basically starting over.

So, as part of the process, it's important to not only get things straightened out (i.e. sort out, set in order, and shine), but to find ways to standardize and sustain the initiative.

A key to long-term success is developing the habit, which I try to impart to my family by telling them that by putting things away immediately after use, there is less work to do later straightening up. I also try to make it a habit to sell, donate, throw out, or recycle anything that is not being used (known in Lean terms as "red-tagging" items), especially when buying a new item that is similar. For example, donate 1–2 pairs of old shoes when you buy a new pair.

The same thing goes for your personal schedule. Being focused, organized, and efficient can help you to get much more accomplished in a day, week, or month, than being a last-minute procrastinator. Trying to develop better time management skills that are focused on value-added activities can help you get a lot more done in a day and lead to more satisfaction, more of a sense of accomplishment, and, ultimately, more success.

Don't Be a Perfectionist Either

Obviously, where you can, you want to make things easier, where possible with the use of visuals—e.g. organize with bins and labels—but that's not always possible.

This type of habit can be useful in organizing your life. A lot of time can be wasted doing things that don't add value to your life, such as searching for information or materials that you already have, but that aren't at your fingertips. So using labels, organized files (paper and electronic), lists, electronic calendar reminders, etc., can save time later.

I've also found that it works best to try not to be too much of a "perfectionist" about everything (i.e. a Felix), as you should try to "take care of the big things up-front and don't sweat the details." A lot of time can be wasted on details in planning for something that may or may not happen. It's best to do a kind of mental risk assessment, thinking about the potential impact and the likelihood of it occurring, before spending a lot of time up-front worrying (another waste of time and energy, as well as a source of stress). The things that have a high potential impact and likelihood of happening should be planned for, the rest can be let go, at least for the time being.

What Adds Value to Your Personal Life?

We talk a lot about value-added versus non-value-added activities in Lean for a business setting. The same goes for your personal life. Do you really need to waste time with activities, or even people, who don't add a lot of value to your life, and just add stress? You need to put some thought into what you really want in life, both short-term and long-term, and then give priority to those things, and try your best to minimize things that don't.

Don't Worry About Things You Can't Control

It is also important to realize that there is no point in worrying or wasting energy on things you can't control, and to spend more time thinking about things you can control.

I have a relative who is a bit of a control freak (another source of waste) who tends to make one bad decision after another, mostly due to a lack of longer-term personal planning. Then later, they blame all the negative things that happen on everyone except the main cause: themselves, and their failure to think things through beforehand.

So, it's important to try to "make things happen" for you through careful, logical planning, rather than "letting things happen," and then complaining about them later.

Set (and Reset) Personal Goals

It is important to set informal personal plans with goals (short- and long-term) that add value to you and those around you, that you can focus on without being distracted. As we may not always hit our goals (e.g. a vacation to Hawaii), we can always modify them (e.g. a vacation in the Caribbean), or delay them.

Health: Physical and Mental

We can't neglect our physical and mental health which can help keep our personal lives "Lean" (figuratively and literally). One also needs to set goals in that regard. I think like other goals in life, it's important that they are realistic, and always keep in mind everything is OK in moderation (exercise, food, etc.). If we don't stick to this, we are creating a lot of waste (excess weight, and mental and physical health issues) in the long-term trying to bring ourselves back to where we feel we should be health-wise.

As they say in sports, it's important to have a "short memory" so you can stay focused on the future. For some that is easy; for others, not so easy. Again, if you have a clear picture of what adds value in your life, it should be easier to at least forget negative things that have occurred in the past, as most didn't add value to your life in the first place.

Another thing to consider is when you want to start a family, as that will of course have a huge impact on your personal life, finances, and career plans. A major thing to consider is are you and your partner ready for that responsibility mentally, physically, and financially? The answer may never be a total "yes," but it is important to consider these things before, and not after the time comes.

FINANCIAL EFFICIENCY: ARE YOU THE TORTOISE OR THE HARE?

While your financial position is also personal and linked to career, I think it deserves its own focus; while money can't necessarily achieve happiness, the lack of it can certainly cause misery.

A Penny Saved...

When we hear that the average American retirement savings of all families is $95,776, and nearly half of families have no retirement account savings at all, according to the Economic Policy Institute (EPI), it starts to hit home how important financial security is. Even more scary is that the median savings at retirement for all families in the U.S. is just $5,000, and the median for families with some savings is $60,000 (Morrissey, 2016).

One thing to be focused on, as my mother always reminded me, is that to start saving early in life (even small amounts) in tax-deferred retirement accounts such as IRAs, 401Ks, etc., can lead to greater security and peace of mind as you reach retirement age. Not to mention that forgoing participation in a company's 401K plan (even with the minimum contribution), means that you are giving away "free" money via company matching in many cases.

One way to get motivated to start saving early in life is to think of the concept of compounding interest. If a 25-year-old started saving the relatively meager amount of $15/day (assuming an average annual return of 6%), they would have $1 million at the age of 67.

The longer you wait, the harder it is too. For example, if you waited until you were 40 years old to start saving for retirement, and had an average remaining lifetime salary of $80,000/year (with the same 6% annual return), you would have to set aside almost 20% of your biweekly paycheck to reach $1 million at age 67 (Elkins, 2017).

This doesn't mean that you should skip all of the "fun" things in life when you are young, but instead focus on planning for and doing things that add value, and not doing things that don't add much value to you personally. It's a bit hard to do at a young, relatively immature age, I know, but again, it's not as hard to imagine when you look at it from this perspective.

Be Organized, Have a Portfolio, and Minimize Debt

The other part of saving and not wasting money on things that don't add value, is the now common idea of having a "portfolio" of savings, with the risk spread out according to age and risk preference. You really don't need to spend a lot of time constantly adjusting your portfolio either, as you need to realize that you are in it for the long-term. It is enough (I've found) to review your savings and investment portfolio annually, and not to panic during a downturn which creates unnecessary worry (and work), at least if you have your risk set according to your comfort level, as most losses will be adjusted in the long-term—at least on funds, as opposed to buying individual stocks and bonds, which is riskier, of course.

Another good old saying is "neither a lender nor a borrower be." So, consider no load funds, no debt, and therefore, no regret. If we try to minimize debt in our lives (other than big ticket item necessities, like a car or house), including credit card debt, you can focus on growing your savings.

What Adds True Value to You in a Financial Sense?

When buying houses and cars, you should really think deeply about value. Do you really need the extra space that you will hardly use in a "McMansion," or a new luxury SUV and working to pay those bills each month, or will you really be just as satisfied (at least after some period of time) living in a comfortable size home and with a nice SUV, and having peace of mind that you are putting away some cash for vacations, emergencies, retirement, and your children's college?

If you're somewhat handy (a "do it yourselfer" or DIY-er) like me, and have the time, then you can save lots of money around the house by fixing and upgrading on your own while gaining the satisfaction that comes with it. I estimate that I've saved around $50,000 in my current home over the past 18 years being a DIY-er. A possible alternative is sourcing your own materials at the best price and hiring a "handyman" to do the work.

Using coupons, discounts, and scouring the web for deals helps as well, as for some (myself included), the process of finding the best deal can be almost as thrilling as the purchase itself. While buying pre-owned isn't for everyone, great deals can be found on new, open-box items (especially electronics on eBay, for example) that come with the same guarantees as new items.

Also consider the saying that "everything is negotiable," which is surprisingly truer than you would think. Whether on a big ticket item or an appliance bought at retail, there is always an opportunity to reduce the price or have something thrown in for "free." For example, I've shopped at large retailer, and asked the manager if I can get a discount for a toaster oven that had been opened (an "open-box return"), but which was new and resealed, and only had instructions missing (which could be downloaded, if needed). I ended up getting a significant discount. So don't be afraid to ask these type of questions, as "the squeeky wheel gets the oil."

We discussed negotiation a bit earlier in this book, and as mentioned, preparation is key to achieving good results during any negotiation, and the availability of information on the internet has made this easier than ever. Try not to be too impulsive (a habit of mine, which I try to minimize), and on bigger items like houses and cars, take multiple visits, as many times things are missed the first or second time around.

CAREER EFFICIENCY, HAPPINESS, AND SUCCESS

When speaking with my junior and senior college students, I always emphasize that they need to put a lot of thought into what they are good at, what they like doing and not doing (e.g. individual contributor versus teamwork), field of choice, and whether the company is a good fit for them (and not just the other way around).

You Can't Pick Your Boss, But You Can Pick Your Job

While we may see surveys showing high rates of job satisfaction, we know that there are many, many people who are not satisfied with, or even hate, their jobs. As we will spend over one-third of our lives (at least Monday–Friday) at work, it's important that we like (and continue to like) our jobs and career paths.

We should also not forget that, while you can't pick your boss, you can certainly pick your job (and company). In my career, every ten years or so, I would take a good hard look at my job and career path, and often "tweak" its direction. I've been lucky enough to have selected a field that I love, supply chain. So, for example, while I worked for many years in industry in the corporate world, I then moved into consulting, started my own supply chain software, consulting, and training business, and then moved into teaching as a full-time university professor.

In some cases, it may even be worth considering a total career change (or "reinventing yourself" as I call it), which, while riskier—and potentially bringing less income in the short term—can add to professional and personal happiness by enabling you to focus on things in your work life that add value to you, and in the long run, will bring you more success anyway.

Whistle While You Work

Besides doing what you are good at and what you like, it's important to be productive in your career for both advancement and personal satisfaction. Again, by focusing on things that add value to your job (per your goals), and not sweating the little things, you can accomplish much more in a day than your colleagues (who are often competitors as well). It is important to not only be productive, but accurate, which helps in decision-making.

Also, when I say to not sweat the little things, it is important to identify what they are, as sometimes what seems like a little thing may in fact be a symptom of something much larger. That's where having good "business sense" comes in. To me, it's like "common sense," combined with a decent understanding of how businesses work, and how functions interact internally and externally.

While it seems like everyone should have good business sense, as with common sense, not everyone has it. To some degree, with age and experience comes wisdom, which contributes to business sense, but that's not always the case. That's why the idea of critical thinking, the objective analysis and evaluation of an issue in order to form a judgment, is so important, and is heavily stressed at today's universities and in industry. In many cases, especially in industry, it can be in short supply, and having that ability can lead to success and satisfaction.

A good saying to keep in mind before making a decision is to "measure twice and cut once," as in many cases, decisions can be irreversible.

While I know that the idea of having a Lean life philosophy may not resonate with everyone, it's something to consider as it may work for you, and it's never too late to change.

References

CHAPTER 1

Burns, S. and Reisman, L. 2005. Lean Sourcing: Creating Sustainable Purchasing Savings. Last accessed at www.aptiumglobal.com, 2016.

Four Principles. Lean Procurement. Last accessed at www.fourprinciples.ae, 2016.

McAvoy, K. 2016. Deloitte's 2016 CPO Survey Points to Investment in Tech. Spend Matters. February 19, 2016. Last accessed at www.spendmatters.com, 2016.

Myerson, P. 2014. "A Lean and Agile Supply Chain: Not an Option, But a Necessity". *Inbound Logistics*, October 16, 2014. Last accessed at www.inboundlogistics.com, 2018.

CHAPTER 2

Atkinson, D. 2012. 10 Guiding Principles for Successful Supplier Relationship Management. Last accessed at www.4pillars.org, 2017.

Deloitte Consulting GmbH. 2015. Supplier Relationship Management (SRM) Redefining the value of strategic supplier collaboration. Last accessed at www2.deloitte.com, 2017.

Lipton, M. 2013. Demand-Driven Supply Chains Are In Demand. *Industry Week* (March 8).

Rawat, N. 2009. Purchasing and Supply Chain: History of Purchasing. Last accessed at http://navpurchasing.blogspot.com/2009/07/history-of-purchasing.html, September 27, 2013.

CHAPTER 3

Allen, G. 2012. Why You Should Consider a Career in Procurement. *The Guardian*, October 10, 2012. Last accessed at www.theguardian.com, 2017.

Houston, P.W. and Hutchens, R. 2009. *Procurement's New Operating Model* (Florham Park, NJ: Booz & Company). Last accessed at www.strategyand.pwc.com, 2017.

Learn.org. 2014. How Can I Become a Certified Purchasing Manager? Last accessed at www.learn.org, 2017.

Murray, M. 2016. Purchasing Organization Structure. The Balance.com, July 11, 2016. Last accessed at www.thebalance.com, 2017.

CHAPTER 4

Blascovich, J., Ferrer, A., Markham, B. 2011. Follow the Procurement Leaders: Seven Ways to Lasting Results, A.T. Kearney's 2011 Assessment of Excellence in Procurement Study. Last accessed at www.atkearney.com, 2017.

Krajewski, L.J., Ritzman, L.P., and Malhotra, M.K. 2013. *Operations Management: Processes and Supply Chains*, 10th edn (Boston: Pearson Higher Education, pp. 11–12.

State of Victoria (Australia). 2014. Identifying Procurement Categories–Procurement Guide. Last accessed at www.procurement.vic.gov.au, 2017.

CHAPTER 5

Deloitte. 2016. The Deloitte Global Chief Procurement Officer Survey 2016. Last accessed at www.deloitte.co.uk/cposurvey2016, 2018.

Kauffman, R.G. and Crimi, T.A. 2005. A Best-Practice Approach for Development of Global Supply Chains. Paper presented at the 90th Annual International Supply Management Conference, Philadelphia, PA (May).

SAP White Paper. 2007. Last accessed at www.sap.com, 2014.

CHAPTER 6

Abilla, P. 2012. How Manufacturing Software Can Adjust to Lean Principles. Shmula. Last accessed at www.shmula.com, 2016.

Aptium Global, Inc. 2005. Lean Sourcing: Creating Sustainable Purchasing Savings. Executive white paper. Last accessed at www.aptiumglobal.com, 2017.

Benton, W.C. 2010. *Purchasing and Supply Management*. 2nd edn (Boston, MA: McGraw-Hill/Irwin), Ch.6.

Benton, W.C., and Shin, H. 1998. Manufacturing Planning and Control: The evolution of MRP and JIT integration. *European Journal of Operational Research* 110:3 (November), 411–440.

Heizer, J. and Render, B. 2011. *Operations Management*. 10th edn (New Jersey: Prentice Hall), 626.

Ptak, C. and Smith, C. 2012. The State of Demand Driven MRP. Demand Driven Institute. Last accessed at www.demanddriveninstitute.com, 2018.

Williams, P. 2013. Waste Not, Want Not – Lean Six Sigma Values for Procurement (September 6). Last accessed at www.capgemini-consulting.com, 2017.

CHAPTER 7

Aptium Global, Inc. 2005. Lean Sourcing: Creating Sustainable Purchasing Savings. Executive white paper. Last accessed at www.aptiumglobal.com, 2017.

Blascovich, J., Ferrer, A., and Markham, B. 2011. 7 Ways to Procurement Excellence. *Supply Chain Management Review* (November). www.scmr.com.

Clegg and Montgomery, "Seven Steps for Sourcing Information Products", *Information Outlook*, December 2005, volume 9, number 12. Last accessed at www.procurement-academy.com, 2017.

PricewaterhouseCoopers LLP. 2014. Sourcing as Strategy, Advisory Services Manufacturing (August). Last accessed at www.pwc.com, 2017.

Source One Management Services LLC. Strategic Sourcing MRO Case Study by Source One, Case Studies and Examples. Last accessed at www.sourceoneinc.com, 2017.

CHAPTER 8

Dominick, C. 2015. Ten Types of Procurement Software (July 1). College Planning & Management. Last accessed at www.webcpm.com, 2017.

Oracle. 2006. Lean Procurement: The Future of Supply Chain Management in a Demand-Driven World, An Oracle White Paper Written in Collaboration with CSS International, Inc. (June). Last accessed at www.oracle.com, 2017.

Scapa Case Study, Consumers Interstate Corporation. Last accessed at www.leanprocurement.com, 2017.

Staff contributors, iValue. 2016. Achieve Lean in Procurement: Eliminate Waste but Don't Neglect to Add Value (June 13). Last accessed at blog.ivalua.com, 2018.

Thomson, J. 2015. Lean Review of Procurement Arrangements: A Case Study (June 17). Last accessed at www.scott-moncrief.com, 2018.

CHAPTER 9

Chen, J.C. and Cox, R.A. 2012. Value Stream Management for Lean Office—A Case Study, *American Journal of Industrial and Business Management*, 2(17–29). Last accessed at http://dx.doi.org/10.4236/ajibm.2012.22004, 2017.

EPA Office of Policy. 2014. Lean Government Region 1 Laboratory Purchasing Process Lean Event Case Study (December). Last accessed at www.epa.gov, 2017.

Torvatn, T., Pedersen, A.-C., and Holmen, E. 2016. Chapter 18: Lean Purchasing. In *The Routledge Companion to Lean Management*, ed. Netland, T. and Powell, D. (New York: Routledge).

CHAPTER 10

Abilla, P. 2012. How Manufacturing Software Can Adjust to Lean Principles. Shmula. Last accessed at www.shmula.com, 2016.

Accurate Gauge Gains a Strategic Business Advantage from MSC ControlPoint Inventory Management, Customer Success Story. Last accessed at www.mscdirect.com, 2017.

Benton, W.C., and Hojung S. 1998. Manufacturing Planning and Control: The evolution of MRP and JIT integration, *European Journal of Operational Research*, 110(3) (November): 411–440.

IFS Software. 2004. Gables Engineering: Case Study. Last accessed at www.top10erp.org, 2016.

Leaning Out the MRO Supply Chain, White Paper written by Penton Manufacturing and Supply Group and MH&L magazine and sponsored by MSC Direct. Last accessed at https://cdn.mscdirect.com/global/media/pdf/solutions/lean-mro-white-paper.pdf, 2017.

Ptak, C. and Smith, C. 2012. The State of Demand Driven MRP, Demand Driven Institute. Last accessed at www.demanddriveninstitute.com, 2018.

CHAPTER 11

Barve, A. 2002. Six Best Practices in Cost Management (July 12). Special Collections Research Center at North Carolina State University. Last accessed at www.ncsu.edu, 2017.

CIPS (Chartered Institute of Purchasing and Supply). 2013. Costing and pricing – what the buyer needs to know. CIPS Knowledge Insight. Last accessed at www.cips.org, 2017.

Genpact. 2011.Case Study – Supply Chain Decision Services. Last accessed at www.japan.genpact.com, 2017.

Guttman Development Strategies. Win-Win Negotiation, Case Studies – Leadership Development. Last accessed at www.guttmandev.com, 2017.

McCrea, B. 2013. 6 Steps to More Effective Supplier Negotiations – How to create win-win negotiation outcomes every time you sit down to talk price with your suppliers. Digi-Key Electronics article library, November 07. Last accessed at www.digikey.com, 2017.

Tate, W. 2011. The Essentials of Supply Chain Management Strategic Sourcing: Cost Management. *Supply Chain Management Review* (May 16).

Watershed Associates, LLC. YEAR. Negotiation Stages Introduction. Last accessed at www.watershedassociates.com, 2017.

CHAPTER 12

Elsey, R.D. 2013. Contract Management Guide, Knowledge Insight. CIPS (Chartered Institute of Purchasing and Supply) Knowledge. 2013. Last accessed at www.cips.org, 2017.

Sheffield, Y., and Rice Jr., J., 2005. A Supply Chain View of the Resilient Enterprise, *MIT Sloan Management Review*, Fall, Vol. 47, No. 1, 41–48.

United Nations, 2012. United Nations Procurement Practitioner's Handbook, Revision 1.1 (September). Last accessed at www.unmg.org, 2017.

CHAPTER 13

Basware. New Purchase-to-Pay System Allows Smarter Processes at Atea, Basware software case study. Last accessed at www.basware.com, 2016.

Dominick, C. 2015. Ten Types of Procurement Software (July 1). College Planning & Management. Last accessed at www.webcom.com, 2016.

Heizer, J. and Render, B. 2011. *Operations Management*. 10th edn (New Jersey: Prentice Hall), 626.

JDA. Enabling Online Supplier Collaboration at Toshiba Semiconductor Company, JDA software case study. Last accessed at www.jda.com, 2016.

SAP. Clariant cuts costs with Ariba solutions – Automating and enhancing procurement processes, SAP software case study. Last accessed at www.sap.com, 2016.

CHAPTER 14

Department for Children, Schools and Families. Strategic procurement – an overview. Last accessed at www.yor-ok.org.uk/CommissioningNatDocs/3%20Strategic%20 procurement.doc, 2018.

Henshall, D. 2015. Develop a Procurement Analytics Strategy - Beyond simple spend data towards strategic decisions (October 1). CPP Purchasing Practice. Last accessed at www.purchasingpractice.com, 2018.

Steele, P.T. and Court, B.H. 1996. *Profitable purchasing strategies: a manager's guide for improving organizational competitiveness through the skills of purchasing* (London: McGraw-Hill Book Company).

Wheatley, M. 2013. Guide to Procurement Analytics. Data Informed (May 3). Last accessed at www.data-informed.com, 2018.

CHAPTER 15

BD Global Procurement. Providing Sourcing, Strategy and Value. Last accessed at https:// www.bd.com/en-us/company/trading-partners/bd-suppliers/global-procurement, 2018.

Christopher, M. and Peck, H. 2004. Building the Resilient Supply Chain. *International Journal of Logistics Management*, Vol. 15, No. 2, 1–13.

Heizer, J. and Render, B. 2013. *Operations Management*, 11th edn (Pearson), p. 438.

Kauffman, R.G. and Crimi, T.A. 2005. A Best-Practice Approach for Development of Global Supply Chains. Paper presented at the 90th Annual International Supply Management Conference, Philadelphia, PA, May 2005.

Portioli Staudacher, A., and Tantardini, M. 2009. Global Sourcing: lessons from lean companies to improve supply chain performances. Paper presented at the 3rd International Conference on Industrial Engineering and Industrial Management (XIII Congreso de Ingeniería de Organización), Barcelona-Terrassa (September 2–4). Last accessed at www.adingor.es, 2018.

PwC and the MIT Forum for Supply Chain Innovation. 2013. Making the right risk decisions to strengthen operations performance. Last accessed at www.pwc.com, 2014.

SC Digest Editorial Staff. 2010. The Five Challenges of Today's Global Supply Chains (August 12). Last accessed at www.scdigest.com, 2014.

Sheffield, Y., and Rice Jr., J., 2005. A Supply Chain View of the Resilient Enterprise, *MIT Sloan Management Review*, Fall, Vol. 47, No. 1, 41–48.

CHAPTER 16

Burnson, P. 2018. Creating a True Digital Procurement Supply Chain (May 15). Supply Chain 247. Last accessed at www.supplychain247.com, 2018.

De Backer, K., Mercker, B-U., Moder, M., and Spiller, P. 2017Purchasing power: Lean management creates new value in procurement, Insights on Operations (July). McKinsey & Company. Last accessed at www.mckinsey.com, 2018.

Source One Management Services, LLC. What's Next for Procurement: 8 Trends to Watch in 2018. Last accessed at www.sourceoneinc.com, 2018.

SpendEdge Procurement Research. 2018. Top 10 Procurement Trends In 2018. Last accessed at www.spendedge.com, 2018.

APPENDIX A

Elkins, K. 2017. These 4 charts will totally change how you think about saving money (September 27). CNBC Money. Last accessed at www.cnbc.com, 2018.

Morrissey, M. 2016. The State of American Retirement–How 401(k)s have failed most American workers (March 3). Last accessed at www.epi.org, 2018.

Index

A

Accurate Gauge, MSC controlpoint
        inventory management, 147–148
    approach, 147–148
    challenge, 147
Advanced planning and scheduling (APS)
        system, 76
Advanced strategic sourcing, 18
AEP, see Assessment of excellence in
        procurement (AEP)
Agile procurement process, 5–6, 18
Agile supply chain, 5
APS, see Advanced planning and
        scheduling (APS) system
Ariba software, 111
Artificial intelligence, 235
Assessment of excellence in procurement
        (AEP), 94
Atea
    approach, 191–192
    challenge, 191

B

BATNA, see Best alternative to a
        negotiated agreement (BATNA)
BD, see Becton Dickinson (BD)
Becton Dickinson (BD), 216–218
    continuous improvement
        programs, 218
    functional capabilities and culture, 218
    process efficiency, 217
    supplier relationship and risk
        management, 217–218
Benchmarking, 18
Best alternative to a negotiated agreement
        (BATNA), 93
Bid and auction, 120, 184
Big data, 234
Bill of materials (BOM), 128, 131
Blockchain, 234
BOM, see Bill of materials (BOM)

Bullwhip effect, 9, 10, 55
Buyer-based pricing, 157

C

Capacity requirement planning (CRP),
        134, 135
Captive pricing, 157
Career efficiency, 242–244
Centralized procurement, 29–30
    advantages of, 29
    disadvantages of, 30
Certified in Production and Inventory
        Management (CPIM)
        program, 36
Certified Professional in Supply
        Management (CPSM), 35
Certified Professional Public Buyer
        (CPPB), 36
Certified Professional Purchasing
        Manager (CPPM), 36
Certified Public Procurement Officer
        (CPPO), 36
Certified purchasing manager (CPM), 35
Certified Purchasing Professional (CPP),
        35–36
Certified Supply Chain Professional
        (CSCP), 36
Chartered Institute of Procurement &
        Supply, 168
CIC, see Consumers Interstate Consulting
        (CIC) group
Clariant, 190–191
    approach, 190
    challenge, 190
Cloud technology, 234
Cognitive procurement, 233–234
Combination solutions, 114
Consumer app-like features, 235
Consumer packaged goods (CPG), 20
Consumers Interstate Consulting (CIC)
        group, 117
Continued technology evolution, 234–235

Contracts
    administration, 178–179
    award stage, 176–177
    business case, preparing, 168
    changes within contract, 177
    compliance, 108
    contract closure, 180
    developing and managing, 167–180
    downstream or post-award activities,
        177–180
    exit strategy, developing, 171
    factor rating method, 174–175
    form of contract, establishing, 172
    management, 113, 167–182
    management approval, securing, 168
    management plan, developing, 171
    negotiation, 175–176
    offers, evaluating, 174–175
    organization's performance and
        effectiveness review, 179–180
    pre-qualification, qualification and
        tendering procedures, 172–173
    project team, assembling, 169
    relationship management, 178
    risk assessment, 169–170, 179
    service delivery management, 177–178
    specifications and requirements,
        drafting, 171–172
    standard terms and conditions of,
        204–205
    strategy, developing, 169
    supplier appraisal, 173–174
    tender documents, drafting, 174
    upstream or pre-award activities,
        168–177
Corporate purchase card, 120–121, 184
Corporate social responsibility (CSR), 232
Cost and price analysis, 156–158
    customer value, maximizing, 157–158
    pricing strategies, 156–157
Cost-cutting methods, 85
Cost management, 151–165
    cost and price analysis, 156–158
    negotiation, 158–162
    procurement practices, annual cost
        savings, 151–153
    segment major purchasing categories,
        153–155
Cost-plus pricing, 156

Costs, 9
    reduction, 11, 67
    savings, 108
    strategy, 39
CPG, see Consumer packaged goods
        (CPG)
CPIM, see Certified in Production and
        Inventory Management (CPIM)
        program
CPM, see Certified purchasing manager
        (CPM)
CPP, see Certified Purchasing Professional
        (CPP)
CPPB, see Certified Professional Public
        Buyer (CPPB)
CPPM, see Certified Professional
        Purchasing Manager (CPPM)
CPPO, see Certified Public Procurement
        Officer (CPPO)
CPSM, Certified Professional in Supply
        Management (CPSM)
Critical decoupling points, 74
CRP, see Capacity requirement planning
        (CRP)
CSCP, see Certified Supply Chain
        Professional (CSCP)
CSR, see Corporate social responsibility
        (CSR)
Current procurement policies, 233
Cyber-security, 234

D

Data analytics, 193–197
    analytics applications, 194–195
    categories of, 193–194
    category management, focus, 197
    data gaps, identifying, 196–197
Data-mining, 18
DDSC, see Demand-driven supply chains
        (DDSC)
Decentralized procurement, 30
Defects, 7
Deloitte Global CPO Survey, 2016, 11
Demand-driven supply chains (DDSC),
        10, 20–22
    agility and flexibility, 21
    data timeliness and granularity, 21
    fast re-planning and what-if analysis, 21

metrics and incentives, alignment, 21–22
multi-tier connectivity and collaboration, 21
Demand "pull" system, 73
Discrete orders, 120, 184
Discriminating pricing, 157
DPS, *see* Dupont Production System (DPS)
Dupont Production System (DPS), 78
Dynamic replenishment, 61

E

E-commerce, 62–63
Economic order quantity (EOQ) model, 134, 135–138
assumptions, 136
basic EOQ calculation, 137–138
production order quantity model, 137
quantity discount model, 137
EDI, *see* Electronic data interchange (EDI)
EFT, *see* Electronic funds transfer (EFT)
E-Invoicing, 114
Electronic data interchange (EDI), 121, 184
Electronic funds transfer (EFT), 121, 185
End-to-end solutions, 235
Enterprise cost, 13
Enterprise resource planning (ERP) system, 57
EOQ, *see* Economic order quantity (EOQ) model
EPA lean review, 126–127
approach, 126–127
challenge, 126
EPayment, 114
E-procurement, 120, 183–192
EProcurement, 113
ERP, *see* Enterprise resource planning (ERP) system
ERP software modules, 121
Erskine Hospital Limited, 115–116
approach, 115–116
challenge, 115
recommendations for, 116
ESourcing, 113
Ethics, 167–182
codes of conduct, 182

concepts, principles and risks, 182
in contract management, 181–182
in procurement, 181–182

F

Financial efficiency, 240–242
Flexibility strategy, 39

G

Gables Engineering, MRP system, 146–147
approach, 146
challenge, 146
Global energy supplier, 162–164
approach, 163–164
challenge, 162–163
Globalization, growth of, 211–218
communications, improvements, 213
factors influencing, 211–213
freedom of trade, 212–213
labor availability and skills, 213
reasons, for company, 213–215
transnational corporations, 213
transportation, improvements, 212
Global procurement, 211–227
globalization, growth of, 211–218
global supply chain risks and challenges, 220–222
risk management, 222–227
Global supply chain, 53–54, 220–222
key challenges, 222
questions to consider, 221–222
risks and challenges, 220–222
strategy development, 54–55
Going rate pricing, 156

H

Hybrid supply chain strategy, 5–6
"Hybrid" type manufacturing environment, 75

I

IBP, *see* Integrated business planning (IBP) model
Indirect procurement, 131–150

Institute for Supply Management (ISM), 35
Integrated business planning (IBP)
	model, 58
Integrated supply management, 19
Internet, 62–63
Internet
	negotiation, 92
Internet of Things (IoT), 234
Inventory, 6
Inventory accuracy improvements, 9
Invoicing processes, 61
IoT, *see* Internet of Things (IoT)
ISM, *see* Institute for Supply Management
	(ISM)

J

Just-in-time (JIT) production, 8, 17, 59, 67
	and MRP systems, 70–76
	purchasing characteristics, 68–70

K

Kanban process, 59, 73
Key performance indicators (KPIs), 40, 108
KPIs, *see* Key performance indicators (KPIs)

L

Lead-timee, 9
Lean factors, 13
Lean (philosophy) for life, 237–244
	career efficiency, happiness, and
		success, 242–244
	financial efficiency, 240–242
	personal efficiency and happiness,
		237–240
	physical and mental health, 239–240
Lean global procurement, 215–216
Lean manufacturing, 74
Lean office
	approach, 128
	challenge, 127
	creating, 127–129
Lean procurement process, 4, 5–6, 8,
		67–85, 109–111, 232
	core principles of, 110–111
	defects, 82

demand-driven, 9–11
eight wastes, 81–83
examples of improvements, 8–9
future of, 229–236
inventory, 81
journey, 236
lean purchasing, 68–78
motion, 81
organizations, 13
over-processing, 82
overproduction, 82
people and, 230–231
procurement technology, 81
skills (or people waste), 82–83
strategic sourcing *versus* lean sourcing,
		83–85
strategy, 12–14
technology, 233–235
and technology case studies, 189–192
technology opportunity, 11–12
technology to enhance, 112–114
transportation waste, 81
waiting, 82
Lean purchasing, 123–126
	flow concept, 124–125
	perfection, 126
	pull strategy, 125
	specify value, 123–124
	value stream, 124
Lean purchasing, 68–78
	benefits, 69–70
	challenges in implementing, 76–78
	JIT and MRP systems, 70–76
	JIT purchasing characteristics, 68–70
Lean Six Sigma, 57
Lean sourcing, 83–85
	journey, 95–96
	maturity model, 96
Lean strategic sourcing, 94–95
	approach, 97
	challenge, 96
	MRO–case study, 96–98
	seven characteristics of, 94–95
Lean supply chain, 5
Lean thinking, 3, 4
Lean tools, 8, 11, 110
"Leveraging" effect, 18, 19
Low-cost country sourcing, 17

M

Maintenance, repair and operating (MRO), 131
Marginal pricing, 156
Market penetration pricing, 156
Market-skimming, 156
Mass customizer, 5
Master production schedule (MPS), 131
Material requirements planning (MRP) systems, 9, 70–76, 119, 131–135
  costs, minimizing, 135–142
  economic order quantity model, 135–138
  lean and, 142–143
  leaning out MRO inventory, 143–146
  lot-sizing techniques, 134–135
  MPS and, 132–134
  reorder point models, 138–142
McKinsey & Company, 236
MNCs, *see* Multinational corporations (MNCs)
Motion (or movement), 6
MPS, *see* Master production schedule (MPS)
MRO, *see* Maintenance, repair and operating (MRO)
MRP, *see* Material requirements planning (MRP) systems
Multinational corporations (MNCs), 213

N

Needs analysis, 90
Negotiation, 158–162
  effective and efficient, 161–162
  stages of, 159–161
Next-gen analytics, 235

O

Oil embargo, 17
One-piece-flow, 8
Organizational structure, 27–30
Outsourced manufacturer collaboration, 61
Outsourcing, procurement strategy, 43–44

benefits of, 43
disadvantages or risks, 43–44
Over-processing, 7
Overproduction, 7
Ownership, cost of, 18, 19–20

P

Paradigm shift, 19, 136
Performance management, 167–182
Performance monitoring, 167
Periodic order quantity (POQ), 134
Personal organization, 237–238
POQ, *see* Periodic order quantity (POQ)
Premium pricing, 156
Pre-negotiated blanket, 120, 184
Price, 107, 108
Pricewaterhouse Coopers (PwC), 98
Procurement, operating model, 31–34
  execution processes, 32–33
  organization, 32
  performance management, 33–34
  procure-to-pay processes, 33
  sourcing strategy processes, 32
  supplier and customer management, 33
  technology, 33
Procurement department organizational structure, 28
Procurement executives, challenges, 64–65
  cost reduction, 64
  digital journey, 64–65
  outsourcing, strategy, 65
  skills gap, 65
  supplier relationships, 65
Procurement process, 4, 101–107; *see also* Lean procurement
  analysis, tools, and techniques, 193–207
  category management, 199–200
  collaborative procurement, 198
  competition, 203–204
  cost reduction, 19
  direct procurement, 102–103
  distributed and integrative negotiations, 107
  documents and processes, automation, 183–185

e-procurement, 204
Erskine lean review of, 115–116
establish specifications, 103–104
focus areas, 6–8
framework contracts and
        agreements, 205
history of, 16
identify and review requirements,
        102–103
identify and select suppliers, 104–106
indirect procurement, 103
key metrics, 107–109
negotiations, 106–107
organization, 4
outsourcing, 17
process and technology, 183–185
right price, determine, 106–107
spend analysis, 198
standalone procurement solutions,
        187–189
strategic procurement tools and
        techniques, 198–207
strategy and plan, 199
supplier lists, preferred, 206
supplier preferencing, 201–202
supplier relationship management,
        200–202
supply chain value analysis, 202–203
sustainable procurement, 206
total quality management, 206–207
value stream mapping, 202–203
Procurement software, 112, 186–189
Procurement strategy, 40–46
    align with business, 41
    best practices, 41–42
    competitive advantage, supply chain
        strategy, 38–39
    development and application, 37–51
    few or many suppliers, 45
    insourcing, 44
    joint ventures, 45
    make or buy decision, 42–43
    near-sourcing, 44
    organizational and supply chain
        strategy, 37–38
    outsourcing, 43–44
    risk, managing, 41
    supplier relationship management, 42
    tailor category strategies, 42

    tailored procurement category
        strategies, 46–51
    top and bottom lines, contribution, 41
    vertical integration, 44–45
    virtual companies, 45–46
    war for talent, 42
Procurement technology, 111–114,
        186–189
    improvements, 17
Procure-to-pay solution, 187
Purchase orders, issuing, 119–121
Purchase-to-pay system, 191–192
Purchasing function, 4, 15, 18–19, 119–129
    correct delivery, follow-up, 121–122
    EPA lean review, 126–127
    goods, receive and accept, 122
    invoice for payment, approving, 122–123
    process, 119
    purchase orders, issuing, 119–121
PwC, *see* Pricewaterhouse Coopers (PwC)

Q

Quality, data, 8, 9
Quality strategy, 39

R

Relationship pricing, 157
Reorder point (ROP) models, 138–142
    fixed period model, 141
    fixed quantity model, 138–139
    safety stock, 139–140
    single period model, 141–142
Request for proposal (RFP), 92
Requests for information (RFIs), 92
Return on investment (ROI), 108
RFIs, *see* Requests for information (RFIs)
RFP, *see* Request for proposal (RFP)
Risk management, 222–227
    external risks, 224–225
    internal risks, 223–224
    potential risk identification and
        impact, 223
    risk mitigation, 226–227
    sources of risk, 223–225
    supply chain disruptions, 225–226
ROI, *see* Return on investment (ROI)
ROP, *see* Reorder point (ROP) models

S

Safety stock
  probabilistic, 139–140
  rules of thumb, 140
Scapa Group
  approach, 117
  challenge, 117
Segment major purchasing categories,
    153–155
  bottleneck purchases, 155
  leveraging purchases, 154–155
  non-critical purchases, 154
  strategic purchases, 155
Skills, 7–8
Source One, 97
Sourcing, as strategy
  approach, 98–99
  case study, 98–99
  challenge, 98
Sourcing strategies, 91
Spend analysis, 11, 17, 113
Spending analysis, 90
SPM, *see* Supplier performance
    management (SPM)
SRM, *see* Supplier relationship
    management (SRM)
SRM governance, 23
Strategic planning, 17
Strategic sourcing, 12, 13, 83–85, 89–99
  processes, 89–93
Strategic sourcing concept, 17
Supplier development, 24, 124, 152, 173
Supplier discovery, 113
Supplier information management, 113
Supplier management, 114
Supplier performance management
    (SPM), 23, 167
Supplier relationship management (SRM),
    22–26
  challenges, overcome, 24–25
  collaborating with suppliers, 22–25
  conformance with supplier audits, 24
  guiding principles for, 25–26
  mutually-beneficial relationships,
    suppliers, 23
  strategy to action, 25
  supply risks, 24
  sustainable value, 23–24

traditional perspectives, 23
Supplier segmentation, 23
Supply chain costs, 3
Supply chain integration and
    collaboration, 55–62
  benefits to, 56
  customer collaboration, 61–62
  external integration, 59–62
  internal integration, 56–58
  sales and operations planning, 58
  supplier collaboration, 59–61
Supply chain leveraging effect, 18
Supply chain organization, 17
Supply chain strategy
  company and functional objectives, 38
  for competitive advantage, 38–39
  mission statement, 37–38
Supply management, 3, 17
  centralized procurement, 29–30
  certifications, 35–36
  decentralized procurement, 30
  education and certifications, 35–36
  globalization growth, 54–55
  global supply chain, 53–54
  internet and e-commerce, 62–63
  issues and opportunities in, 53–65
  organizational structure, 27–30
  organization and structure, 27–36
  people and careers, 34–36
  procurement, operating model for,
    31–34
  procurement executives, challenges
    for, 64–65
  quality and safety, 63–64
  supply chain integration and
    collaboration, 55–62
  technologies, 183–192
Supply market analysis, 90
Supply market globalization, 17

T

Tailored procurement category strategies,
    46–51
  best practice categorization process,
    49–51
  direct *vs.* indirect procurement, 46–48
  identifying procurement categories,
    48–49

Technology opportunity, 11–12
Time strategy, 39
Toshiba Semiconductor Company,
    189–190
  approach, 189
  challenge, 189
  JDA solutions, 190
Total quality management (TQM),
    206–207
TQM, *see* Total quality management
    (TQM)
Transportation, 6

V

Value-added networks (VANs), 121, 185
Value-addition, personal life, 239
Value stream mapping (VSM), 8, 82–83,
    124, 126, 128

VANs, *see* Value-added networks (VANs)
Vendor-managed inventory (VMI), 59,
    120, 184
VMI, *see* Vendor-managed inventory
    (VMI)
VSM, *see* Value stream mapping (VSM)

W

Waiting, 6–7
Waste reduction, 84, 125
Wastes of Lean, 6–8
Win–win negotiation, electronic
    components manufacturer,
    164–165
  approach, 164–165
  challenge, 164
WIP, *see* Work in process (WIP) inventory
Work in process (WIP) inventory, 71, 119